INCREDIBLE
HUNTING
STORIES

INCREDIBLE HUNTING STORIES

CLASSIC TALES FROM THE FIELD

EDITED BY JAY CASSELL

Skyhorse Publishing

Skyhorse Publishing books may be purchased in bulk at special discounts for sales promotion, corporate gifts, fund-raising, or educational purposes. Special editions can also be created to specifications. For details, contact the Special Sales Department, Skyhorse Publishing, 307 West 36th Street, 11th Floor, New York, NY 10018 or info@skyhorsepublishing.com.

Skyhorse® and Skyhorse Publishing® are registered trademarks of Skyhorse Publishing, Inc.®, a Delaware corporation.

Visit our website at www.skyhorsepublishing.com.

10 9 8 7 6 5

All stories are reprinted by permission of the author, unless otherwise indicated.

The authors and texts included in this book represent more than a century of literature. The integrity of their individual styles, including spelling, grammar, and punctuation, has been respected. The stories reflect the attitudes of their times, and do not necessarily represent the opinions or views of Skyhorse Publishing, Inc.

This book is a condensation of the previously published volume *The Gigantic Book of Hunting Stories*.

Library of Congress Cataloging-in-Publication Data is available on file.

"To Hunt: The Question of Killing" reprinted with the permission of the author.

Cover design by Tom Lau
Cover photo credit: Ernest Hemingway Photograph Collection. John F. Kennedy Presidential Library and Museum, Boston.

Print ISBN: 978-1-5107-1378-9
Ebook ISBN: 978-1-5107-1383-3

Printed in China

TABLE OF CONTENTS

INTRODUCTION

The sport of hunting has a rich history of finely told adventure tales—stories of charging elephants in the African bush, enraged grizzlies defending their cubs in Alaska, or of man-eating tigers deep in the Indian jungle, stalking unwitting villagers while at the same time being pursued by a professional hunter. The list of such stories is long and vast, with great writers current and past all adding to the body of work.

Introspective pieces abound—with hunters pondering the meaning of life and death, with anthropomorphic animals interpreting what it's like to be hunted ("Trail's End," by Sigurd Olsen) or even mountains observing the relationship between deer and wolves ("Thinking Like a Mountain," by Aldo Leopold). Writers who write about hunting are apt to make observations from a variety of perspectives, again, all adding to an incredibly diverse body of literature.

Many tales revolve around experiences afield, with a hunter either successfully getting his game or not. Success or failure isn't based on a downed bird or animal, however, but on how the day went, how the hunting was, how friends interacted with each other during the day afield. Tales of hunting turkeys, quail, and grouse, of deer hunting from a tree stand while thinking of family and friends, or of gazing into a log fire, thinking how fires can bring together good friends ("Log Fires," Gene Hill), they're all part of it.

James Kilgo wrote a compelling little book titled *Deep Enough for Ivorybills* back in 1988. The book is not just about hunting and fishing, but about rediscovering how life is an integral part of the larger rhythms of nature and the seasons. It seems he had gotten away from life oriented toward the outdoors, but then came back to it. "Hunting brought me a deeply satisfying relationship with other men and with the woods," he wrote. He sums it up what he learned with this: "Whether or not I really want to go kill the buck, I am not yet willing to forego the company of men who hunt."

Hunting literature. It can reconnect you with what is deep in your soul, it can keep you connected with the past and the present. In this book, *Incredible Hunting Tales*, we've selected a number of classic tales with a number of current ones, the whole idea being that we're once again adding to the work.

—Jay Cassell
Katonah, NY
Fall 2016

SECTION ONE
CLASSIC TALES

CHAPTER 1

A MAN-KILLING BEAR

by Theodore Roosevelt

Almost every trapper past middle age who has spent his life in the wilderness has stories to tell about exceptionally savage bears. One of these stories was told in my ranch house one winter evening by an old mountain hunter, clad in fur cap, buckskin hunting shirt and leather trousers, who had come to my ranch at nightfall, when the cowboys were returning from their day's labor.

The old fellow, who was known by the nickname of "Buckskin," had camped for several months in the Bad Lands but a score of miles away from my ranch. Most of his previous life had been spent among the main chains of the Rockies. After supper the conversation drifted to bears, always a favorite subject of talk in frontier cabins, and some of my men began to recount their own adventures with these great, clumsy-looking beasts.

This at once aroused the trapper's interest. He soon had the conversation to himself, telling us story after story of the bears he had killed and the escapes he had met with in battling against them.

In particular he told us of one bear which, many years before, had killed the partner with whom at the time he was trapping.

The two men were camped in a high mountain valley in northwestern Wyoming, their camp being pitched at the edge of a "park country"—that is, a region where large glades and groves of tall evergreen trees alternate.

They had been trapping beaver, the animal which, on account of its abundance and the value of the fur, was more eagerly followed than any other by the old-time plains and mountain trappers. They had with them four shaggy pack ponies, such as most of these hunters use, and as these ponies were not needed at the moment, they had been turned loose to shift for themselves in the open glade country.

Late one evening three of the ponies surprised the trappers by galloping up to the campfire and there halting. The fourth did not make his appearance. The trappers knew that some wild beast must have assailed the animals and had probably caught one and caused the others to flee toward the place which they had learned to associate with safety.

Before dawn the next morning the two men started off to look for the lost horse. They skirted several great glades, following the tracks of the ponies that had come to the fire the previous evening. Two miles away, at the edge of a tall pine wood, they found the body of the lost horse, already partially eaten.

The tracks round about showed that the assailant was a grizzly of uncommon size, which had evidently jumped at the horses just after dusk, as they fed up to the edge of the woods. The owner of the horse decided to wait by the carcass for the bear's return, while old Buckskin went off to do the day's work in looking after traps, and the like.

Buckskin was absent all day, and reached camp after nightfall. His friend had come in ahead of him, having waited in vain for the bear. As

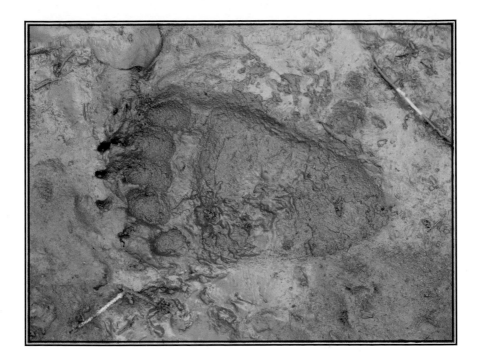

there was no moon he had not thought it worthwhile to stay by the bait during the night.

The next morning they returned to the carcass and found that the bear had returned and eaten his full, after which he had lumbered off up the hill side. They took up his tracks and followed him for some three hours; but the wary old brute was not to be surprised. When they at last reached the spot where he had made his bed, it was only to find that he must have heard them as they approached, for he had evidently left in a great hurry.

After following the roused animal for some distance they found they could not overtake him. He was in an ugly mood, and kept halting every mile or so to walk to and fro, bite and break down the saplings, and paw the earth and dead logs; but in spite of this bullying he would not absolutely await their approach, but always shambled off before they came in sight.

At last they decided to abandon the pursuit. They then separated, each to make an afternoon's hunt and return to camp by his own way.

Our friend reached camp at dusk, but his partner did not turn up that evening at all. However, it was nothing unusual for either one of the two to be off for a night, and Buckskin thought little of it.

Next morning he again hunted all day, and returned to camp fully expecting to see his friend there, but found no sign of him. The second night passed, still without his coming in.

The morning after, the old fellow became uneasy and started to hunt him up. All that day he searched in vain, and when, on coming back to camp, there was still no trace of him, he was sure that some accident had happened.

The next morning he went back to the pine grove in which they had separated on leaving the trail of the bear. His friend had worn hobnail boots instead of moccasins, and this made it much easier to follow his tracks. With some difficulty the old hunter traced him for some four miles, until he came to a rocky stretch of country, where all sign of the footprints disappeared.

However, he was a little startled to observe footprints of a different sort. A great bear, without doubt the same one that had killed the horse, had been travelling in a course parallel to that of the man.

Apparently the beast had been lurking just in front of his two pursuers the day they followed him from the carcass; and from the character of the "sign" Buckskin judged that as soon as he separated from his friend, the bear had likewise turned and had begun to follow the trapper.

The bear had not followed the man into the rocky piece of ground, and when the old hunter failed in his efforts to trace up his friend, he took the trail of the bear instead.

Three-quarters of a mile on, the bear, which had so far been walking, broke into a gallop, the claws making deep scratches here and there in the patches of soft earth. The trail then led into a very thick and dark wood, and here the footprints of the man suddenly reappeared.

For some little time the old hunter was unable to make up his mind with certainty as to which one was following the other; but finally, in the decayed mold by a rotten log, he found unmistakable sign where the print of the bear's foot overlaid that of the man. This put the matter beyond doubt. The bear was following the man.

For a couple of hours more the hunter slowly and with difficulty followed the dim trail.

The bear had apparently not cared to close in, but had slouched along some distance behind the man. Then in a marshy thicket where a mountain stream came down, the end had come.

Evidently at this place the man, still unconscious that he was followed, had turned and gone upward, and the bear, altering his course to an oblique angle, had intercepted him, making his rush just as he came through a patch of low willows. The body of the man lay under the willow branches beside the brook, terribly torn and disfigured.

Evidently the bear had rushed at him so quickly that he could not fire his gun, and had killed him with its powerful jaws. The unfortunate man's body was almost torn to pieces. The killing had evidently been done purely for malice, for the remains were uneaten, nor had the bear returned to them.

Angry and horrified at his friend's fate, old Buckskin spent the next two days in looking carefully through the neighboring groves for fresh tracks of the cunning and savage monster. At last he found an open spot of ground where the brute was evidently fond of sunning himself in the early morning, and to this spot the hunter returned before dawn the following day.

He did not have long to wait. By sunrise a slight crackling of the thick undergrowth told him that the bear was approaching. A few minutes afterward the brute appeared. It was a large beast with a poor coat, its head scarred by teeth and claw marks gained in many a combat with others of its own kind.

It came boldly into the opening and lay down, but for some time kept turning its head from side to side so that no shot could be obtained.

At last, growing impatient, the hunter broke a stick. Instantly the bear swung his head around sidewise, and in another moment a bullet crashed into its skull at the base of the ear, and the huge body fell limply over on its side, lifeless.

CHAPTER 2

THE GAME OF THE HIGH PEAKS: THE WHITE GOAT

By Theodore Roosevelt

In the fall of 1886 I went far west to the Rockies and took a fortnight's hunting trip among the northern spurs of the Cœur d'Alêne, between the towns of Heron and Horseplains in Montana. There are many kinds of game to be found in the least known or still untrodden parts of this wooded mountain wilderness—caribou, elk, ungainly moose with great shovel horns, cougars, and bears. But I did not have time to go deeply into the heart of the forest-clad ranges, and devoted my entire energies to the chase of but one animal, the white antelope-goat, then the least known and rarest of all American game.

We started from one of those most dismal and forlorn of all places, a dead mining town, on the line of the Northern Pacific Railroad. My foreman,

Merrifield, was with me, and for guide I took a tall, lithe, happy-go-lucky mountaineer, who, like so many of the restless frontier race, was born in Missouri. Our outfit was simple, as we carried only blankets, a light wagon sheet, the ever-present camera, flour, bacon, salt, sugar, and coffee: canned goods are very unhandy to pack about on horseback. Our rifles and ammunition, with the few cooking-utensils and a book or two, completed the list. Four solemn ponies and a ridiculous little mule named Walla Walla bore us and our belongings. The Missourian was an expert packer, versed in the mysteries of the "diamond hitch," the only arrangement of the ropes that will insure a load staying in its place. Driving a pack train through the wooded paths and up the mountain passes that we had to traverse is hard work anyhow, as there are sure to be accidents happening to the animals all the time, while their packs receive rough treatment from jutting rocks and overhanging branches, or from the half-fallen tree-trunks under which the animals wriggle; and if the loads are continually coming loose, or slipping so as to gall the horses' backs and make them sore, the labor and anxiety are increased tenfold.

In a day or two we were in the heart of the vast wooded wilderness. A broad, lonely river ran through its midst, cleaving asunder the mountain chains. Range after range, peak upon peak, the mountains towered on every side, the lower timbered to the top, the higher with bare crests of gray crags, or else hooded with fields of shining snow. The deep valleys lay half in darkness, hemmed in by steep, timbered slopes and straight rock walls. The torrents, broken into glittering foam masses, sprang down through the chasms that they had rent in the sides of the high hills, lingered in black pools under the shadows of the scarred cliffs, and reaching the rank, tree-choked valleys, gathered into rapid streams of clear brown water, that drenched the drooping limbs of the tangled alders. Over the whole land lay like a shroud the mighty growth of the unbroken evergreen forest—spruce and hemlock, fir, balsam, tamarack, and lofty pine.

Yet even these vast wastes of shadowy woodland were once penetrated by members of that adventurous and now fast vanishing folk, the American frontiersmen. Once or twice, while walking silently over the spongy moss

beneath the somber archways of the pines, we saw on a tree-trunk a dim, faint ax-scar, the bark almost grown over it, showing where, many years before, some fur-trapper had chopped a deeper blaze than usual in making out a "spotted line"—man's first highway in the primeval forest; or on some hill-side we would come to the more recent, but already half-obliterated, trac-es of a miner's handiwork. The trapper and the miner were the pioneers of the mountains, as the hunter and the cowboy have been the pioneers of the plains: they are all of the same type, these sinewy men of the border, fearless and self-reliant, who are ever driven restlessly onward through the wilderness by the half-formed desires that make their eyes haggard and eager. There is no plain so lonely that their feet have not trodden it; no mountain so far off that their eyes have not scanned its grandeur.

We took nearly a week in going to our hunting-grounds and out from them again. This was tedious work, for the pace was slow, and it was accom-panied with some real labor. In places the mountain paths were very steep and the ponies could with difficulty scramble along them; and once or twice they got falls that no animals less tough could have survived. Walla Walla being the unfortunate that suffered most. Often, moreover, we would come to a windfall, where the fallen trees lay heaped crosswise on one another in the wildest confusion, and a road had to be cleared by ax work. It was marvelous to see the philosophy with which the wise little beasts behaved, picking their way gingerly through these rough spots, hopping over fallen tree-trunks, or stepping between them in places where an Eastern horse would have snapped a leg short off, and walking composedly along narrow ledges with steep precipices below. They were tame and friendly, being turned loose at night, and not only staying near by, but also allowing themselves to be caught without difficulty in the morning; industriously gleaning the scant food to be found in the burnt places or along the edges of the brooks, and often in the evening standing in a patient, solemn semicircle round the camp fire, just beyond where we were seated. Walla Walla, the little mule, was always in scrapes. Once we spent a morning of awkward industry in washing our clothes; having finished, we spread the half-cleansed array upon the bushes and departed on a hunt. On returning, to our horror we spied the miserable Walla Walla shamefacedly shambling off from the neighborhood of the wash, having partly chewed up every individual garment and completely undone all our morning's labor.

At first we did not have good weather. The Indians, of whom we met small band—said to be Flatheads or their kin, on a visit from the coast region—had set fire to the woods not far away, and the smoke became so dense as to hurt our eyes, to hide the sun at midday, and to veil all objects from our sight as completely as if there had been a heavy fog. Then we had two days of incessant rain, which rendered our camp none too comfortable; but when it cleared we found that it had put out the fire and settled all the smoke, leaving a brilliant sky overhead.

We first camped in a narrow valley, surrounded by mountains so tall that except at noonday it lay in the shadow; and it was only when we were out late on the higher foot-hills that we saw the sun sink in a flame behind the distant ranges. The trees grew tall and thick, the underbrush choking the ground between their trunks, and their branches interlacing so that the sun's rays hardly came through them. There were very few open glades, and these were not more than a dozen rods or so across. Even on the mountains it was only when we got up very high indeed, or when we struck an occasional bare spur, or shoulder, that we could get a glimpse into the open. Elsewhere we could never see a hundred yards ahead of us, and like all plainsmen or mountaineers we at times felt smothered under the trees, and longed to be where we could look out far and wide on every side; we felt as if our heads were in hoods. A broad brook whirled and eddied past our camp, and a little below us was caught in a deep, narrow gorge, where the strangling rocks churned its swift current into spray and foam, and changed its murmurous humming and splashing into an angry roar. Strange little water wrens—the water-ousel of the books—made this brook their home. They were shaped like thrushes, and sometimes warbled sweetly, yet they lived right in the torrent, not only flitting along the banks and wading in the edges, but plunging boldly into midstream, and half walking, half flying along the bottom, deep under water, and perching on the slippery, spray-covered rocks of the waterfall or skimming over and through the rapids even more often than they ran along the margins of the deep, black pools.

White-tail deer were plentiful, and we kept our camp abundantly supplied with venison, varying it with all the grouse that we wanted, and with quantities of fresh trout. But I myself spent most of my time after the quarry I had come to get—the white goat.

White goats have been known to hunters ever since Lewis and Clarke crossed the continent, but they have always ranked as the very rarest and most difficult to get of all American game. This reputation they owe to the nature of their haunts, rather than to their own wariness, for they have been so little disturbed that they are less shy than either deer or sheep. They are found here and there on the highest, most inaccessible mountain peaks down even to Arizona and New Mexico; but being fitted for cold climates, they are extremely scarce everywhere south of Montana and northern Idaho, and the great majority even of the most experienced hunters have hardly so much as heard of their existence. In Washington Territory, northern Idaho, and north-western Montana they are not uncommon, and are plentiful in parts of the mountain ranges of British America and Alaska. Their preference for the highest peaks is due mainly to their dislike of warmth, and in the north—even south of the Canadian line—they are found much lower down the mountains than is the case farther south. They are very conspicuous animals, with their snow-white coats and polished black horns, but their pursuit necessitates so much toil and hardship that not one in ten of the professional hunters has ever killed one; and I know of but one or two Eastern sportsmen who can boast a goat's head as a trophy. But this will soon cease to be the case: for the Canadian Pacific Railway has opened the haunts where the goats are most plentiful, and any moderately adventurous and hardy rifleman can be sure of getting one by taking a little time, and that, too, whether he is a skilled hunter or not, since at present the game is not difficult to approach. The white goat will be common long after the elk has vanished, and it has already outlasted the buffalo. Few sportsmen henceforth—indeed, hardly any—will ever boast a buffalo head of their own killing: but the number of riflemen who can place to their credit the prized white fleeces and jet-black horns will steadily increase.

The Missourian, during his career as a Rocky Mountain hunter, had killed five white goats. The first he had shot near Canyon City, Colorado, and never having heard of any such animal before had concluded afterward that it was one of a flock of recently imported Angora goats, and accordingly, to avoid trouble, buried it where it lay: and it was not until fourteen years later, when he came up to the Cœur d'Alêne and shot another, that he became aware of what he had killed. He described them as being bold, pugnacious animals, not easily startled, and extremely tenacious of life. Once he had set a large hound at one which he came across while descending an ice-swollen river in early spring. The goat made no attempt to flee or to avoid the hound, but coolly awaited its approach and killed it with one wicked thrust of the horns; for the latter are as sharp as needles, and are used for stabbing, not butting. Another time he caught a goat in a bear trap set on a game trail. Its leg was broken, and he had to pack it out on pony-back, a two-days journey, to the settlement; yet in spite of such rough treatment it lived a week after it got there, when, unfortunately, the wounded leg mortified. It fought most determinedly, but soon became reconciled to captivity, eating with avidity all the grass it was given, recognizing its keeper, and grunting whenever be brought it food or started to walk away before it had had all it wished. The goats he had shot lived in ground where the walking was tiresome to the last degree, and where it was almost impossible not to make a good deal of noise: and nothing but their boldness and curiosity enabled him ever to kill any. One he shot while waiting at a pass for deer. The goat, an old male, came up, and fairly refused to leave the spot, walking round in the underbrush and finally mounting a great fallen log, where he staid snorting and stamping angrily until the Missourian lost patience and killed him.

For three or four days I hunted steadily and without success, and it was as hard work as any that I had ever undertaken. Both Merrifield and I were accustomed to a life in the saddle, and although we had varied it with an occasional long walk after deer or sheep, yet we were utterly unable to cope with the Missourian when it came to mountaineering. When we had previously hunted, in the Big Horn Mountains, we had found stout moccasins most comfortable, and extremely useful for still-hunting through the great woods and among the open glades; but the multitudinous sharp rocks and sheer, cliff-like slopes of the Cœur d'Alêne rendered our moccasins absolutely useless, for the first day's tramp bruised our feet till they were sore and slit our foot-gear into ribbons, besides tearing our clothes. Merrifield was then crippled, having nothing else but his cowboy boots; fortunately, I had taken in addition a pair of shoes with soles thickly studded with nails.

We would start immediately after breakfast each morning, carrying a light lunch in our pockets, and go straight up the mountain sides for hours at a time, varying it by skirting the broad, terrace-like ledges, or by clambering along the cliff crests. The climbing was very hard. The slope was so steep that it was like going up stairs; now through loose earth, then through a shingle of pebbles or sand, then over rough rocks, and again over a layer of pine needles as smooth and slippery as glass, while brittle, dry sticks that snapped at a touch, and loose stones that rattled down if so much as brushed, strewed the ground everywhere, the climber stumbling and falling over them and finding it almost absolutely impossible to proceed without noise, unless at a rate of progress too slow to admit of getting anywhere. Often, too, we would encounter dense underbrush, perhaps a thicket of little burnt balsams, as prickly and brittle as so much coral; or else a heavy growth of laurel, all the branches pointing downward, and to be gotten through only by main force. Over all grew the vast evergreen forest, except where an occasional cliff jutted out, or where there were great land-slides, each perhaps half a mile long and a couple of hundred yards across, covered with loose slates or granite bowlders.

We always went above the domain of the deer, and indeed saw few evidences of life. Once or twice we came to the round foot-prints of cougars, which are said to be great enemies of the goats, but we never caught a glimpse of the sly beasts themselves. Another time I shot a sable from a spruce, up which the little fox-headed animal had rushed with the agility of a squirrel. There were plenty of old tracks of bear and elk, but no new ones; and occasionally we saw the foot-marks of the great timber wolf.

But the trails at which we looked with the most absorbed interest were those that showed the large, round hoof-marks of the white goats. They had worn deep paths to certain clay licks in the slides, which they must have visited often in the early spring, for the trails were little traveled when we were in the mountains during September. These clay licks were mere holes in the banks, and were in spring-time visited by other animals besides goats; there were old deer trails to them. The clay seemed to contain something that both birds and beasts were fond of, for I frequently saw flocks of cross-bills light in the licks and stay there for many minutes at a time, scratching the smooth surface with their little claws and bills. The goat trails led away in every direction from the licks, but usually went up-hill, zigzagging or in a straight line, and continually growing fainter as they went farther off, where the animals scattered to their feeding-grounds. In the spring-time the goats are clad with a dense coat of long white wool, and there were shreds and tufts of this on all the twigs of the bushes under which the paths passed; in the early fall the coat is shorter and less handsome.

Although these game paths were so deeply worn, they yet showed very little fresh goat sign; in fact, we came across the recent trails of but two of the animals we were after. One of these we came quite close to, but never saw it, for we must have frightened it by the noise we made; it certainly, to judge by its tracks, which we followed for a long time, took itself straight out of the country. The other I finally got, after some heart-breaking work and a complicated series of faults committed and misfortunes endured.

I had been, as usual, walking and clambering over the mountains all day long, and in mid-afternoon reached a great slide, with half-way across it a tree. Under this I sat down to rest, my back to the trunk, and had been there but a few minutes when my companion, the Missourian, suddenly whispered to me that a goat was coming down the slide at its edge, near the woods. I was in a most uncomfortable position for a shot. Twisting my head round, I could see the goat waddling down-hill, looking just like a handsome tame billy, especially when at times he stood upon a stone to glance around, with all four feet close together. I cautiously tried to shift my position, and at once dislodged some pebbles, at the sound of which the goat sprang promptly up on the bank, his whole mien changing into one of alert, alarmed curiosity. He was less than a hundred yards off, so I risked a shot, all cramped and twisted though I was. But my bullet went low; I only broke his left fore-leg, and he disappeared over the bank like a flash. We raced and scrambled after him, and the Missourian, an excellent tracker, took up the bloody trail. It went along the hill-side for nearly a mile, and then turned straight up the mountain, the Missourian leading with his long, free gait, while I toiled after him at a dogged trot. The trail went up the sharpest and steepest places, skirting the cliffs and precipices. At one spot I nearly came to grief for good and all, for in running along a shelving ledge, covered with loose slates, one of these slipped as I stepped on it, throwing me clear over the brink. However, I caught in a pine top, bounced down through it, and brought up in a balsam with my rifle all right, and myself unhurt except for the shaking. I scrambled up at once and raced on after my companion, whose limbs and wind seemed alike incapable of giving out. This work lasted for a couple of hours.

The trail came into a regular game path and grew fresher, the goat having stopped to roll and wallow in the dust now and then. Suddenly, on the top of the mountain, we came upon him close up to us. He had just risen from rolling and stood behind a huge fallen log, his back barely showing above it as he turned his head to look at us. I was completely winded, and had lost my strength as well as my breath, while great bead-like drops of sweat stood in my eyes; but I steadied myself as well as I could and aimed to break the backbone, the only shot open to me, and not a difficult one at such a short distance. However, my bullet went just too high, cutting the skin above the long spinal bones over the shoulders; and the speed with which that three-legged goat went down the precipitous side of the mountain would have done credit to an antelope on the level.

Weary and disgusted, we again took up the trail. It led straight down-hill, and we followed it at a smart pace. Down and down it went, into the valley and straight to the edge of the stream, but half a mile above camp. The goat had crossed the water on a fallen tree-trunk, and we took the same path. Once across, it had again gone right up the mountain. We followed it as fast as we could, although pretty nearly done out, until it was too dark to see the blood stains any longer, and then returned to camp, dispirited and so tired that we could hardly drag ourselves along, for we had been going to speed for five hours, up and down the roughest and steepest ground.

But we were confident that the goat would not travel far with such a wound after he had been chased as we had chased him. Next morning at daybreak we again climbed the mountain and took up the trail. Soon it led into others and we lost it, but we kept up the hunt nevertheless for hour after hour, making continually wider and wider circles. At last, about midday, our perseverance was rewarded, for coming silently out on a great bare cliff shoulder, I spied the goat lying on a ledge below me and some seventy yards off. This time I shot true, and he rose only to fall back dead; and a minute afterward we were standing over him, handling the glossy black horns and admiring the snow-white coat.

After this we struck our tent and shifted camp some thirty miles to a wide valley through whose pine-clad bottom flowed a river, hurrying on to the Pacific between unending forests. On one hand the valley was hemmed in by an unbroken line of frowning cliffs, and on the other by chains of lofty mountains in whose sides the ravines cut deep gashes.

The clear weather had grown colder. At night the frost skimmed with thin ice the edges of the ponds and small lakes that at long intervals dotted the vast reaches of woodland. But we were very comfortable, and hardly needed our furs, for as evening fell we kindled huge fires, to give us both light and warmth; and even in very cold weather a man can sleep out comfortably enough with no bedding if he lights two fires and gets in between them, or finds a sheltered nook or corner across the front of which a single great blaze can be made. The long walks and our work as cragsmen hardened our thews, and made us eat and sleep as even our life on the ranch could hardly do: the mountaineer must always be more sinewy than the horseman. The clear, cold water of the swift streams too was a welcome change from the tepid and muddy currents of the rivers of the plains; and we heartily enjoyed the baths, a plunge into one of the icy pools making us gasp for breath and causing the blood to tingle in our veins with the shock.

Our tent was pitched in a little glade, which was but a few yards across, and carpeted thickly with the red kinnikinic berries, in their season beloved of bears, and from the leaves of which bush the Indians make a substitute for tobacco. Little three-toed woodpeckers with yellow crests scrambled about over the trees near by, while the great log-cocks hammered and rattled on the tall dead trunks. Jays that were dark blue all over came familiarly round camp in company with the ever-present moose-birds or whisky jacks. There were many grouse in the woods, of three kinds—blue, spruce,

and ruffed—and these varied our diet and also furnished us with some sport with our rifles, as we always shot them in rivalry. That is, each would take a shot in turn, aiming at the head of the bird, as it perched motionless on the limb of a tree or stopped for a second while running along the ground; then if he missed or hit the bird anywhere but in the head, the other scored one and took the shot. The resulting tally was a good test of comparative skill; and rivalry always tends to keep a man's shooting up to the mark.

Once or twice, when we had slain deer, we watched by the carcasses, hoping that they would attract a bear, or perhaps one of the huge timber wolves whose mournful, sinister howling we heard each night. But there were no bears in the valley; and the wolves, those cruel, crafty beasts, were far too cunning to come to the bait while we were there. We saw nothing but crowds of ravens, whose hoarse barking and croaking filled the air as they circled around overhead, lighted in the trees, or quarreled over the carcass. Yet although we saw no game it was very pleasant to sit out, on the still evenings, among the tall pines or on the edge of a great gorge, until the afterglow of the sunset was dispelled by the beams of the frosty moon. Now and again the hush would be suddenly broken by the long howling of a wolf, that echoed and rang under the hollow woods and through the deep chasms until they resounded again, while it made our hearts bound and the blood leap in our veins. Then there would be silence once more, broken only by the rush of the river and the low moaning and creaking of the pines; or the strange calling of the owls might be answered by the far-off, unearthly laughter of a loon, its voice carried through the stillness a marvelous distance from the little lake on which it was swimming.

One day, after much toilsome and in places almost dangerous work, we climbed to the very top of the nearest mountain chain, and from it looked out over a limitless, billowy field of snow-capped ranges. Up above the timber line were snow-grouse and huge, hoary-white woodchucks, but no trace of the game we were after; for, rather to our surprise, the few goat signs that we saw were in the timber. I did not catch another glimpse of the animals themselves until my holiday was almost over and we were preparing to break camp. Then I saw two. I had spent a most laborious day on the mountain as usual, following the goat paths, which were well-trodden trails leading up the most inaccessible places; certainly the white goats are marvelous climbers, doing it all by main strength and perfect command over their muscles, for they are heavy, clumsy seeming animals, the reverse of graceful, and utterly without any look of light agility. As usual, towards evening I was pretty well tired out, for it would be difficult to imagine harder work than to clamber unendingly up and down the huge cliffs. I came down along a great jutting spur, broken by a series of precipices, with flat terraces at their feet, the terraces being covered with trees and bushes, and running, with many breaks and interruptions, parallel to each other across the face of the mountains. On one of these terraces was a space of hard clay ground beaten perfectly bare of vegetation by the hoofs of the goats, and, in the middle, a hole, two or three feet in width, that was evidently in the spring used as a lick. Most of the tracks were old, but there was one trail coming diagonally down the side of the mountain on which there were two or three that were very fresh. It was getting late, so I did not stay long, but continued the descent. The terrace on which the lick was situated lay but a few hundred yards above the valley, and then came a level, marshy plain a quarter of a mile broad, between the base of the mountain and the woods. Leading down to this plain was another old goat-trail, which went to a small, boggy pool, which the goats must certainly have often visited in the spring; but it was then unused.

When I reached the farther side of the plain and was about entering the woods, I turned to look over the mountain once more, and my eye was immediately caught by two white objects which were moving along the terrace, about half a mile to one side of the lick. That they were goats was evident at a glance, their white bodies contrasting sharply with the green vegetation. They came along very rapidly, giving me no time to get back over the plain, and stopped for a short time at the lick, right in sight from where I was, although too far off for me to tell anything about their size. I think they smelt my footprints in the soil; at any rate they were very watchful, one of them always jumping up on a rock or fallen log to mount guard when the other halted to browse. The sun had just set; it was impossible to advance

The Rocky Mountains

across the open plain, which they scanned at every glance; and to skirt it and climb up any other place than the pass down which I had come—itself a goat-trail—would have taken till long after nightfall. All that I could do was to stay where I was and watch them, until in the dark I slipped off unobserved and made the best of my way to camp, resolved to hunt them up on the morrow.

Shortly after noon next day we were at the terrace, having approached with the greatest caution, and only after a minute examination, with the field-glasses, of all the neighboring mountain. I wore moccasins, so as to make no noise. We soon found that one of the trails was evidently regularly traveled, probably every evening, and we determined to lie in wait by it, so as either to catch the animals as they came down to feed, or else to mark them if they got out on some open spot on the terraces where they could be stalked. As an ambush we chose a ledge in the cliff below a terrace, with, in front, a breastwork of the natural rock some five feet high. It was perhaps fifty yards from the trail. I hid myself on this ledge, having arranged on the rock breast-work a few pine branches through which to fire, and waited, hour after hour, continually scanning the mountain carefully with the glasses. There was very little life. Occasionally a chickaree or chipmunk scurried out from among the trunks of the great pines to pick up the cones which he had previously bitten off from the upper branches; a noisy Clarke's crow clung for some time in the top of a hemlock; and occasionally flocks of cross-bill went by, with swift undulating flight and low calls. From time to time I peeped cau-tiously over the pine branches on the breastwork; and the last time I did this I suddenly saw two goats, that had come noiselessly down, standing motion-less directly opposite to me, their suspicions evidently aroused by something. I gently shoved the rifle over one of the boughs; the largest goat turned its head sharply round to look, as it stood quartering to me, and the bullet went fairly through the lungs. Both animals promptly ran off along the terrace, and I raced after them in my moccasins, skirting the edge of the cliff, where there were no trees or bushes. As I made no noise and could run very swiftly on the bare cliff edge, I succeeded in coming out into the first little glade, or break, in the terrace at the same time that the goats did. The first to come out of the bushes was the big one I had shot at, an old she, as it turned out; while the other, a yearling ram, followed. The big one turned to look at me as she mounted a fallen tree that lay across a chasm-like rent in the terrace; the light red frothy blood covered her muzzle, and I paid no further heed to her as she slowly walked along the log, but bent my attention towards the yearling, which was galloping and scrambling up an almost perpendicular path that led across the face of the cliff above. Holding my rifle just over it, I fired, breaking the neck of the goat, and it rolled down some fifty or sixty yards, almost to where I stood. I then went after the old goat, which had lain down; as I approached she feebly tried to rise and show fight, but her strength was spent, her blood had ebbed away, and she fell back lifeless in the effort. They were both good specimens, the old one being unusually large, with fine horns. White goats are squat, heavy beasts; not so tall as black-tail deer, but weighing more.

Early next morning I came back with my two men to where the goats were lying, taking along the camera. Having taken their photographs and skinned them we went back to camp, hunted up the ponies and mules, who had been shifting for themselves during the past few days, packed up our tent, trophies, and other belongings, and set off for the settlements, well pleased with our trip.

All mountain game yields noble sport, because of the nerve, daring, and physical hardihood implied in its successful pursuit. The chase of the white goat involves extraordinary toil and some slight danger on account of the extreme roughness and inaccessibility of its haunts; but the beast itself is less shy than the mountain sheep. How the chase of either compares in difficulty with that of the various Old World mountain game it would be hard to say. Men who have tried both say that, though there is not in Europe the chance to try the adventurous, wandering life of the wilderness so beloved by the American hunter, yet when it comes to comparing the actual chase of the game of the two worlds, it needs greater skill, both as cragsman and still-hunter, to kill ibex and chamois in the Alps or Pyrenees—by fair stalking I mean; for if they are driven to the guns, as is sometimes done, the sport is of a very inferior kind, not rising above the methods of killing white-tail in the Eastern States, or of driving deer in Scotland. I myself have had no experience of Old World mountaineering, beyond two perfectly conventional trips up the Matterhorn and Jungfrau—on the latter, by the way, I saw three chamois a long way off.

My brother has done a good deal of ibex, mountain sheep, and mark hoor shooting in Cashmere and Thibet, and I suppose the sport to be had among the tremendous mountain masses of the Himalayas must stand above all other kinds of hill shooting; yet, after all, it is hard to believe that it can yield much more pleasure than that felt by the American hunter when he follows the lordly elk and the grizzly among the timbered slopes of the Rockies, or the big-horn and the white-fleeced, jet-horned antelope-goat over their towering and barren peaks.

CHAPTER 3

ELEPHANT HUNTING ON MOUNT KENIA

By Theodore Roosevelt

Theodore Roosevelt with bull elephant. Photo courtesy of the
Library of Congress

On July 24th, in order to ship our fresh accumulations of specimens
and trophies, we once more went into Nairobi. It was a pleasure
again to see its tree-bordered streets and charming houses bowered
in vines and bushes, and to meet once more the men and women who dwelt
in the houses. I wish it were in my power to thank individually the members
of the many East African households of which I shall always cherish warm
memories of friendship and regard.

At Nairobi I saw Selous, who had just returned from a two months'
safari with McMillan, Williams, and Judd. Their experience shows how large
the element of luck is in lion hunting. Selous was particularly anxious to kill
a good lion; there is nowhere to be found a more skilful or more hardwork-
ing hunter; yet he never even got a shot. Williams, on the other hand, came
across three. Two he killed easily. The third charged him. He was carrying a
double-barrelled .450, but failed to stop the beast; it seized him by the leg,
and his life was saved by his Swahili gun-bearer, who gave the lion a fatal shot
as it stood over him. He came within an ace of dying; but when I saw him,
at the hospital, he was well on the road to recovery. One day Selous while
on horseback saw a couple of lionesses, and galloped after them, followed
by Judd, seventy or eighty yards behind. One lioness stopped and crouched
under a bush, let Selous pass, and then charged Judd. She was right alongside
him, and he fired from the hip; the bullet went into her eye; his horse jumped
and swerved at the shot, throwing him off, and he found himself sitting on
the ground, not three yards from the dead lioness. Nothing more was seen of
the other.

Continually I met men with experiences in their past lives which showed
how close the country was to those primitive conditions in which warfare
with wild beasts was one of the main features of man's existence. At one dinner my host and two of my fellow-guests had been within a year or eighteen
months severely mauled by lions. All three, by the way, informed me that the
actual biting caused them at the moment no pain whatever; the pain came
later. On meeting Harold Hill, my companion on one of my Kapiti Plains
lion hunts, I found that since I had seen him he had been roughly handled
by a dying leopard. The government had just been obliged to close one of the
trade routes to native caravans because of the ravages of a man-eating lion,
which carried men away from the camps. A safari which had come in from
the north had been charged by a rhino, and one of the porters tossed and
killed, the horn being driven clear through his loins. At Heatley's farm three
buffalo (belonging to the same herd from which we had shot five) rushed
out of the papyrus one afternoon at a passing buggy, which just managed to

escape by a breakneck run across the level plain, the beasts chasing it for a mile. One afternoon, at Government House, I met a government official who had once succeeded in driving into a corral seventy zebras, including more stallions than mares; their misfortune in no way abated their savagery toward one another, and as the limited space forbade the escape of the weaker, the stallions fought to the death with teeth and hoofs during the first night, and no less than twenty were killed outright or died of their wounds.

Most of the time in Nairobi we were the guests of ever-hospitable Mc-Millan, in his low, cool house, with its broad, vine-shaded veranda, running around all four sides, and its garden, fragrant and brilliant with innumerable flowers. Birds abounded, singing beautifully; the bulbuls were the most noticeable singers, but there were many others. The dark ant-eating chats haunted the dusky roads on the outskirts of the town, and were interesting birds; they were usually found in parties, flirted their tails up and down as they sat on bushes or roofs or wire, sang freely in chorus until after dusk, and then retired to holes in the ground for the night. A tiny owl with a queer little voice called continually not only after nightfall, but in the bright afternoons. Shrikes spitted insects on the spines of the imported cactus in the gardens.

It was race week, and the races, in some of which Kermit rode, were capital fun. The white people—army officers, government officials, farmers from the country roundabout, and their wives—rode to the races on ponies or even on camels, or drove up in rickshaws, in gharries, in bullock tongas, occasionally in automobiles, most often in two-wheel carts or rickety hacks drawn by mules and driven by a turbaned Indian or a native in a cotton shirt. There were Parsees, and Goanese dressed just like the Europeans. There were many other Indians, their picturesque womenkind gaudy in crimson, blue, and saffron. The constabulary, Indian and native, were in neat uniforms and well set up, though often barefooted. Straight, slender Somalis with clear-cut features were in attendance on the horses. Native negroes, of many different tribes, flocked to the race-course and its neighborhood. The Swahilis, and those among the others who aspired toward civilization, were well clad, the men in half European costume, the women in flowing, parti-colored robes. But most of them were clad, or unclad, just as they always had been. Wakamba, with filed teeth, crouched in circles on the ground. Kikuyu passed, the men each with a blanket hung round the shoulders, and girdles of chains, and armlets and anklets of solid metal; the older women bent under burdens they carried on the back, half of them in addition with babies slung somewhere round them, while now and then an unmarried girl would have her face painted with ochre and vermilion. A small party of Masai warriors kept close together, each clutching his shining, long-bladed war spear, their hair daubed red and twisted into strings. A large band of Kavirondo, stark naked, with shield and spear and head-dress of nodding plumes, held a dance near the race-track. As for the races themselves, they were carried on in the most sporting spirit, and only the Australian poet Patterson could adequately write of them.

On August 4th I returned to Lake Naivasha, stopping on the way at Kijabe to lay the corner-stone of the new mission building. Mearns and Loring had stayed at Naivasha and had collected many birds and small mammals. That night they took me out on a springhaas hunt. Thanks to Kermit we had discovered that the way to get this curious and purely nocturnal animal was by "shining" it with a lantern at night, just as in our own country deer, coons, owls, and other creatures can be killed. Springhaas live in big burrows, a number of them dwelling together in one community, the holes close to one another, and making what in the West we would call a "town" in speaking of prairie dogs. At night they come out to feed on the grass. They are as heavy as a big jack-rabbit, with short forelegs, and long hind legs and tail, so that they look and on occasion move like miniature kangaroos, although in addition to making long hops or jumps, they often run almost like an ordinary rat or rabbit. They are pretty creatures, fawn-colored above, and white beneath, with the terminal half of the tail very dark. In hunting them we simply walked over the flats for a couple of hours, flashing the bull's eye lantern on all sides, until we saw the light reflected back by a springhaas's eyes. Then I would approach to within range, and hold the lantern in my left hand so as to shine both on the sight and on the eyes in front, resting my gun on my left wrist. The number 3 shot, in the Fox double-barrel, would always do the business, if I

Lake Naivasha

held straight enough. There was nothing but the gleam of the eyes to shoot at; and this might suddenly be raised or lowered as the intently watching animal crouched on all-fours or raised itself on its hind legs. I shot half a dozen, all that the naturalists wanted. Then I tried to shoot a fox; but the moon had risen from behind a cloud bank; I had to take a long shot and missed; but my companions killed several, and found that they were a new species of the peculiar African long-eared fox.

While waiting for the safari to get ready, Kermit went off on a camping trip and shot two bushbuck, while I spent a couple of days trying for singing waterbuck on the edge of the papyrus. I missed a bull, and wounded another which I did not get. This was all the more exasperating because interspersed with the misses were some good shots: I killed a fine waterbuck cow at a hundred yards, and a buck tommy for the table at two hundred and fifty; and, after missing a handsome black and white, red-billed and red-legged jabiru, or saddle-billed stork, at a hundred and fifty yards, as he stalked through the meadow after frogs, I cut him down on the wing at a hundred and eighty, with the little Springfield rifle. The waterbuck spent the daytime outside, but near the edge of, the papyrus; I found them grazing or resting, in the open, at all times between early morning and late afternoon. Some of them spent most of the day in the papyrus, keeping to the watery trails made by the hippos and by themselves; but this was not the general habit, unless they had been persecuted. When frightened they often ran into the papyrus, smashing the dead reeds and splashing the water in their rush. They are noble-looking antelope, with long, shaggy hair, and their chosen haunts beside the lake were very attractive. Clumps of thorn-trees and flowering bushes grew at the edge of the tall papyrus here and there, and often formed a matted jungle, the trees laced together by creepers, many of them brilliant in their bloom. The climbing morning-glories sometimes completely covered a tree with their pale-purple flowers; and other blossoming vines spangled the green over which their sprays were flung with masses of bright yellow.

Four days' march from Naivasha, where we again left Mearns and Loring, took us to Neri. Our line of march lay across the high plateaus and mountain chains of the Aberdare range. The steep, twisting trail was slippery with mud. Our last camp, at an altitude of about ten thousand feet, was so cold that the water froze in the basins and the shivering porters slept in numbed discomfort. There was constant fog and rain, and on the highest plateau the bleak landscape, shrouded in driving mist, was northern to all the senses. The ground was rolling, and through the deep valleys ran brawling brooks of clear water; one little foaming stream, suddenly tearing down a hill-side, might have been that which Childe Roland crossed before he came to the dark tower.

There was not much game, and it generally moved abroad by night. One frosty evening we killed a duiker by shining its eyes. We saw old elephant tracks. The high, wet levels swarmed with mice and shrews, just as our arctic and alpine meadows swarm with them. The species were really widely different from ours, but many of them showed curious analogies in form and habits; there was a short-tailed shrew much like our mole shrew, and a longhaired, short-tailed rat like a very big meadow mouse. They were so plentiful that we frequently saw them, and the grass was cut up by their runways. They were abroad during the day, probably finding the nights too cold, and in an hour Heller trapped a dozen or two individuals belonging to seven species and five different genera. There were not many birds so high up. There were deer ferns; and Spanish moss hung from the trees and even from the bamboos. The flowers included utterly strange forms, as for instance giant lobelias ten feet high. Others we know in our gardens: geraniums and red-hot-pokers, which in places turned the glades to a fire color. Yet others either were like, or looked like, our own wild flowers: orange lady-slippers, red gladiolas on stalks six feet high, pansy-like violets, and blackberries and yellow raspberries. There were stretches of bushes bearing masses of small red or large white flowers shaped somewhat like columbines, or like the garden balsam; the red flower bushes were under the bamboos, the white at lower level. The crests and upper slopes of the mountains were clothed in the green uniformity of the bamboo forest, the trail winding dim under its dark archway of tall, close-growing stems. Lower down were junipers and yews, and then many other trees, with among them tree ferns and strange dragon trees with lily-like frondage. Zone succeeded zone from top to bottom, each marked by a different plant life.

In this part of Africa, where flowers bloom and birds sing all the year round, there is no such burst of bloom and song as in the northern spring and early summer. There is nothing like the mass of blossoms which carpet the meadows of the high mountain valleys and far northern meadows, during their brief high tide of life, when one short joyous burst of teeming and vital beauty atones for the long death of the iron fall and winter. So it is with the bird songs. Many of them are beautiful, though to my ears none quite as beautiful as the best of our own bird songs. At any rate there is nothing that quite corresponds to the chorus that during May and June moves northward from the Gulf States and southern California to Maine, Minnesota, and Oregon, to Ontario and Saskatchewan; when there comes the great vernal burst of bloom and song; when the mayflower, bloodroot, wake-robin, anemone, adder's tongue, liverwort, shadblow, dogwood, and redbud gladden the woods; when mocking-birds and cardinals sing in the magnolia groves of the South, and hermit thrushes, winter wrens, and sweetheart sparrows in the spruce and hemlock forests of the North; when bobolinks in the East and meadowlarks East and West sing in the fields; and water ousels by the cold streams of the Rockies, and canyon wrens in their sheer gorges; when from the Atlantic seaboard to the Pacific wood thrushes, veeries, rufous-backed thrushes, robins, bluebirds, orioles, thrashers, cat-birds, house finches, song sparrows—some in the East, some in the West, some both East and West—and many, many other singers thrill the gardens at sunrise; until the long days begin to shorten, and tawny lilies burn by the roadside, and the indigo buntings trill from the tops of little trees throughout the hot afternoons.

We were in the Kikuyu country. On our march we met several parties of natives. I had been much inclined to pity the porters, who had but one blanket apiece; but when I saw the Kikuyus, each with nothing but a smaller blanket, and without the other clothing and the tents of the porters, I realized how much better off the latter were simply because they were on a white man's safari. At Neri boma we were greeted with the warmest hospitality by the District Commissioner, Mr. Browne. Among other things, he arranged a great Kikuyu dance in our honor. Two thousand warriors, and many women, came in; as well as a small party of Masai moran. The warriors were naked, or half-naked; some carried gaudy blankets, others girdles of leopard skin; their ox-hide shields were colored in bold patterns, their long-bladed spears quivered and gleamed. Their faces and legs were painted red and yellow; the faces of the young men who were about to undergo the rite of circumcision were stained a ghastly white, and their bodies fantastically painted. The warriors wore bead necklaces and waist belts and armlets of brass and steel, and spurred anklets of monkey skin. Some wore head-dresses made out of a lion's mane or from the long black and white fur of the Colobus monkey; others had plumes stuck in their red-daubed hair. They chanted in unison a deep-toned chorus, and danced rhythmically in rings, while the drums throbbed and the horns blared; and they danced by us in column, springing and chanting. The women shrilled applause, and danced in groups by themselves. The Masai circled and swung in a panther-like dance of their own, and the measure, and their own fierce singing and calling, maddened them until two of their number, their eyes staring, their faces working, went into fits of berserker frenzy, and were disarmed at once to prevent mischief. Some of the tribesmen held wilder dances still in the evening, by the light of fires that blazed in a grove where their thatched huts stood.

The second day after reaching Neri the clouds lifted and we dried our damp clothes and blankets. Through the bright sunlight we saw in front of us the high rock peaks of Kenia, and shining among them the fields of everlasting snow which feed her glaciers; for beautiful, lofty Kenia is one of the glacier-bearing mountains of the equator. Here Kermit and Tarlton went northward on a safari of their own, while Cuninghame, Heller, and I headed for Kenia itself. For two days we travelled through a well-peopled country. The fields of corn—always called mealies in Africa—of beans, and sweet potatoes, with occasional plantations of bananas, touched one another in almost uninterrupted succession. In most of them we saw the Kikuyu women at work with their native hoes; for among the Kikuyus, as among other savages, the woman is the drudge and beast of burden. Our trail led by clear, rushing streams, which formed the head-waters of the Tana; among the trees fringing their banks were graceful palms, and there were groves of tree ferns here and there on the sides of the gorges.

On the afternoon of the second day we struck upward among the steep foot-hills of the mountain, riven by deep ravines. We pitched camp in an open glade, surrounded by the green wall of tangled forest, the forest of the tropical mountain sides.

The trees, strange of kind and endless in variety, grew tall and close, laced together by vine and creeper, while underbrush crowded the space between their mossy trunks, and covered the leafy mould beneath. Toward dusk crested ibis flew overhead with harsh clamor, to seek their night roosts; parrots chattered, and a curiously home-like touch was given by the presence of a thrush in color and shape almost exactly like our robin. Monkeys called in the depths of the forest, and after dark tree-frogs piped and croaked, and the tree hyraxes uttered their wailing cries.

Elephants dwelt permanently in this mountainous region of heavy woodland. On our march thither we had already seen their traces in the "shambas," as the cultivated fields of the natives are termed; for the great beasts are fond of raiding the crops at night, and their inroads often do serious damage. In this neighborhood their habit is to live high up in the mountains, in the bamboos, while the weather is dry; the cow and calves keeping closer to the bamboos than the bulls. A spell of wet weather, such as we had fortunately been having, drives them down in the dense forest which covers the lower slopes. Here they may either pass all their time, or at night they may go still further down, into the open valley where the shambas lie; or they may occasionally still do what they habitually did in the days before the white hunter came, and wander far away, making migrations that are sometimes seasonal, and sometimes irregular and unaccountable.

No other animal, not the lion himself, is so constant a theme of talk, and a subject of such unflagging interest round the camp-fires of African hunters and in the native villages of the African wilderness, as the elephant. Indeed the elephant has always profoundly impressed the imagination of mankind. It is, not only to hunters, but to naturalists, and to all people who possess any curiosity about wild creatures and the wild life of nature, the most interesting of all animals. Its huge bulk, its singular form, the value of its ivory, its great intelligence—in which it is only matched, if at all, by the highest apes, and possibly

by one or two of the highest carnivores—and its varied habits, all combine to give it an interest such as attaches to no other living creature below the rank of man. In line of descent and in physical formation it stands by itself, wholly apart from all the other great land beasts, and differing from them even more widely than they differ from one another. The two existing species—the African, which is the larger and finer animal, and the Asiatic—differ from one another as much as they do from the mammoth and similar extinct forms which were the contemporaries of early man in Europe and North America. The carvings of our palaeolithic forefathers, etched on bone by cavern dwellers, from whom we are sundered by ages which stretch into an immemorial past, show that in their lives the hairy elephant of the north played the same part that his remote collateral descendant now plays in the lives of the savages who dwell under a vertical sun beside the tepid waters of the Nile and the Congo.

In the first dawn of history, the sculptured records of the kings of Egypt, Babylon, and Nineveh show the immense importance which attached in the eyes of the mightiest monarchs of the then world to the chase and the trophies of this great strange beast. The ancient civilization of India boasts as one of its achievements the taming of the elephant, and in the ancient lore of that civilization the elephant plays a distinguished part.

The elephant is unique among the beasts of great bulk in the fact that his growth in size has been accompanied by growth in brain power. With other beasts growth in bulk of body has not been accompanied by similar growth of mind. Indeed sometimes there seems to have been mental retrogression. The rhinoceros, in several different forms, is found in the same regions as the elephant, and in one of its forms it is in point of size second only to the elephant among terrestrial animals. Seemingly the ancestors of the two creatures, in that period, separated from us by uncounted hundreds of thousand of years, which we may conveniently designate as late miocene or early pliocene, were substantially equal in brain development. But in one case increase in bulk seems to have induced lethargy and atrophy of brain power, while in the other case brain and body have both grown. At any rate the elephant is now one of the wisest and the rhinoceros one of the stupidest of big mammals. In consequence the elephant outlasts the rhino, although he is the largest, carries infinitely more valuable spoils, and is far more eagerly and persistently hunted. Both animals wandered freely over the open country of East Africa thirty years ago. But the elephant learns by experience infinitely more readily than the rhinoceros. As a rule, the former no longer lives in the open plains, and in many places now crosses them if possible only at night. But those rhinoceros which formerly dwelt in the plains for the most part continued to dwell there until killed out. So it is at the present day. Not the most foolish elephant would under similar conditions behave as the rhinos that we studied and hunted by Kilimakiu and in the Sotik behaved. No elephant, in regions where they have been much persecuted by hunters, would habitually spend its days lying or standing in the open plain; nor would it, in such places, repeatedly, and in fact, uniformly, permit men to walk boldly up to it without heeding them until in its immediate neighborhood. The elephant's sight is bad, as is that of the rhinoceros; but a comparatively brief experience with rifle-bearing man usually makes the former take refuge in regions where scent and hearing count for more than sight; while no experience has any such effect on the rhino. The rhinos that now live in the bush are the descendants of those which always lived in the bush; and it is in the bush that the species will linger long after it has vanished from the open; and it is in the bush that it is most formidable.

Elephant and rhino differ as much in their habits as in their intelligence. The former is very gregarious, herds of several hundred being sometimes found, and is of a restless, wandering temper, often shifting his abode and sometimes making long migrations. The rhinoceros is a lover of solitude; it is usually found alone, or a bull and cow, or cow and calf may be in company; very rarely are as many as half a dozen found together. Moreover, it is comparatively stationary in its habits, and as a general thing stays permanently in one neighborhood, not shifting its position for very many miles unless for grave reasons.

The African elephant has recently been divided into a number of sub-species; but as within a century its range was continuous over nearly the whole continent south of the Sahara, and as it was given to such extensive occasional

wanderings, it is probable that the examination of a sufficient series of specimens would show that on their confines these races grade into one another.
In its essentials the beast is almost everywhere the same, although, of course,
there must be variation of habit with any animal which exists throughout so
wide and diversified a range of territory; for in one place it is found in high
mountains, in another in a dry desert, in another in low-lying marshes or wet
and dense forests.

In East Africa the old bulls are usually found singly or in small parties
by themselves. These have the biggest tusks; the bulls in the prime of life, the
herd bulls or breeding bulls, which keep in herds with the cows and calves,
usually have smaller ivory. Sometimes, however, very old but vigorous bulls
are found with the cows; and I am inclined to think that the ordinary herd
bulls at times also keep by themselves, or at least in company with only a few
cows, for at certain seasons, generally immediately after the rains, cows, most
of them with calves, appear in great numbers at certain places, where only a
few bulls are ever found. Where undisturbed elephant rest, and wander about
at all times of the day and night, and feed without much regard to fixed
hours. Morning or evening, noon or midnight, the herd may be on the move,
or its members may be resting; yet, during the hottest hours of noon they seldom feed, and ordinarily stand almost still, resting—for elephant very rarely
lie down unless sick. Where they are afraid of man, their only enemy, they
come out to feed in thinly forested plains, or cultivated fields, when they do
so at all, only at night, and before daybreak move back into the forest to rest.
Elsewhere they sometimes spend the day in the open, in grass or low bush.
Where we were, at this time, on Kenia, the elephants sometimes moved down
at night to feed in the shambas, at the expense of the crops of the natives, and
sometimes stayed in the forest, feeding by day or night on the branches they
tore off the trees, or, occasionally, on the roots they grubbed up with their
tusks. They work vast havoc among the young or small growth of a forest, and
the readiness with which they uproot, overturn, or break off medium sized
trees conveys a striking impression of their enormous strength. I have seen a
tree a foot in diameter thus uprooted and overturned.

The African elephant has never, like his Indian kinsman, been trained to man's use. There is still hope that the feat may be performed; but hitherto its probable economic usefulness has for various reasons seemed so questionable that there has been scant encouragement to undergo the necessary expense and labor. Up to the present time the African elephant has yielded only his ivory as an asset of value. This, however, has been of such great value as well-nigh to bring about the mighty beast's utter extermination. Ivory hunters and ivory traders have penetrated Africa to the haunts of the elephant since centuries before our era, and the elephant boundaries have been slowly receding throughout historic time; but during the century just passed its process has been immensely accelerated, until now there are but one or two out-of-the-way nooks of the Dark Continent to the neighborhood of which hunter and trader have not penetrated. Fortunately the civilized powers which now divide dominion over Africa have waked up in time, and there is at present no danger of the extermination of the lord of all four-footed creatures. Large reserves have been established on which various herds of elephants now live what is, at least for the time being, an entirely safe life. Furthermore, over great tracts of territory outside the reserves regulations have been promulgated which, if enforced as they are now enforced, will present any excessive diminution of the herds. In British East Africa, for instance, no cows are allowed to be shot save for special purposes, as for preservation in a museum, or to safeguard life and property; and no bulls with tusks weighing less than thirty pounds apiece. This renders safe almost all the females and an ample supply of breeding males. Too much praise cannot be given the governments and the individuals who have brought about this happy result; the credit belongs especially to England and to various Englishmen. It would be a veritable and most tragic calamity if the lordly elephant, the giant among existing four-footed creatures, should be permitted to vanish from the face of the earth.

But of course protection is not permanently possible over the greater part of that country which is well fitted for settlement; nor anywhere, if the herds grow too numerous. It would be not merely silly, but worse than silly, to try to stop all killing of elephants. The unchecked increase of any big and formidable wild beast, even though not a flesh eater, is incompatible with the existence of man when he has emerged from the state of lowest savagery. This is not a matter of theory, but of proved fact. In place after place in Africa where protection has been extended to hippopotamus or buffalo, rhinoceros or elephant, it has been found necessary to withdraw it because the protected animals did such damage to property, or became such menaces to human life. Among all four species cows with calves often attack men without provocation, and old bulls are at any time likely to become infected by a spirit of wanton and ferocious mischief and apt to become mankillers. I know settlers who tried to preserve the rhinoceros which they found living on their big farms, and who were obliged to abandon the attempt, and themselves to kill the rhinos because of repeated and wanton attacks on human beings by the latter. Where we were by Neri, a year or two before our visit, the rhinos had become so dangerous, killing one white man and several natives, that the District Commissioner who preceded Mr. Browne was forced to undertake a crusade against them, killing fifteen. Both in South Africa and on the Nile protection extended to hippopotamus has in places been wholly withdrawn because of the damage done by the beast to the crops of the natives, or because of their unprovoked assaults on canoes and boats. In one instance a last surviving hippo was protected for years, but finally grew bold because of immunity, killed a boy in sheer wantonness, and had to be himself slain. In Uganda the buffalo were for years protected, and grew so bold, killed so many natives, and ruined so many villages that they are now classed as vermin and their destruction in every way encouraged. In the very neighborhood where I was hunting at Kenia but six weeks before my coming, a cow buffalo had wandered down into the plains and run amuck, had attacked two villages, had killed a man and a boy, and had then been mobbed to death by the spearmen. Elephant, when in numbers, and when not possessed of the fear of man, are more impossible neighbors than hippo, rhino, or buffalo; but they are so eagerly sought after by ivory hunters that it is only rarely that they get the chance to become really dangerous to life, although in many places their ravages among the crops are severely felt by the unfortunate natives who live near them.

The chase of the elephant, if persistently followed, entails more fatigue and hardship than any other kind of African hunting. As regards risk, it is hard to say whether it is more or less dangerous than the chase of the lion and the buffalo. Both Cuninghame and Tarlton, men of wide experience, ranked elephant hunting, in point of danger, as nearly on the level with lion hunting, and as more dangerous than buffalo hunting; and all three kinds as far more dangerous than the chase of the rhino. Personally, I believe the actual conflict with a lion, where the conditions are the same, to be normally the more dangerous sport; though far greater demands are made by elephant hunting on the qualities of personal endurance and hardihood and resolute perseverance in the face of disappointment and difficulty. Buffalo, seemingly, do not charge as freely as elephant, but are more dangerous when they do charge. Rhino when hunted, though at times ugly customers, seem to me certainly less dangerous than the other three; but from sheer stupid truculence they are themselves apt to take the offensive in unexpected fashion, being far more prone to such aggression than are any of the others—man-eating lions always excepted.

Very few of the native tribes in Africa hunt the elephant systematically. But the 'Ndorobo, the wild bush people of East Africa, sometimes catch young elephants in the pits they dig with slow labor, and very rarely they kill one with a kind of harpoon. The 'Ndorobo are doubtless in part descended from some primitive bush people, but in part also derive their blood from the more advanced tribes near which their wandering families happen to live; and they grade into the latter, by speech and through individuals who seem to stand half-way between. Thus we had with us two Masai 'Ndorobo, true wild people, who spoke a bastard Masai; who had formerly hunted with Cuninghame, and who came to us because of their ancient friendship with him. These shy wood creatures were afraid to come to Neri by daylight, when we were camped there, but after dark crept to Cuninghame's tent. Cuninghame gave them two fine red blankets, and put them to sleep in a little tent, keeping their spears in his own tent, as a matter of precaution to prevent their running away. The elder of the two, he informed me, would certainly have a fit of hysterics when we killed our elephant! Cuninghame was also joined by other old friends of former hunts, Kikuyu 'Ndorobo these, who spoke Kikuyu like the people who cultivated the fields that covered the river-bottoms and hill-sides of the adjoining open country, and who were, indeed, merely outlying, forest-dwelling members of the lowland tribes. In the deep woods we met one old Dorobo, who had no connection with any more advanced tribe, whose sole belongings were his spear, skin cloak, and fire stick, and who lived purely on honey and game; unlike the bastard 'Ndorobo, he was ornamented with neither paint nor grease. But the 'Ndorobo who were our guides stood farther up in the social scale. The men passed most of their time in the forest, but up the mountain sides they had squalid huts on little clearings, with shambas, where their wives raised scanty crops. To the 'Ndorobo, and to them alone, the vast, thick forest was an open book; without their aid as guides both Cuninghame and our own gun-bearers were at fault, and found their way around with great difficulty and slowness. The bush people had nothing in the way of clothing save a blanket over the shoulders, but wore the usual paint and grease and ornaments; each carried a spear which might have a long and narrow, or short and broad blade; two of them wore head-dresses of tripe—skull-caps made from the inside of a sheep's stomach.

For two days after reaching our camp in the open glade on the mountain side it rained. We were glad of this, because it meant that the elephants would not be in the bamboos, and Cuninghame and the 'Ndorobo went off to hunt for fresh signs. Cuninghame is as skilful an elephant hunter as can be found in Africa, and is one of the very few white men able to help even the wild bushmen at their work. By the afternoon of the second day they were fairly well satisfied as to the whereabouts of the quarry.

The following morning a fine rain was still falling when Cuninghame, Heller, and I started on our hunt but by noon it had stopped. Of course we went in single file and on foot; not even a bear hunter from the cane-brakes of the lower Mississippi could ride through that forest. We left our home camp standing, taking blankets and a coat and a change of underclothing for each of us, and two small Whymper tents, with enough food for three days; I also

took my wash kit and a book from the Pigskin Library. First marched the
'Ndorobo guides, each with his spear, his blanket round his shoulders, and
a little bundle of corn and sweet potato. Then came Cuninghame, followed
by his gun-bearer. Then I came, clad in khaki-colored flannel shirt and khaki
trousers buttoning down the legs, with hob-nailed shoes and a thick slouch
hat; I had intended to wear rubber-soled shoes, but the soaked ground was
too slippery. My two gun-bearers followed, carrying the Holland and the
Springfield. Then came Heller, at the head of a dozen porters and skinners;
he and they were to fall behind when we actually struck fresh elephant spoor,
but to follow our trail by the help of a Dorobo who was left with them.

For three hours our route lay along the edge of the woods. We climbed
into and out of deep ravines in which groves of tree ferns clustered. We waded
through streams of swift water, whose course was broken by cataract and rapid. We passed through shambas, and by the doors of little hamlets of thatched
beehive huts. We met flocks of goats and hairy, fat-tailed sheep guarded by
boys, strings of burden-bearing women stood meekly to one side to let us
pass; parties of young men sauntered by, spear in hand.

Then we struck into the great forest, and in an instant the sun was shut
from sight by the thick screen of wet foliage. It was a riot of twisted vines, interlacing the trees and bushes. Only the elephant paths, which, of every age, crossed
and recrossed it hither and thither, made it passable. One of the chief difficulties
in hunting elephants in the forest is that it is impossible to travel, except very
slowly and with much noise, off these trails, so that it is sometimes very difficult
to take advantage of the wind; and although the sight of the elephant is dull,
both its sense of hearing and its sense of smell are exceedingly acute.

Hour after hour we worked our way onward through tangled forest and
matted jungle. There was little sign of bird or animal life. A troop of long-haired
black and white monkeys bounded away among the tree tops. Here and there
brilliant flowers lightened the gloom. We ducked under vines and climbed over
fallen timber. Poisonous nettles stung our hands. We were drenched by the wet
boughs which we brushed aside. Mosses and ferns grew rank and close. The
trees were of strange kinds. There were huge trees with little leaves, and small

A temperate rainforest in southern Africa

trees with big leaves. There were trees with bare, fleshy limbs, that writhed out through the neighboring branches, bearing sparse clusters of large frondage. In places the forest was low, the trees thirty or forty feet high, the bushes, that choked the ground between, fifteen or twenty feet high. In other places mighty monarchs of the wood, straight and tall, towered aloft to an immense height; among them were trees whose smooth, round boles were spotted like sycamores, while far above our heads their gracefully spreading branches were hung with vines like mistletoe and draped with Spanish moss; trees whose surfaces were corrugated and knotted as if they were made of bundles of great creepers; and giants whose buttressed trunks were four times a man's length across.

Twice we got on elephant spoor, once of a single bull, once of a party of three. Then Cuninghame and the 'Ndorobo redoubled their caution. They would minutely examine the fresh dung; and above all they continually tested the wind, scanning the tree tops, and lighting matches to see from the smoke what the eddies were near the ground. Each time after an hour's stealthy stepping and crawling along the twisted trail a slight shift of the wind in the almost still air gave our scent to the game, and away it went before we could catch a glimpse of it; and we resumed our walk. The elephant paths led up hill and down—for the beasts are wonderful climbers—and wound in and out in every direction. They were marked by broken branches and the splintered and shattered trunks of smaller trees, especially where the elephant had stood and fed, trampling down the bushes for many yards around. Where they had crossed the marshy valleys they had punched big round holes, three feet deep, in the sticky mud.

As evening fell we pitched camp by the side of a little brook at the bottom of a ravine, and dined ravenously on bread, mutton, and tea. The air was keen, and under our blankets we slept in comfort until dawn. Breakfast was soon over and camp struck; and once more we began our cautious progress through the dim, cool archways of the mountain forest.

Two hours after leaving camp we came across the fresh trail of a small herd of perhaps ten or fifteen elephant cows and calves, but including two big herd bulls. At once we took up the trail. Cuninghame and his bush people consulted again and again, scanning every track and mark with minute attention. The signs showed that the elephants had fed in the shambas early in the night, had then returned to the mountain, and stood in one place resting for several hours, and had left this sleeping ground some time before we reached it. After we had followed the trail a short while we made the experiment of trying to force our own way through the jungle, so as to get the wind more favorable but our progress was too slow and noisy, and we returned to the path the elephants had beaten. Then the 'Ndorobo went ahead, travelling noiselessly and at speed. One of them was clad in a white blanket, and another in a red one, which were conspicuous; but they were too silent and cautious to let the beasts see them, and could tell exactly where they were and what they were doing by the sounds. When these trackers waited for us they would appear before us like ghosts; once one of them dropped down from the branches above, having climbed a tree with monkey-like ability to get a glimpse of the great game.

At last we could hear the elephants, and under Cuninghame's lead we walked more cautiously than ever. The wind was right, and the trail of one elephant led close alongside that of the rest of the herd, and parallel thereto. It was about noon. The elephants moved slowly, and we listened to the boughs crack, and now and then to the curious internal rumblings of the great beasts. Carefully, every sense on the alert, we kept pace with them. My double-barrel was in my hands, and, wherever possible, as I followed the trail, I stepped in the huge footprints of the elephant, for where such a weight had pressed there were no sticks left to crack under my feet. It made our veins thrill thus for half an hour to creep stealthily along, but a few rods from the herd, never able to see it, because of the extreme denseness of the cover, but always hearing first one and then another of its members, and always trying to guess what each one might do, and keeping ceaselessly ready for whatever might befall. A flock of hornbills flew up with noisy clamor, but the elephants did not heed them.

At last we came in sight of the mighty game. The trail took a twist to one side, and there, thirty yards in front of us, we made out part of the gray and massive head of an elephant resting his tusks on the branches of a young tree. A couple of minutes passed before, by cautious scrutiny, we were able to tell whether the animal was a cow or a bull, and whether, if a bull, it carried

heavy enough tusks. Then we saw that it was a big bull with good ivory. It turned its head in my direction and I saw its eye; and I fired a little to one side of the eye, at a spot which I thought would lead to the brain. I struck exactly where I aimed, but the head of an elephant is enormous and the brain small, and the bullet missed it. However, the shock momentarily stunned the beast. He stumbled forward, half falling, and as he recovered I fired with the second barrel, again aiming for the brain. This time the bullet sped true, and as I lowered the rifle from my shoulder, I saw the great lord of the forest come crashing to the ground.

But at that very instant, before there was a moment's time in which to reload, the thick bushes parted immediately on my left front, and through them surged the vast bulk of a charging bull elephant, the matted mass of tough creepers snapping like packthread before his rush. He was so close that he could have touched me with his trunk. I leaped to one side and dodged behind a tree trunk, opening the rifle, throwing out the empty shells, and slipping in two cartridges. Meanwhile Cuninghame fired right and left, at the same time throwing himself into the bushes on the other side. Both his bullets went home, and the bull stopped short in his charge, wheeled, and immediately disappeared in the thick cover. We ran forward, but the forest had closed over his wake. We heard him trumpet shrilly, and then all sound ceased.

The 'Ndorobo, who had quite properly disappeared when this second bull charged, now went forward, and soon returned with the report that he had fled at speed, but was evidently hard hit, as there was much blood on the spoor. If we had been only after ivory we should have followed him at once; but there was no telling how long a chase he might lead us; and as we desired to save the skin of the dead elephant entire, there was no time whatever to spare. It is a formidable task, occupying many days, to preserve an elephant for mounting in a museum, and if the skin is to be properly saved, it must be taken off without an hour's unnecessary delay.

So back we turned to where the dead tusker lay, and I felt proud indeed as I stood by the immense bulk of the slain monster and put my hand on the ivory. The tusks weighed a hundred and thirty pounds the pair. There was the usual scene of joyful excitement among the gun-bearers—who had behaved excellently—and among the wild bush people who had done the tracking for us; and, as Cuninghame had predicted, the old Masai Dorobo, from pure delight, proceeded to have hysterics on the body of the dead elephant. The scene was repeated when Heller and the porters appeared half an hour later. Then, chattering like monkeys, and as happy as possible, all, porters, gun-bearers, and 'Ndorobo alike, began the work of skinning and cutting up the quarry, under the leadership and supervision of Heller and Cuninghame, and soon they were all splashed with blood from head to foot. One of the trackers took off his blanket and squatted stark naked inside the carcass the better to use his knife. Each laborer rewarded himself by cutting off strips of meat for his private store, and hung them in red festoons from the branches round about. There was no let up in the work until it was stopped by darkness.

Our tents were pitched in a small open glade a hundred yards from the dead elephant. The night was clear, the stars shone brightly, and in the west the young moon hung just above the line of tall tree tops. Fires were speedily kindled and the men sat around them, feasting and singing in a strange minor tone until late in the night. The flickering light left them at one moment in black obscurity, and the next brought into bold relief their sinewy crouching figures, their dark faces, gleaming eyes, and flashing teeth. When they did sleep, two of the 'Ndorobo slept so close to the fire as to burn themselves; an accident to which they are prone, judging from the many scars of old burns on their legs. I toasted slices of elephant's heart on a pronged stick before the fire, and found it delicious; for I was hungry, and the night was cold. We talked of our success and exulted over it, and made our plans for the morrow; and then we turned in under our blankets for another night's sleep.

Next morning some of the 'Ndorobo went off on the trail of Cuninghame's elephant to see if it had fallen, but found that it had travelled steadily, though its wounds were probably mortal. There was no object in my staying, for Heller and Cuninghame would be busy for the next ten days, and would ultimately have to use all the porters in taking off and curing the skin, and transporting it to Neri; so I made up my mind to go down to the plains for a hunt by myself. Taking one porter to carry my bedding, and with my gun-bearers, and a Dorobo as guide, I struck off through the forest for the main camp, reaching it early in the afternoon. Thence I bundled off a safari to Cuninghame and Heller, with food for a week, and tents and clothing; and then enjoyed the luxury of a shave and a warm bath. Next day was spent in writing and in making preparations for my own trip. A Kikuyu chief, clad in a cloak of hyrax skins, and carrying his war spear, came to congratulate me on killing the elephant and to present me with a sheep. Early the following morning everything was in readiness; the bullnecked porters lifted their loads, I stepped out in front, followed by my led horse, and in ten hours' march we reached Neri boma with its neat building, its trees, and its well-kept flower beds.

My hunting and travelling during the following fortnight will be told in the next chapter. On the evening of September 6th we were all together again at Meru boma, on the north-eastern slopes of Kenia—Kermit, Tarlton, Cuninghame, Heller, and I. Thanks to the unfailing kindness of the Commissioner, Mr. Horne, we were given full information of the elephant in the neighborhood. He had no 'Ndorobo, but among the Wa-Meru, a wild martial tribe, who lived close around him, there were a number of hunters, or at least of men who knew the forest and the game, and these had been instructed to bring in any news.

We had, of course, no idea that elephant would be found close at hand. But next morning, about eleven, Horne came to our camp with four of his black scouts, who reported that three elephants were in a patch of thick jungle beside the shambas, not three miles away. Horne said that the elephants were cows, that they had been in the neighborhood some days, devastating the shambas, and were bold and fierce, having charged some men who sought to drive them away from the cultivated fields; it is curious to see how little heed these elephants pay to the natives. I wished a cow for the museum, and also another bull. So off we started at once, Kermit carrying his camera. I slipped on my rubber-soled shoes, and had my gun-bearers accompany me bare-footed, with the Holland and the Springfield rifles. We followed foot-paths among the fields until we reached the edge of the jungle in which the elephants stood.

This jungle lay beside the forest, and at this point separated it from the fields. It consisted of a mass of rank-growing bushes, allied to the cotton-plant, ten or twelve feet high, with only here and there a tree. It was not good ground in which to hunt elephant, for the tangle was practically impenetrable to a hunter save along the elephant trails, whereas the elephants themselves could move in any direction at will, with no more difficulty than a man would have in a hay-field. The bushes in most places rose just above their backs, so that they were completely hid from the hunter even a few feet away. Yet the cover afforded no shade to the mighty beasts, and it seemed strange that elephants should stand in it at mid-day with the sun out. There they were, however, for, looking cautiously into the cover from behind the bushes on a slight hill crest a quarter of a mile off, we could just make out a huge ear now and then as it lazily flapped.

On account of the wind we had to go well to one side before entering the jungle. Then in we went in single file, Cuninghame and Tarlton leading, with a couple of our naked guides. The latter showed no great desire to get too close, explaining that the elephants were "very fierce." Once in the jungle, we trod as quietly as possible, threading our way along the elephant trails, which crossed and re-crossed one another. Evidently it was a favorite haunt, for the sign was abundant, both old and new. In the impenetrable cover it was quite impossible to tell just where the elephants were, and twice we sent one of the savages up a tree to locate the game. The last time the watcher, who stayed in the tree, indicated by signs that the elephant were not far off; and his companions wished to lead us round to where the cover was a little lower and thinner. But to do so would have given them our wind, and Cuninghame refused, taking into his own hands the management of the stalk. I kept my heavy rifle at the ready, and on we went, in watchful silence, prepared at any moment for a charge. We could not tell at what second we might catch our first glimpse at very close quarters of "the beast that hath between his eyes the serpent for a hand," and when thus surprised the temper of "the huge earth-shaking beast" is sometimes of the shortest.

Cuninghame and Tarlton stopped for a moment to consult; Cuninghame stooped, and Tarlton mounted his shoulders and stood upright, steadying himself by my hand. Down he came and told us that he had seen a small tree shake seventy yards distant; although upright on Cuninghame's shoulder he could not see the elephant itself. Forward we stole for a few yards, and then a piece of good luck befell us, for we came on the trunk of a great fallen tree, and scrambling up, we found ourselves perched in a row six feet above the ground. The highest part of the trunk was near the root, farthest from where the elephants were; and though it offered precarious footing, it also offered the best lookout. Thither I balanced, and looking over the heads of my companions I at once made out the elephant. At first I could see nothing but the shaking branches, and one huge ear occasionally flapping. Then I made out the ear of another beast, and then the trunk of a third was uncurled, lifted, and curled again; it showered its back with earth. The watcher we had left behind in the tree top coughed, the elephants stood motionless, and up went the biggest elephant's trunk, feeling for the wind; the watcher coughed again, and then the bushes and saplings swayed and parted as three black bulks came toward us. The cover was so high that we could not see their tusks, only the tops of their heads and their backs being visible. The leader was the biggest, and at it I fired when it was sixty yards away, and nearly broadside on, but heading slightly toward me. I had previously warned every one to kneel. The recoil of the heavy rifle made me rock, as I stood unsteadily on my perch, and I failed to hit the brain. But the bullet, only missing the brain by an inch or two, brought the elephant to its knees; as it rose I floored it with the second barrel. The blast of the big rifle, by the way, was none too pleasant for the other men on the log and made Cuninghame's nose bleed. Reloading, I fired twice at the next animal, which was now turning. It stumbled and nearly fell, but at the same moment the first one rose again, and I fired both barrels into its head, bringing it once more to the ground. Once again it rose—an elephant's brain is not an easy mark to hit under such conditions—but as it moved slowly off, half stunned, I snatched the little Springfield rifle, and this time shot true, sending the bullet into its brain. As it fell I took another shot at the wounded elephant, now disappearing in the forest, but without effect.

On walking up to our prize it proved to be not a cow, but a good-sized adult (but not old) herd bull, with thick, short tusks weighing about forty pounds apiece. Ordinarily, of course, a bull, and not a cow, is what one desires, although on this occasion I needed a cow to complete the group for the National Museum. However, Heller and Cuninghame spent the next few days in preserving the skin, which I after gave to the University of California; and I was too much pleased with our luck to feel inclined to grumble. We were back in camp five hours after leaving it. Our gun-bearers usually felt it incumbent on them to keep a dignified bearing while in our company. But, the death of an elephant is always a great event; and one of the gun-bearers, as they walked ahead of us campward, soon began to improvise a song, reciting the success of the hunt, the death of the elephant, and the power of the rifles; and gradually, as they got farther ahead, the more lighthearted among them began to give way to their spirits and they came into camp frolicking, gambolling, and dancing as if they were still the naked savages that they had been before they became the white man's followers.

Two days later Kermit got his bull. He and Tarlton had camped about ten miles off in a magnificent forest, and late the first afternoon received news that a herd of elephants was in the neighborhood. They were off by dawn, and in a few hours came on the herd. It consisted chiefly of cows and calves, but there was one big master bull, with fair tusks. It was open forest with long grass. By careful stalking they got within thirty yards of the bull, behind whom was a line of cows. Kermit put both barrels of his heavy double .450 into the tusker's head, but without even staggering him; and as he walked off Tarlton also fired both barrels into him, with no more effect; then, as he slowly turned, Kermit killed him with a shot in the brain from the .405 Winchester. Immediately the cows lifted their ears, and began trumpeting and threatening; if they had come on in a body at that distance, there was not much chance of turning them or of escaping from them: and after standing stock still for a minute or two, Kermit and Tarlton stole quietly off for a hundred yards, and waited until the anger of the cows cooled and they had moved away, before going up to the dead bull. Then they followed the herd again, and Kermit got some photos which, as far as I know, are better than any that have ever been taken of wild elephant. He took them close up; at imminent risk of a charge.

The following day the two hunters rode back to Meru, making a long circle. The elephants they saw were not worth shooting, but they killed the finest rhinoceros we had yet seen. They saw it in an open space of tall grass, surrounded by lantana brush, a flowering shrub with close-growing stems, perhaps twenty feet high and no thicker than a man's thumb; it forms a favorite cover for elephants and rhinoceros, and is well nigh impenetrable to hunters. Fortunately this particular rhino was outside it, and Kermit and Tarlton got up to about twenty-five yards from him. Kermit then put one bullet behind his shoulder, and as he whipped round to charge, another bullet on the point of his shoulder; although mortally wounded, he showed no signs whatever of being hurt, and came at the hunters with great speed and savage desire to do harm. Then an extraordinary thing happened. Tarlton fired, inflicting merely a flesh wound in one shoulder, and the big, fearsome brute, which had utterly disregarded the two fatal shots, on receiving this flesh wound, wheeled and ran. Both firing, they killed him before he had gone many yards. He was a bull, with a thirty-inch horn.

By this time Cuninghame and Heller had finished the skin and skeleton of the bull they were preserving. Near the carcass Heller trapped an old male leopard, a savage beast; its skin was in fine shape, but it was not fat, and weighed just one hundred pounds. Now we all joined, and shifted camp to a point eight or nine miles distant from Meru boma, and fifteen hundred feet lower among the foot-hills. It was much hotter at this lower level; palms were among the trees that bordered the streams. On the day we shifted camp Tarlton and I rode in advance to look for elephants, followed by our gun-bearers and half a dozen wild Meru hunters, each carrying a spear or a bow and arrows. When we reached the hunting grounds, open country with groves of trees and patches of jungle, the Meru went off in every direction to find elephant. We waited their return under a tree, by a big stretch of cultivated ground. The region was well peopled, and all the way down the path had led between fields, which the Meru women were tilling with their adze-like hoes, and banana plantations, where among the bananas other trees had been planted, and the yam vines trained up their trunks. These cool, shady banana plantations, fenced in with tall hedges and bordered by rapid brooks, were really very attractive. Among them were scattered villages of conical thatched huts, and level places plastered with cow dung on which the grain was threshed; it was then stored in huts raised on posts. There were herds of cattle, and flocks of sheep and goats; and among the burdens the women bore we often saw huge bottles of milk. In the shambas there were platforms, and sometimes regular thatched huts, placed in the trees; these were for the watchers, who were to keep the elephants out of the shambas at night. Some of the natives wore girdles of banana leaves, looking, as Kermit said, much like the pictures of savages in Sunday-school books.

Early in the afternoon some of the scouts returned with news that three bull elephants were in a piece of forest a couple of miles distant, and thither we went. It was an open grove of heavy thorn timber beside a strip of swamp; among the trees the grass grew tall, and there were many thickets of abutilon, a flowering shrub a dozen feet high. On this the elephant were feeding. Tarlton's favorite sport was lion hunting, but he was also a first-class elephant hunter, and he brought me up to these bulls in fine style. Although only three hundred yards away, it took us two hours to get close to them. Tarlton and the "shenzis"—wild natives, called in Swahili (a kind of African chinook) "washenzi"—who were with us, climbed tree after tree, first to place the elephants, and then to see if they carried ivory heavy enough to warrant my shooting them. At last Tarlton brought me to within fifty yards of them. Two were feeding in bush which hid them from view, and the third stood between, facing us. We could only see the top of his head and back, and not his tusks, and could not tell whether he was worth shooting. Much puzzled, we stood where we were, peering anxiously at the huge, half-hidden game. Suddenly there was a slight eddy in the wind, up went the elephant's trunk, twisting to and fro in the air; evidently he could not catch a clear scent; but in another moment we saw the three great dark forms moving gently off through the bush. As rapidly as possible, following the trails already trampled by the elephants, we walked forward, and after a hundred yards Tarlton pointed to a big bull with good tusks standing motionless behind some small trees seventy yards distant. As I aimed at his head he started to move off; the first bullet from the heavy Holland brought him to his knees, and as he rose I knocked him flat with the second. He struggled to rise; but, both firing, we kept him down; and I finished him with a bullet in the brain from the little Springfield. Although rather younger than either of the bulls I had already shot, it was even larger. In its stomach were beans from the shambas, abutilon tips, and bark, and especially the twigs, leaves, and white blossoms of the smaller shrub. The tusks weighed a little over a hundred pounds the pair.

We still needed a cow for the museum; and a couple of days later, at noon, a party of natives brought in word that they had seen two cows in a spot five miles away. Piloted by a naked spearman, whose hair was done into a cue, we rode toward the place. For most of the distance we followed old elephant trails, in some places mere tracks beaten down through stiff grass which stood above the head of a man on horseback, in other places paths rutted deep into the earth. We crossed a river, where monkeys chattered among the tree tops. On an open plain we saw a rhinoceros cow trotting off with her calf. At last we came to a hill-top with, on the summit, a noble fig-tree, whose giant limbs were stretched over the palms that clustered beneath. Here we left our horses and went forward on foot, crossing a palm-fringed stream in a little valley. From the next rise we saw the backs of the elephants as they stood in a slight valley, where the rank grass grew ten or twelve feet high. It was some time before we could see the ivory so as to be sure of exactly what we were shooting. Then the biggest cow began to move slowly forward, and we walked nearly parallel to her, along an elephant trail, until from a slight knoll I got a clear view of her at a distance of eighty yards. As she walked leisurely along, almost broadside to me, I fired the right barrel of the Holland into her head, knocking her flat down with the shock; and when she rose I put a bullet from the left barrel through her heart, again knocking her completely off her feet; and this time she fell permanently. She was a very old cow, and her ivory was rather better than in the average of her sex in this neighborhood, the tusks weighing about eighteen pounds apiece. She had been ravaging the shambas over night—which accounted in part for the natives being so eager to show her to me—and in addition to leaves and grass, her stomach contained quantities of beans. There was a young one—just out of calfhood, and quite able to take care of itself—with her; it ran off as soon as the mother fell.

Early next morning Cuninghame and Heller shifted part of the safari to the stream near where the dead elephant lay, intending to spend the following three days in taking off and preparing the skin. Meanwhile Tarlton, Kermit, and I were to try our luck in a short hunt on the other side of Meru boma, at a little crater lake called Lake Ingouga. We could not get an early start, and reached Meru too late to push on to the lake the same day.

The following morning we marched to the lake in two hours and a half. We spent an hour in crossing a broad tongue of woodland that stretched down from the wonderful mountain forest lying higher on the slopes. The trail was blind in many places because elephant paths of every age continually led along and across it, some of them being much better marked than the trail itself, as it twisted through the sun-flecked shadows underneath the great trees. Then we came out on high downs, covered with tall grass and littered with volcanic stones; and broken by ravines which were choked with dense underbrush. There were high hills, and to the left of the downs, toward Kenia, these were clad in forest. We pitched our tents on a steep cliff overlooking the crater lake—or pond, as it might more properly be called. It was bordered with sedge, and through the water-lilies on its surface we saw the reflection of the new moon after nightfall. Here and there thick forest came down to the brink, and through this, on opposite sides of the pond, deeply worn elephant paths, evidently travelled for ages, wound down to the water.

That evening we hunted for bushbuck, but saw none. While sitting on a hillock at dusk, watching for game, a rhino trotted up to inspect us, with ears cocked forward and tail erect. A rhino always has something comic about it, like a pig, formidable though it at times is. This one carried a poor horn, and therefore we were pleased when at last it trotted off without obliging us to shoot it. We saw new kinds of whydah birds, one with a yellow breast, one with white in its tail; at this altitude the cocks were still in full plumage, although it was just past the middle of September; whereas at Naivasha they had begun to lose their long tail feathers nearly two months previously.

On returning to camp we received a note from Cuninghame saying that Heller had been taken seriously sick, and Tarlton had to go to them. This left Kermit and me to take our two days' hunt together.

One day we got nothing. We saw game on the open downs, but it was too wary, and though we got within twenty-five yards of eland in thick cover, we could only make out a cow, and she took fright and ran without our ever getting a glimpse of the bull that was with her. Late in the afternoon we saw an elephant a mile and a half away, crossing a corner of the open downs. We followed its trail until the light grew too dim for shooting, but never overtook it, although at the last we could hear it ahead of us breaking the branches; and we made our way back to camp through the darkness.

The other day made amends. It was Kermit's turn to shoot an elephant, and mine to shoot a rhinoceros; and each of us was to act as the backing gun for the other. In the forenoon, we saw a bull rhino with a good horn walking over the open downs. A convenient hill enabled us to cut him off without difficulty, and from its summit we killed him at the base, fifty or sixty yards off. His front horn was nearly twenty-nine inches long; but though he was an old bull, his total length, from tip of nose to tip of tail, was only twelve feet, and he was, I should guess, not more than two-thirds the bulk of the big bull I killed in the Sotik.

We rested for an hour or two at noon, under the shade of a very old tree with glossy leaves, and orchids growing on its gnarled, hoary limbs, while the unsaddled horses grazed, and the gun-bearers slept near by, the cool mountain air, though this was midday under the equator, making them prefer the sunlight to the shade. When we moved on it was through a sea of bush ten or fifteen feet high, dotted here and there with trees; and riddled in every direction by the trails of elephant, rhinoceros, and buffalo. Each of these animals frequents certain kinds of country to which the other two rarely or never penetrate; but here they all three found ground to their liking. Except along their winding trails, which were tunnels where the jungle was tall, it would have been practically impossible to traverse the thick and matted cover in which they had made their abode.

We could not tell what moment we might find ourselves face to face with some big beast at such close quarters as to insure a charge, and we moved in cautious silence, our rifles in our hands. Rhinoceros were especially plentiful, and we continually came across not only their tracks, but the dusty wallows in which they rolled, and where they came to deposit their dung. The fresh sign of elephant, however, distracted our attention from the lesser game, and we followed the big footprints eagerly, now losing the trail, now finding it again. At last near a clump of big trees we caught sight of three huge, dark bodies ahead of us. The wind was right, and we stole toward them, Kermit leading, and I immediately behind. Through the tangled branches their shapes loomed in vague outline; but we saw that one had a pair of long tusks, and our gun-bearers unanimously pronounced it a big bull, with good ivory. A few more steps gave Kermit a chance at its head, at about sixty yards, and with a bullet from his .405 Winchester he floored the mighty beast. I rose, and we both fired in unison, bringing it down again; but as we came up it struggled to get on its feet, roaring savagely, and once more we both fired together. This finished it. We were disappointed at finding that it was not a bull; but it was a large cow, with tusks over five feet long—a very unusual length for a cow—one weighing twenty-five, and the other twenty-two pounds.

Our experience had convinced us that both the Winchester .405, and the Springfield .300 would do good work with elephants; although I kept to my belief that, for such very heavy game, my Holland .500-.450 was an even better weapon.

Not far from where this elephant fell Tarlton had, the year before, witnessed an interesting incident. He was watching a small herd of elephants, cows and calves, which were in the open, when he saw them begin to grow uneasy. Then, with a shrill trumpet, a cow approached a bush, out of which bounded a big lion. Instantly all the cows charged him, and he fled as fast as his legs could carry him for the forest, two hundred yards distant. He just managed to reach the cover in safety; and then the infuriated cows, in their anger at his escape, demolished the forest for several rods in every direction.

CHAPTER 4

PHINEAS FINN

By Anthony Trollope

The Willingford Bull

PHINEAS left London by a night mail train on Easter Sunday, and found himself at the Willingford Bull about half an hour after midnight. Lord Chiltern was up and waiting for him, and supper was on the table. The Willingford Bull was an English inn of the old stamp, which had now, in these latter years of railway travelling, ceased to have a road business—for there were no travellers on the road, and but little posting—but had acquired a new trade as a dépôt for hunters and hunting men. The landlord let out horses and kept hunting stables, and the house was generally filled from the beginning of November till the middle of April. Then it became a desert in the summer, and no guests were seen there, till the pink coats flocked down again into the shires.

'How many days do you mean to give us?' said Lord Chiltern, as he helped his friend to a devilled leg of turkey.

'I must go back on Wednesday,' said Phineas.

'That means Wednesday night. I'll tell you what we'll do. We've the Cottesmore to-morrow. We'll get into Tailby's country on Tuesday, and Fitzwilliam will be only twelve miles off on Wednesday. We shall be rather short of horses.'

'Pray don't let me put you out. I can hire something here, I suppose?'

'You won't put me out at all. There'll be three between us each day, and we'll run our luck. The horses have gone on to Empingham for to-morrow. Tailby is rather a way off—at Somerby; but we'll manage it. If the worst comes to the worst, we can get back to Stamford by rail. On Wednesday we shall have everything very comfortable. They're out beyond Stilton and will draw home our way. I've planned it all out. I've a trap with a fast stepper, and if we start to-morrow at half-past nine, we shall be in plenty of time. You shall ride Meg Merrilies, and if she don't carry you, you may shoot her.'

'Is she one of the pulling ones?'

'She is heavy in hand if you are heavy at her, but leave her mouth alone and she'll go like flowing water. You'd better not ride more in a crowd than you can help. Now what'll you drink?'

They sat up half the night smoking and talking, and Phineas learned more about Lord Chiltern then than ever he had learned before. There was brandy and water before them, but neither of them drank. Lord Chiltern, indeed, had a pint of beer by his side from which he sipped occasionally. 'I've taken to beer,' he said, 'as being the best drink going. When a man hunts six days a week he can afford to drink beer. I'm on an allowance,—three pints a day. That's not too much.'

'And you drink nothing else?'

'Nothing when I'm alone,—except a little cherry-brandy when I'm out. I never cared for drink;—never in my life. I do like excitement, and have been less careful than I ought to have been as to what it has come from. I could give up drink to-morrow, without a struggle—if it were worth my while to make up my mind to do it. And it's the same with gambling. I never do gamble now, because I've got no money; but I own I like it better than anything in the world. While you are at it, there is life in it.'

'You should take to politics, Chiltern.'

'And I would have done so, but my father would not help me. Never mind, we will not talk about him. How does Laura get on with her husband?'

'Very happily, I should say.'

'I don't believe it,' said Lord Chiltern. 'Her temper is too much like mine to allow her to be happy with such a log of wood as Robert Kennedy. It is such men as he who drive me out of the pale of decent life. If that is decency, I'd sooner be indecent. You mark my words. They'll come to grief. She'll never be able to stand it.'

'I should think she had her own way in everything,' said Phineas.

'No, no. Though he's a prig, he's a man; and she will not find it easy to drive him.'

'But she may bend him.'

'Not an inch—that is if I understand his character. I suppose you see a good deal of them?'

'Yes—pretty well. I'm not there so often as I used to be in the Square.'

'You get sick of it, I suppose. I should. Do you see my father often?'

'Only occasionally. He is always very civil when I do see him.'

'He is the very pink of civility when he pleases, but the most unjust man I ever met.'

'I should not have thought that.'

'Yes, he is,' said the Earl's son, and all from lack of judgment to discern the truth. He makes up his mind to a thing on insufficient proof, and then nothing will turn him. He thinks well of you—would probably believe your word on any indifferent subject without thought of a doubt; but if you were to tell him that I didn't get drunk every night of my life and spend most of my time in thrashing policemen, he would not believe you. He would smile incredulously and make you a little bow. I can see him do it.'

'You are too hard on him, Chiltern.'

'He has been too hard on me, I know. Is Violet Effingham still in Grosvenor Place?'

'No; she's with Lady Baldock.'

'That old grandmother of evil has come to town—has she? Poor Violet! When we were young together we used to have such fun about that old woman.'

'The old woman is an ally of mine now,' said Phineas.

'You make allies everywhere. You know Violet Effingham of course?'

'Oh yes. I know her.'

'Don't you think her very charming?' said Lord Chiltern.

'Exceedingly charming.'

'I have asked that girl to marry me three times, and I shall never ask her again. There is a point beyond which a man shouldn't go. There are many reasons why it would be a good marriage. In the first place, her money would be serviceable. Then it would heal matters in our family, for my father is as prejudiced in her favour as he is against me. And I love her dearly. I've loved her all my life—since I used to buy cakes for her. But I shall never ask her again.'

'I would if I were you,' said Phineas—hardly knowing what it might be best for him to say.

'No; I never will. But I'll tell you what. I shall get into some desperate scrape about her. Of course she'll marry, and that soon. Then I shall make a fool of myself. When I hear that she is engaged I shall go and quarrel with the man, and kick him—or get kicked. All the world will turn against me, and I shall be called a wild beast.'

'A dog in the manger is what you should be called.'

'Exactly—but how is a man to help it? If you loved a girl, could you see another man take her?' Phineas remembered of course that he had lately come through this ordeal. 'It is as though he were to come and put his hand upon me, and wanted my own heart out of me. Though I have no property in her at all, no right to her—though she never gave me a word of encouragement, it is as though she were the most private thing in the world to me. I should be half mad, and in my madness I could not master the idea that I was being robbed. I should resent it as a personal interference.'

'I suppose it will come to that if you give her up yourself,' said Phineas.

'It is no question of giving up. Of course I cannot make her marry me. Light another cigar, old fellow.'

Phineas, as he lit the other cigar, remembered that he owed a certain duty in this matter to Lady Laura. She had commissioned him to persuade her brother that his suit with Violet Effingham would not be hopeless, if he could only restrain himself in his mode of conducting it. Phineas was disposed to do his duty, although he felt it to be very hard that he should be called upon to be eloquent against his own interest. He had been thinking for the last quarter of an hour how he must bear himself if it might turn out that he should be the man whom Lord Chiltern was resolved to kick. He looked at his friend and host, and became aware that a kicking-match with such a one would not be pleasant pastime. Nevertheless, he would be happy enough to be subject to Lord Chiltern's wrath for such a reason. He would do his duty by Lord Chiltern; and then, when that had been adequately done, he would, if occasion served, fight a battle for himself.

'You are too sudden with her, Chiltern,' he said, after a pause.

'What do you mean by too sudden?' said Lord Chiltern, almost angrily.

'You frighten her by being so impetuous. You rush at her as though you wanted to conquer her by a single blow.'

'So I do.'

'You should be more gentle with her. You should give her time to find out whether she likes you or not.'

'She has known me all her life, and has found that out long ago. Not but what you are right. I know you are right. If I were you, and had your skill in pleasing, I should drop soft words into her ear till I had caught her. But I have no gifts in that way. I am as awkward as a pig at what is called flirting. And I have an accursed pride which stands in my own light. If she were in this house this moment, and if I knew she were to be had for asking, I don't think I could bring myself to ask again. But we'll go to bed. It's half-past two, and we must be off at half-past nine, if we're to be at Exton Park gates at eleven.'

Phineas, as he went up-stairs, assured himself that he had done his duty. If there ever should come to be anything between him and Violet Effingham, Lord Chiltern might quarrel with him—might probably attempt that kicking encounter to which allusion had been made—but nobody could justly say that he had not behaved honourably to his friend.

On the next morning there was a bustle and a scurry, as there always is on such occasions, and the two men got off about ten minutes after time. But Lord Chiltern drove hard, and they reached the meet before the master had moved off. They had a fair day's sport with the Cottesmore; and Phineas, though he found that Meg Merrilies did require a good deal of riding, went through his day's work with credit. He had been riding since he was a child, as is the custom with all boys in Munster, and had an Irishman's natural aptitude for jumping. When they got back to the Willingford Bull he felt pleased with the day and rather proud of himself. 'It wasn't fast, you know,' said Chiltern, 'and I don't call that a stiff country. Besides, Meg is very handy when you've got her out of the crowd. You shall ride Bonebreaker to-morrow at Somerby, and you'll find that better fun.'

'Bonebreaker? Haven't I heard you say he rushes like mischief?'

'Well, he does rush. But, by George! you want a horse to rush in that country. When you have to go right through four or five feet of stiff green wood, like a bullet through a target, you want a little force, or you're apt to be left up a tree.'

'And what do you ride?'

'A brute I never put my leg on yet. He was sent down to Wilcox here, out of Lincolnshire, because they couldn't get anybody to ride him there. They say he goes with his head up in the air, and won't look at a fence that isn't as high as his breast. But I think he'll do here. I never saw a better made beast, or one with more power. Do you look at his shoulders. He's to be had for seventy pounds, and these are the sort of horses I like to buy.'

Again they dined alone, and Lord Chiltern explained to Phineas that he rarely associated with the men of either of the hunts in which he rode. 'There is a set of fellows down here who are poison to me, and there is another set, and I am poison to them. Everybody is very civil, as you see, but I have no associates. And gradually I am getting to have a reputation as though I were the devil himself. I think I shall come out next year dressed entirely in black.'

'Are you not wrong to give way to that kind of thing?'

'What the deuce am I to do? I can't make civil little speeches. When once a man gets a reputation as an ogre, it is the most difficult thing in the world to drop it. I could have a score of men here every day if I liked it—my title would do that for me—but they would be men I should loathe, and I should be sure to tell them so, even though I did not mean it. Bonebreaker, and the new horse, and another, went on at twelve to-day. You must expect hard work to-morrow, as I daresay we shan't be home before eight.'

The next day's meet was in Leicestershire, not far from Melton, and they started early. Phineas, to tell the truth of him, was rather afraid of Bonebreaker, and looked forward to the probability of an accident. He had neither wife nor child, and nobody had a better right to risk his neck. 'We'll put a gag on 'im,' said the groom, 'and you'll ride 'im in a ring,—so that you may well-nigh break his jaw; but he is a rum un, sir.' 'I'll do my best,' said Phineas. 'He'll take all that,' said the groom. 'Just let him have his own way at everything,' said Lord Chiltern, as they moved away from the meet to Pickwell Gorse; 'and if you'll only sit on his back, he'll carry you through as safe as a church.' Phineas could not help thinking that the counsels of the master and of the groom were very different. 'My idea is,' continued Lord Chiltern, that in hunting you should always avoid a crowd. I don't think a horse is worth riding that will go in a crowd. It's just like yachting,—you should have plenty of sea-room. If you're to pull your horse up at every fence till somebody else is over, I think you'd better come out on a donkey.' And so they went away to Pickwell Gorse.

There were over two hundred men out, and Phineas began to think that it might not be so easy to get out of the crowd. A crowd in a fast run no doubt

Foxhunting: Clearing a Ditch by John Frederick Herring, 1839

quickly becomes small by degrees and beautifully less; but it is very difficult, especially for a stranger, to free himself from the rush at the first start. Lord Chiltern's horse plunged about so violently, as they stood on a little hill-side looking down upon the cover, that he was obliged to take him to a distance, and Phineas followed him. 'If he breaks down wind,' said Lord Chiltern, 'we can't be better than we are here. If he goes up wind, he must turn before long, and we shall be all right.' As he spoke an old hound opened true and sharp,— an old hound whom all the pack believed,—and in a moment there was no doubt that the fox had been found. 'There are not above eight or nine acres in it,' said Lord Chiltern, 'and he can't hang long. Did you ever see such an un-easy brute as this in your life? But I feel certain he'll go well when he gets away.'

Phineas was too much occupied with his own horse to think much of that on which Lord Chiltern was mounted. Bonebreaker, the very moment that he heard the old hound's note, stretched out his head, and put his mouth upon the bit, and began to tremble in every muscle. 'He's a great deal more anxious for it than you and I are,' said Lord Chiltern. 'I see they've given you that gag. But don't you ride him on it till he wants it. Give him lots of room, and he'll go in the snaffle.' All which caution made Phineas think that any insurance office would charge very dear on his life at the present moment.

The fox took two rings of the gorse, and then he went—up wind. 'It's not a vixen, I'll swear,' said Lord Chiltern. 'A vixen in cub never went away like that yet. Now then, Finn, my boy, keep to the right.' And Lord Chiltern, with the horse out of Lincolnshire, went away across the brow of the hill, leaving the hounds to the left, and selected, as his point of exit into the next field, a stiff rail, which, had there been an accident, must have put a very wide margin of ground between the rider and his horse. 'Go hard at your fences, and then you'll fall clear,' he had said to Phineas. I don't think, however, that he would have ridden at the rail as he did, but that there was no help for him. 'The brute began in his own way, and carried on after in the same fashion all through,' he said afterwards. Phineas took the fence a little lower down, and what it was at which he rode he never knew. Bonebreaker sailed over it, whatever it was, and he soon found himself by his friend's side.

The ruck of the men were lower down than our two heroes, and there were others far away to the left, and others, again, who had been at the end of the gorse, and were now behind. Our friends were not near the hounds, not within two fields of them, but the hounds were below them, and therefore could be seen. 'Don't be in a hurry, and they'll be round upon us,' Lord Chiltern said. 'How the deuce is one to help being in a hurry?' said Phineas, who was doing his very best to ride Bonebreaker with the snaffle, but had already began to feel that Bonebreaker cared nothing for that weak instrument. 'By George, I should like to change with you,' said Lord Chiltern. The Lincolnshire horse was going along with his head very low, boring as he galloped, but throwing his neck up at his fences, just when he ought to have kept himself steady. After this, though Phineas kept near Lord Chiltern throughout the run, they were not again near enough to exchange words; and, indeed, they had but little breath for such purpose.

Lord Chiltern rode still a little in advance, and Phineas, knowing his friend's partiality for solitude when taking his fences, kept a little to his left. He began to find that Bonebreaker knew pretty well what he was about. As for not using the gag rein, that was impossible. When a horse puts out what strength he has against a man's arm, a man must put out what strength he has against the horse's mouth. But Bonebreaker was cunning, and had had a gag rein on before. He contracted his lip here, and bent out his jaw there, till he had settled it to his mind, and then went away after his own fashion. He seemed to have a passion for smashing through big, high-grown ox-fences, and by degrees his rider came to feel that if there was nothing worse coming, the fun was not bad.

The fox ran up wind for a couple of miles or so, as Lord Chiltern had prophesied, and then turned,—not to the right, as would best have served him and Phineas, but to the left,—so that they were forced to make their way through the ruck of horses before they could place themselves again. Phineas found himself crossing a road, in and out of it, before he knew where he was, and for a while he lost sight of Lord Chiltern. But in truth he was leading now, whereas Lord Chiltern had led before. The two horses having been together all the morning, and on the previous day, were willing enough to remain in company, if they were allowed to do so. They both crossed the road, not very far from each other, going in and out amidst a crowd of horses, and before long were again placed well, now having the hunt on their right, whereas hitherto it had been on their left. They went over large pasture fields, and Phineas began to think that as long as Bonebreaker would be able to go through the thick grown-up hedges, all would be right. Now and again he came to a cut fence, a fence that had been cut and laid, and these were not so pleasant. Force was not sufficient for them, and they admitted of a mistake. But the horse, though he would rush at them unpleasantly, took them when they came without touching them. It might be all right yet,—unless the beast should tire with him; and then, Phineas thought, a misfortune might probably occur. He remembered, as he flew over one such impediment, that he rode a stone heavier than his friend. At the end of forty-five minutes Bone-breaker also might become aware of the fact.

The hounds were running well in sight to their right, and Phineas began to feel some of that pride which a man indulges when he becomes aware that he has taken his place comfortably, has left the squad behind, and is going well. There were men nearer the hounds than he was, but he was near enough even for ambition. There had already been enough of the run to make him sure that it would be a 'good thing', and enough to make him aware also that probably it might be too good. When a run is over, men are very apt to regret the termination, who a minute or two before were anxiously longing that the hounds might pull down their game. To finish well is everything in hunting. To have led for over an hour is nothing, let the pace and country have been

Foxhunting: Encouraging Hounds by John Frederick Herring, 1839

what they might, if you fall away during the last half mile. Therefore it is that those behind hope that the fox may make this or that cover, while the forward men long to see him turned over in every field. To ride to hounds is very glorious; but to have ridden to hounds is more glorious still. They had now crossed another road, and a larger one, and had got into a somewhat closer country. The fields were not so big, and the fences were not so high. Phineas got a moment to look about him, and saw Lord Chiltern riding without his cap. He was very red in the face, and his eyes seemed to glare, and he was tugging at his horse with all his might. But the animal seemed still to go with perfect command of strength, and Phineas had too much work on his own hands to think of offering Quixotic assistance to anyone else. He saw some one, a farmer, as he thought, speak to Lord Chiltern as they rode close together; but Chiltern only shook his head and pulled at his horse.

There were brooks in those parts. The river Eye forms itself thereabouts, or some of its tributaries do so; and these tributaries, though small as rivers, are considerable to men on one side who are called by the exigencies of the occasion to place themselves quickly on the other. Phineas knew nothing of these brooks; but Bonebreaker had gone gallantly over two, and now that there came a third in the way, it was to be hoped that he might go gallantly over that also. Phineas, at any rate, had no power to decide otherwise. As long as the brute would go straight with him he could sit him; but he had long given up the idea of having a will of his own. Indeed, till he was within twenty yards of the brook, he did not see that it was larger than the others. He looked around, and there was Chiltern close to him, still fighting with his horse—but the farmer had turned away. He thought that Chiltern nodded to him, as much as to tell him to go on. On he went at any rate. The brook, when he came to it, seemed to be a huge black hole, yawning beneath him. The banks were quite steep, and just where he was to take off there was an ugly stump. It was too late to think of anything. He stuck his knees against his saddle—and in a moment was on the other side. The brute, who had taken off a yard before the stump, knowing well the danger of striking it with his foot, came down with a grunt, and did, I think, begin to feel the weight of that extra stone. Phineas, as soon as he was safe, looked back, and there was Lord Chiltern's horse in the very act of his spring—higher up the rivulet, where it was even broader. At that distance Phineas could see that Lord Chiltern was wild with rage against the beast. But whether he wished to take the leap or wished to avoid it, there was no choice left to him. The animal rushed at the brook, and in a moment the horse and horseman were lost to sight. It was well then that that extra stone should tell, as it enabled Phineas to arrest his horse and to come back to his friend.

The Lincolnshire horse had chested the further bank, and of course had fallen back into the stream. When Phineas got down he found that Lord Chiltern was wedged in between the horse and the bank, which was better, at any rate, than being under the horse in the water. 'All right, old fellow,' he said, with a smile, when he saw Phineas. 'You go on; it's too good to lose.' But he was very pale, and seemed to be quite helpless where he lay. The horse did not move—and never did move again. He had smashed his shoulder to pieces against a stump on the bank, and was afterwards shot on that very spot.

When Phineas got down he found that there was but little water where the horse lay. The depth of the stream had been on the side from which they had taken off, and the thick black mud lay within a foot of the surface, close to the bank against which Lord Chiltern was propped. 'That's the worst one I ever was on,' said Lord Chiltern; 'but I think he's gruelled now.'

'Are you hurt?'

'Well;—I fancy there is something amiss. I can't move my arms; and I catch my breath. My legs are all right if I could get away from this accursed brute.'

'I told you so,' said the farmer, coming and looking down upon them from the bank. 'I told you so, but you wouldn't be said.' Then he too got down, and between them both they extricated Lord Chiltern from his position, and got him on to the bank.

'That un's a dead un,' said the farmer, pointing to the horse.

'So much the better,' said his lordship. 'Give us a drop of sherry, Finn.'

He had broken his collar-bone and three of his ribs. They got a farmer's trap from Wissindine and took him into Oakham. When there, he insisted on being taken on through Stamford to the Willingford Bull before he would have his bones set,—picking up, however, a surgeon at Stamford. Phineas remained with him for a couple of days, losing his run with the Fitzwilliams and a day at the potted peas, and became very fond of his patient as he sat by his bedside.

'That was a good run, though, wasn't it?' said Lord Chiltern as Phineas took his leave. 'And, by George, Phineas, you rode Bonebreaker so well, that you shall have him as often as you'll come down. I don't know how it is, but you Irish fellows always ride.

CHAPTER 5

RED LETTER DAYS IN BRITISH COLUMBIA

By Lieutenant Townsend Whelen

In the month of July, 1901, my partner, Bill Andrews, and I were at a small Hudson Bay post in the northern part of British Columbia, outfitting for a long hunting and exploring trip in the wild country to the North. The official map showed this country as "unexplored," with one or two rivers shown by dotted lines. This map was the drawing card which had brought us thousands of miles by rail, stage and pack train to this out-of-the-way spot. By the big stove in the living room of the factor's house we listened to weird tales of this north country, of its enormous mountains and glaciers, its rivers and lakes and of the quantities of game and fish. The factor told us of three men who had tried to get through there in the Klondike rush several years before and had not been heard from yet. The trappers and Siwashes could tell us of trails which ran up either side of the Scumscum, the river on which the post stood, but no one knew what lay between that and the Yukon to the north.

We spent two days here outfitting and on the morning of the third said goodbye to the assembled population and started with our pack train up the east bank of the Scumscum. We were starting out to live and travel in an unknown wilderness for over six months and our outfit may perhaps interest my readers: We had two saddle horses, four pack horses and a dog. A small tent formed one pack cover. We had ten heavy army blankets, which we used for saddle blankets while traveling, they being kept clean by using canvas sweat pads under them. We were able to pack 150 pounds of grub on each horse, divided up as nearly as I can remember as follows: One hundred and fifty pounds flour, 50 pounds sugar, 30 pounds beans, 10 pounds rice, 10 pounds dried apples, 20 pounds prunes, 30 pounds corn meal, 20 pounds oatmeal, 30 pounds potatoes, 10 pounds onions, 50 pounds bacon, 25 pounds salt, 1 pound pepper, 6 cans baking powder, 10 pounds soap, 10 pounds tobacco, 10 pounds tea, and a few little incidentals weighing probably 10 pounds. We took two extra sets of shoes for each horse, with tools for shoeing, 2 axes, 25 boxes of wax matches, a large can of gun oil, canton flannel for gun rags, 2 cleaning rods, a change of underclothes, 6 pairs of socks and 6 moccasins each, with buckskin for resoling, toilet articles, 100 yards of fishing line, 2 dozen fish hooks, an oil stove, awl, file, screw-driver, needles and thread, etc.

For cooking utensils we had 2 frying pans, 3 kettles to nest, 2 tin cups, 3 tin plates and a gold pan. We took 300 cartridges for each of our rifles. Bill carried a .38–55 Winchester, model '94, and I had my old .40–72 Winchester, model '95, which had proved too reliable to relinquish for a high-power small bore. Both rifles were equipped with Lyman sights and carefully sighted. As a precaution we each took along extra front sights, firing pins and main-springs, but did not have a chance to use them. I loaded the ammunition for both rifles myself, with black powder, smokeless priming, and lead bullets. Both rifles proved equal to every emergency.

Where the post stood the mountains were low and covered for the most part with sage brush, with here and there a grove of pines or quaking aspen. As our pack train wound its way up the narrow trail above the river bank we saw many Siwashes spearing salmon, a very familiar sight in that country. These gradually became fewer and fewer, then we passed a miner's cabin and a Siwash village with its little log huts and its hay fields, from which grass is cut for the winter consumption of the horses. Gradually all signs of civilization disappeared, the mountains rose higher and higher, the valley became a canon, and the roar of the river increased, until finally the narrowing trail wound around an outrageous corner with the river a thousand feet below, and looming up in front of us appeared a range of snow-capped mountains, and thus at last we were in the haven where we would be.

That night we camped on one of the little pine-covered benches above the canon. My, but it was good to get the smell of that everlasting sage out of our nostrils, and to take long whiffs of the balsam-ladened air! Sunset comes very late at this latitude in July, and it was an easy matter to wander up a little draw at nine in the evening and shoot the heads of three grouse. After supper it was mighty good to lie and smoke and listen to the tinkle of the horse bells as they fed on the luscious mountain grass. We were old campmates, Bill and I, and it took us back to many trips we had had before, which were, however, to be surpassed many times by this one. I can well remember how as a boy, when I first took to woods loafing, I used to brood over a little work which we all know so well, entitled, "Woodcraft," by that grand old man, "Nessmuk," and particularly that part where he relates about his eight-day tramp through the then virgin wilderness of Michigan. But here we were, starting out on a trip which was to take over half a year, during which time we were destined to cover over 1,500 miles of unexplored mountains, without the sight of a human face or an axe mark other than our own.

The next day after about an hour's travel, we passed the winter cabin of an old trapper, now deserted, but with the frames for stretching bear skins and boards for marten pelts lying around—betokening the owner's occupation. The dirt roof was entirely covered with the horns of deer and mountain sheep, and we longed to close our jaws on some good red venison. Here the man-made trails came to an end, and henceforth we used the game trails entirely. These intersect the country in every direction, being made by the deer, sheep and caribou in their migrations between the high and low altitudes. In some places they were hardly discernible, while in others we followed them for days, when they were as plainly marked as the bridle paths in a city park. A little further on we saw a whole family of goats sunning themselves on a high bluff across the river, and that night we dined on the ribs of a fat little spike buck which I shot in the park where we pitched our tent.

To chronicle all the events which occurred on that glorious trip would, I fear, tire my readers, so I will choose from the rich store certain ones which have made red-letter days in our lives. I can recollect but four days when we were unable to kill enough game or catch enough fish to keep the table well supplied, and as luck would have it, those four days came together, and we nearly starved. We had been camped for about a week in a broad wooded valley, having a glorious loaf after a hard struggle across a mountain pass, and were living on trout from a little stream alongside camp, and grouse which were in the pine woods by the thousands. Tiring of this diet we decided to take a little side trip and get a deer or two, taking only our three fattest horses and leaving the others behind to fatten up on the long grass in the valley, for they had become very poor owing to a week's work high up above timber line. The big game here was all high up in the mountains to escape the heat of the valley. So we started one morning, taking only a little tea, rice, three bannocks, our bedding and rifles, thinking that we would enjoy living on meat straight for a couple of days. We had along with us a black mongrel hound named Lion, belonging to Bill. He was a fine dog on grouse but prone to chase a deer once in a while.

About eight miles up the valley could be seen a high mountain of green serpentine rock and for many days we had been speculating on the many fine bucks which certainly lay in the little ravines around the base, so we chose this for our goal. We made the top of the mountain about three in the afternoon, and gazing down on the opposite side we saw a little lake with good horse feed around it and determined to camp there. About half way down we jumped a doe and as it stood on a little hummock Bill blazed away at it and undershot. This was too much for Lion, the hound, and he broke after the deer, making the mountainside ring with his baying for half an hour. Well, we hunted all the next day, and the next, and never saw a hair. That dog had chased the deer all out of the country with his barking.

By this time our little grub-stake of rice, bannocks and tea was exhausted, and, to make things worse, on the third night we had a terrific hail storm, the stones covering the ground three inches deep. Breakfast the next morning consisted of tea alone and we felt pretty glum as we started out, determining that if we did not find game that day we would pull up stakes for our big camp in the valley. About one o'clock I struck a fresh deer trail and had not followed it long before three or four others joined it, all traveling on a game trail which led up a valley. This valley headed up about six miles from our camp in three little ravines, each about four miles long. When I got to the junction of these ravines it was getting dark and I had to make for camp. Bill was there before me and had the fire going and some tea brewing, but nothing else. He had traveled about twenty miles that day and had not seen a thing. I can still see the disgusted look on his face when he found I had killed nothing. We drank our tea in silence, drew our belts tighter and went to bed.

The next morning we saddled up our horses and pulled out. We had not tasted food for about sixty hours and were feeling very faint and weak. I can remember what an effort it was to get into the saddle and how sick and weak I felt when old Baldy, my saddle horse, broke into a trot. Our way back led near the spot where I had left the deer trail the night before, and we determined to ride that way hoping that perhaps we might get a shot at them. Bill came first, then Loco, the pack horse, and I brought up the rear. As we were crossing one of the little ravines at the head of the main valley Loco bolted and Bill took after him to drive him back into the trail. I sat on my horse idly watching the race, when suddenly I saw a mouse-colored flash and then another and heard the thump, thump of cloven feet. Almost instantly the whole ravine seemed to be alive with deer. They were running in every direction. I leaped from my horse and cut loose at the nearest, which happened to be a doe. She fell over a log and I could see her tail waving in little circles and knew I had her. Then I turned on a big buck on the other side of the ravine and at the second shot he stumbled and rolled into the little stream. I heard Bill shooting off to the left and yelled to him that we had enough, and he soon joined me, saying he had a spike buck down. It was the work of but a few minutes to dress the deer and soon we had a little fire going and the three livers hanging in little strips around it. Right here we three, that is, Bill, the dog and myself, disposed of a liver apiece, and my! how easily and quickly it went—the first meat in over a week. Late that night we made our horse camp in the lower valley, having to walk all the way as our horses packed the meat. The next day was consumed entirely with jerking meat, cooking and eating. We consumed half the spike buck that day. When men do work such as we were doing their appetites are enormous, even without a fast of four days to sharpen them up.

One night I well remember after a particularly hard day with the pack train through a succession of wind-falls. We killed a porcupine just before camping and made it into a stew with rice, dough balls, onions and thick gravy, seasoned with curry. It filled the kettle to within an inch of the top and we ate the whole without stopping, whereat Bill remarked that it was enough for a whole boarding-house. According to the catalogue of Abercrombie and Fitch that kettle held eight quarts.

We made it the rule while our horses were in condition, to travel four days in the week, hunt two and rest one. Let me chronicle a day of traveling; it may interest some of you who have never traveled with a pack train. Arising at the first streak of dawn, one man cooked the breakfast while the other drove in the horses. These were allowed to graze free at every camping place, each horse having a cow bell around its neck, only Loco being hobbled, for he had a fashion of wandering off on an exploring expedition of his own and leading all the other horses with him. The horses were liable to be anywhere within two miles of camp, and it was necessary to get behind them to drive them in. Four miles over these mountains would be considered a pretty good day's work in the East. Out here it merely gave one an appetite for his breakfast. If you get behind a pack of well-trained horses they will usually walk right straight to camp, but on occasions I have walked, thrown stones and cussed from seven until twelve before I managed to get them in. Sometimes a bear will run off a pack of horses. This happened to us once and it took two days to track them to the head of a canon, fifteen miles off, and then we had to break Loco all over again.

Breakfast and packing together would take an hour, so we seldom got started before seven o'clock. One of us rode first to pick out the trail, then followed the four pack horses and the man in the rear, whose duty it was to keep them in the trail and going along. Some days the trail was fine, running along the grassy south hillsides with fine views of the snowcapped ranges, rivers, lakes and glaciers; and on others it was one continual struggle over fallen logs, boulders, through ice-cold rivers, swifter than the Niagara rapids, and

Mountain overlook, British Columbia

around bluffs so high that we could scarcely distinguish the outlines of the trees below. Suppose for a minute that you have the job of keeping the horses in the trail. You ride behind the last horse, lazily watching the train. You do not hurry them as they stop for an instant to catch at a whiff of bunch grass beside the trail. Two miles an hour is all the speed you can hope to make. Suddenly one horse will leave the trail enticed by some particularly green grass a little to one side, and leaning over in your saddle you pick up a stone and hurl it at the delinquent, and he falls into line again. Then everything goes well until suddenly one of the pack horses breaks off on a faint side trail going for all he is worth. You dig in your spurs and follow him down the mountain side over rocks and down timber until he comes to a stop half a mile below in a thicket of quaking aspen. You extricate him and drive him back. The next thing you know one of the horses starts to buck and you notice that his pack is turning; then everything starts at once. The pack slides between the horse's legs, he bucks all the harder, the frying pan comes loose, a side pack comes off and the other horses fly in every direction. Perhaps in an hour you have corralled the horses, repacked the cause of your troubles and are hitting the trail again. In another day's travel the trail may lead over down timber and big boulders and for eight solid hours you are whipping the horses to make them jump the obstructions, while your companion is pulling at the halters.

Rustling with a pack train is a soul-trying occupation. Where possible we always aimed to go into camp about three in the afternoon. Then the horses got a good feed before dark—they will not feed well at night—and we had plenty of time to make a comfortable camp and get a good supper. We seldom pitched our tent on these one-night camps unless the weather looked doubtful, preferring to make a bed of pine boughs near the fire. The blankets were laid on top of a couple of pack sheets and the tent over all.

For several days we had been traveling thus, looking for a pass across a long snow-capped mountain range which barred our way to the north. Finally we found a pass between two large peaks where we thought we could get through, so we started up. When we got up to timber-line the wind was blowing so hard that we could not sit on our horses. It would take up large

stones the size of one's fist and hurl them down the mountain side. It swept by us cracking and roaring like a battery of rapid-fire guns. To cross was impossible, so we back-tracked a mile to a spot where a little creek crossed the trail, made camp and waited. It was three days before the wind went down enough to allow us to cross.

The mountain sheep had made a broad trail through the pass and it was easy to follow, being mostly over shale rock. That afternoon, descending the other side of the range, we camped just below timber line by a little lake of the most perfect emerald hue I have ever seen. The lake was about a mile long. At its head a large glacier extended way up towards the peaks. On the east was a wall of bright red rock, a thousand feet high, while to the west the hillside was covered with dwarf pine trees, some of them being not over a foot high and full-grown at that. Below our camp the little stream, the outlet of the lake, bounded down the hillside in a succession of waterfalls. A more beautiful picture I have yet to see. We stayed up late that night watching it in the light of the full moon and thanked our lucky stars that we were alive. It was very cold; we put on all the clothes we owned and turned in under seven blankets. The heavens seemed mighty near, indeed, and the stars crackled and almost exploded with the still silver mountains sparkling all around. We could hear the roar of the waterfalls below us and the bells of the horses on the hillside above. Our noses were very cold. Far off a coyote howled and so we went to sleep—and instantly it was morning.

I arose and washed in the lake. It was my turn to cook, but first of all I got my telescope and looked around for signs of game. Turning the glass to the top of the wooded hillside, I saw something white moving, and getting a steady position, I made it out to be the rump of a mountain sheep. Looking carefully I picked out four others. Then I called Bill. The sheep were mine by right of discovery, so we traded the cook detail and I took my rifle and belt, stripped to trousers, moccasins and shirt, and started out, going swiftly at first to warm up in the keen mountain air. I kept straight up the hillside until I got to the top and then started along the ridge toward the sheep. As I crossed a little rise I caught sight of them five hundred yards ahead, the band numbering about fifty. Some were feeding, others were bedded down in some shale. From here on it was all stalking, mostly crawling through the small trees and bushes which were hardly knee high. Finally, getting within one hundred and fifty yards, I got a good, steady prone position between the bushes, and picking out the largest ram, I got the white Lyman sight nicely centered behind his shoulder and very carefully and gradually I pressed the trigger. The instant the gun went off I knew he was mine, for I could call the shot exactly. Instantly the sheep were on the move. They seemed to double up bunch and then vanish. It was done so quickly that I doubt if I could have gotten in another shot even if I had wished it. The ram I had fired at was knocked completely off its feet, but picked himself up instantly and started off with the others; but after he had run about a hundred yards I saw his head drop and turning half a dozen somersaults, he rolled down the hill and I knew I had made a heart shot. His horns measured 16½ inches at the base, and the nose contained an enormous bump, probably caused in one of his fights for the supremacy of the herd.

I dressed the ram and then went for the horses. Bill, by this time, had everything packed up, so after going up the hill and loading the sheep on my saddle horse, we started down the range for a region where it was warmer and less strenuous and where the horse feed was better. That night we had mountain sheep ribs—the best meat that ever passed a human's mouth—and I had a head worth bringing home. A 16½-inch head is very rare in these days. I believe the record head measured about 19 inches. I remember distinctly, however, on another hunt in the Lillooet district of British Columbia, finding in the long grass of a valley the half-decayed head of an enormous ram. I measured the pith of the skull where the horn had been and it recorded 18 inches. The horn itself must have been at least 21 inches. The ram probably died of old age or was unable to get out of the high altitude when the snow came.

We journeyed on and on, having a glorious time in the freedom of the mountains. We were traveling in a circle, the diameter of which was about three hundred miles. One day we struck an enormous glacier and had to bend way off to the right to avoid it. For days as we travelled that glacier kept us company. It had its origin way up in a mass of peaks and perpetual snow, being fed from a dozen valleys. At least six moraines could be distinctly seen on its surface, and the air in its vicinity was decidedly cool. Where we first struck it it was probably six miles wide and I believe it was not a bit less than fifty miles long. We named it Chilco glacier, because it undoubtedly drained into a large lake of that name near the coast. At this point we were not over two hundred miles from the Pacific Ocean.

As the leaves on the aspen trees started to turn we gradually edged around and headed toward our starting point, going by another route, however, trusting to luck and the careful map we had been making to bring us out somewhere on the Scum-scum river above the post. The days were getting short now and the nights very cold. We had to travel during almost all the daylight and our horses started to get poor. The shoes we had taken for them were used up by this time and we had to avoid as much as possible the rocky country. We travelled fast for a month until we struck the headwaters of the Scum-scum; then knowing that we were practically safe from being snowed up in the mountain we made a permanent camp on a hillside where the horsefeed was good and started to hunt and tramp to our hearts' delight, while our horses filled up on the grass. We never killed any more game than we could use, which was about one animal every ten days. In this climate meat will keep for a month if protected from flies in the daytime and exposed to the night air after dark.

We were very proud of our permanent camp. The tent was pitched under a large pine tree in a thicket of willows and quaking aspen. All around it was built a windbreak of logs and pine boughs, leaving in front a yard, in the center of which was our camp fire. The windbreak went up six feet high and when a fire was going in front of the tent we were as warm as though in a cabin, no matter how hard the wind blew. Close beside the tent was a little spring, and a half a mile away was a lake full of trout from fifteen pounds down. We spent three days laying in a supply of firewood. Altogether it was the best camp I ever slept in. The hunting within tramping distance was splendid. We rarely hunted together, each preferring to go his own way. When we did not need meat we hunted varmints, and I brought in quite a number of prime coyote pelts and one wolf. One evening Bill staggered into camp with a big mountain lion over his shoulders. He just happened to run across it in a little pine thicket. That was the only one we saw on the whole trip, although their tracks were everywhere and we frequently heard their mutterings in the still evenings. The porcupines at this camp were unusually numerous. They would frequently get inside our wind break and had a great propensity for eating our soap. Lion, the hound, would not bother them; he had learned his lesson well. When they came around he would get an expression on his face as much as to say, "You give me a pain."

The nights were now very cold. It froze every night and we bedded ourselves down with lots of skins and used enormous logs on the fire so that it would keep going all night. We shot some marmots and made ourselves fur caps and gloves and patched up our outer garments with buckskin. And still the snow did not come.

One day while out hunting I saw a big goat on a bluff off to my right and determined to try to get him for his head, which appeared through my telescope to be an unusually good one. He was about half a mile off when I first spied him and the bluff extended several miles to the southwest like a great wall shutting off the view in that direction. I worked up to the foot of the bluffs and then along; climbing up several hundred feet I struck a shelf which appeared to run along the face at about the height I had seen the goat. It was ticklish work, for the shelf was covered with slide rock which I had to avoid disturbing, and then, too, in places it dwindled to a ledge barely three feet wide with about five hundred feet of nothing underneath. After about four hundred yards of this work I heard a rock fall above me and looking up saw the billy leaning over an outrageous corner looking at me. Aiming as nearly as I could straight up I let drive at the middle of the white mass. There was a grunt, a scramble and a lot of rocks, and then down came the goat, striking in between the cliff and a big boulder and not two feet from me. I fairly shivered for fear he would jump up and butt me off the ledge, but he only gave one quiver and lay still. The 330-grain bullet entering the stomach, had broken the spine and killed instantly. He was an old grandfather and had a splen-did head, which I now treasure very highly. I took the head, skin, fat and some of the meat back to camp that night, having to pack it off the bluff in sections. The fat rendered out into three gold-pans full of lard. Goat-fat is excellent for frying and all through the trip it was a great saving on our bacon.

Then one night the snow came. We heard it gently tapping on the tent, and by morning there was three inches in our yard. The time had come only too soon to pull out, which we did about ten o'clock, bidding good-bye to our permanent camp with its comfortable windbreak, its fireplace, table and chairs. Below us the river ran through a canon and we had to cross quite a high mountain range to get through. As we ascended the snow got deeper and deeper. It was almost two feet deep on a level on top of the range. We had to go down a very steep hog-back, and here had trouble in plenty. The horses' feet balled up with snow and they were continually sliding. A pack horse slid down on top of my saddle horse and started him. I was on foot in front and they knocked me down and the three of us slid until stopped by a fallen tree. Such a mess I never saw. One horse was on top of another. The pack was loose and frozen ropes tangled up with everything. It took us half an hour to straighten up the mess and the frozen lash ropes cut our hands frightfully. My ankle had become slightly strained in the mix-up and for several days I suffered agonies with it. There was no stopping—we had to hit the trail hard or get snowed in. One day we stopped to hunt. Bill went out while I nursed my leg. He brought in a fine seven-point buck.

Speaking of the hunt he said: "I jumped the buck in a flat of down timber. He was going like mad about a hundred yards off when I first spied him. I threw up the old rifle and blazed away five times before he tumbled. Each time I pulled I was conscious that the sights looked just like that trademark of the Lyman sight showing the running deer and the sight. When I went over to look at the buck I had a nice little bunch of five shots right behind the shoulder. Those Lyman sights are surely the sights for a hunting rifle." Bill was one of the best shots on game I ever saw. One day I saw him cut the heads off of three grouse in trees while he sat in the saddle with his horse walking up hill. Both our rifles did mighty good work. The more I use a rifle the more I become convinced of the truth of the saying, "Beware of the man with one gun." Get a good rifle to suit you exactly. Fix the trigger pull and sights exactly as you wish them and then stick to that gun as long as it will shoot accurately and you will make few misses in the field.

Only too soon we drove our pack-train into the post. As we rode up two men were building a shack. One of them dropped a board and we nearly jumped out of our skins at the terrific noise. My! how loud everything sounded to our ears, accustomed only to the stillness of those grand mountains. We stayed at the post three days, disposing of our horses and boxing up our heads and skins, and then pulled out for civilization. Never again will such experiences come to us. The day of the wilderness hunter has gone for good. And so the hunt of our lives came to an end.

CHAPTER 6

THE HUNT FOR THE MAN-EATERS OF TSAVO

By Lt. Col. J. H. Patterson, D. S. O.

Editor's Note: When assigned to help supervise the building of a Uganda Railroad bridge over the Tsavo River in east Africa in March, 1898, Lt. Col. J. H. Patterson, D. S. O., had little idea of the magnitude of the adventure upon which he was embarking. The site of the bridge, which is today a part of Kenya, became the scene of savage attacks by man-eating lions preying on the workers. Lt. Col. Patterson's stirring book, *The Man-Eaters of Tsavo*, remains in print to this day. The drama was also captured quite well in the film *The Ghost and the Darkness*, starring Val Kilmer and Michael Douglas.

Unfortunately this happy state of affairs did not continue for long, and our work was soon interrupted in a rude and startling manner. Two most voracious and insatiable man-eating lions appeared upon the scene, and for over nine months waged an intermittent warfare against the railway and all those connected with it in the vicinity of Tsavo. This culminated in a perfect reign of terror in December, 1898, when they actually succeeded in bringing the railway works to a complete standstill for about three weeks. At first they were not always successful in their efforts to carry off a victim, but as time went on they stopped at nothing and indeed braved any danger in order to obtain their favourite food. Their methods then became so uncanny, and their man-stalking so well-timed and so certain of success, that the workmen firmly believed that they were not real animals at all, but devils in lions' shape. Many a time the coolies solemnly assured me that it was absolutely useless to attempt to shoot them. They were quite convinced that the angry spirits of two departed native chiefs had taken this form in order to protect against a railway being made through their country, and by stopping its progress to avenge the insult thus shown to them.

I had only been a few days at Tsavo when I first heard that these brutes had been seen in the neighbourhood. Shortly afterwards one or two coolies mysteriously disappeared, and I was told that they had been carried off by night from their tents and devoured by lions. At the time I did not credit this story, and was more inclined to believe that the unfortunate men had been the victims of foul play at the hands of some of their comrades. They were, as it happened, very good workmen, and had each saved a fair number of rupees, so I thought it quite likely that some scoundrels from the gangs had murdered them for the sake of their money. This suspicion, however, was very soon dispelled. About three weeks after my arrival, I was roused one morning about daybreak and told that one of my jemadars, a fine powerful Sikh named Ungan Singh, had been seized in his tent during the night, and dragged off and eaten.

Naturally I lost no time in making an examination of the place, and was soon convinced that the man had indeed been carried off by a lion, and its

The Tsavo River, Uganda

"pug" marks were plainly visible in the sand, while the furrows made by the heels of the victim showed the direction in which he had been dragged away. Moreover, the jemadar shared his tent with half a dozen other workmen, and one of his bedfellows had actually witnessed the occurrence. He graphically described how, at about midnight, the lion suddenly put its head in at the open tent door and seized Ungan Singh—who happened to be nearest the opening—by the throat. The unfortunate fellow cried out "Choro" ("Let go"), and threw his arms up round the lion's neck. The next moment he was gone, and his panic-stricken companions lay helpless, forced to listen to the terrible struggle which took place outside. Poor Ungan Singh must have died hard; but what chance had he? As a coolie gravely remarked, "Was he not fighting with a lion?"

On hearing this dreadful story I at once set out to try to track the animal, and was accompanied by Captain Haslem, who happened to be staying at Tsavo at the time, and who, poor fellow, himself met with a tragic fate very shortly afterwards. We found it an easy matter to follow the route taken by the lion, as he appeared to have stopped several times before beginning his meal. Pools of blood marked these halting-places, where he doubtless indulged in the man-eaters' habit of licking the skin off so as to get at the fresh blood. (I have been led to believe that this is their custom from the appearance of two half-eaten bodies which I subsequently rescued: the skin was gone in places, and the flesh looked dry, as if it had been sucked.) On reaching the spot where the body had been devoured, a dreadful spectacle presented itself. The ground all round was covered with blood and morsels of flesh and bones, but the unfortunate jemadar's head had been left intact, save for the holes made by the lion's tusks on seizing him, and lay a short distance away from the other remains, the eyes staring wide open with a startled, horrified look in them. The place was considerably cut up, and on closer examination we found that two lions had been there and had probably struggled for possession of the body. It was the most gruesome sight I had ever seen. We collected the remains as well as we could and heaped stones on them, the head with its fixed, terrified stare seeming to watch us all the time, for it we did not bury, but took back to camp for identification before the Medical Officer.

Thus occurred my first experience of man-eating lions, and I vowed there and then that I would spare no pains to rid the neighbourhood of the brutes. I little knew the trouble that was in store for me, or how narrow were to be my own escapes from sharing poor Ungan Singh's fate.

That same night I sat up in a tree close to the late jemadar's, tent, hoping that the lions would return to it for another victim. I was followed to my perch by a few of the more terrified coolies, who begged to be allowed to sit up in the tree with me; all the other workmen remained in their tents, but no more doors were left open. I had with me my .303 and 12-bore shot gun, one barrel loaded with ball and the other with slug. Shortly after settling down to my vigil, my hopes of bagging one of the brutes were raised by the sound of their ominous roaring coming closer and closer. Presently this ceased, and quiet reigned for an hour or two, as lions always stalk their prey in complete silence. All at once, however, we heard a great uproar and frenzied cries coming from another camp about half a mile away; we knew then that the lions had seized a victim there, and that we should see or hear nothing further of them that night.

Next morning I found that one of the brutes had broken into a tent at Railhead Camp—whence we had heard the commotion during the night—and had made off with a poor wretch who was lying there asleep. After a night's rest, therefore, I took up my position in a suitable tree near this tent. I did not at all like the idea of walking the half-mile to the place after dark, but all the same I felt fairly safe, as one of my men carried a bright lamp close behind me. He in his turn was followed by another leading a goat, which I tied under my tree in the hope that the lion might be tempted to seize it instead of a coolie. A steady drizzle commenced shortly after I had settled down to my night of watching, and I was soon thoroughly chilled and wet. I stuck to my uncomfortable post, however, hoping to get a shot, but I well remember the feeling of impotent disappointment I experienced when about midnight I heard screams and cries and a heartrending shriek, which told me that the man-eaters had again eluded me and had claimed another victim elsewhere.

At this time the various camps for the workmen were very scattered, so that the lions had a range of some eight miles on either side of Tsavo to work upon; and as their tactics seemed to be to break into a different camp each night, it was most difficult to forestall them. They almost appeared, too, to have an extraordinary and uncanny faculty of finding out our plans beforehand, so that no matter in how likely or how tempting a spot we lay in wait for them, they invariably avoided that particular place and seized their victim for the night from some other camp. Hunting them by day moreover, in such a dense wilderness as surrounded us, was an exceedingly tiring and really foolhardy undertaking. In a thick jungle of the kind round Tsavo the hunted animal has every chance against the hunter, as however careful the latter may be, a dead twig or something of the sort is sure to crackle just at the critical moment and so give the alarm. Still I never gave up hope of some day finding their lair, and accordingly continued to devote all my spare time to crawling about through the undergrowth. Many a time when attempting to force my way through this bewildering tangle I had to be released by my gun-bearer from the fast clutches of the "wait-a-bit"; and often with immense pains I succeeded in tracing the lions to the river after they had seized a victim, only to lose the trail from there onwards, owing to the rocky nature of the ground which they seemed to be careful to choose in retreating to their den.

At this early stage of the struggle, I am glad to say, the lions were not always successful in their efforts to capture a human being for their nightly meal, and one or two amusing incidents occurred to relieve the tension from which our nerves were beginning to suffer. On one occasion an enterprising bunniah (Indian trader) was riding along on his donkey late one night, when suddenly a lion sprang out on him knocking over both man and beast. The donkey was badly wounded, and the lion was just about to seize the trader, when in some way or other his claws became entangled in a rope by which two empty oil tins were strung across the donkey's neck. The rattle and clatter made by these as he dragged them after him gave him such a fright that he turned tail and bolted off into the jungle, to the intense relief of the terrified bunniah, who quickly made his way up the nearest tree and remained there, shivering with fear, for the rest of the night.

Shortly after this episode, a Greek contractor named Themistocles Pappadimitrini had an equally marvellous escape. He was sleeping peacefully in his tent one night, when a lion broke in, and seized and made off with the mattress on which he was lying. Though rudely awakened, the Greek was quite unhurt and suffered from nothing worse than a bad fright. This same man, however, met with a melancholy fate not long afterwards. He had been to the Kilima N'jaro district to buy cattle, and on the return journey attempted to take a short cut across country to the railway, but perished miserably of thirst on the way.

On another occasion fourteen coolies who slept together in a large tent were one night awakened by a lion suddenly jumping on to the tent and breaking through it. The brute landed with one claw on a coolie's shoulder, which was badly torn; but instead of seizing the man himself, in his hurry he grabbed a large bag of rice which happened to be lying in the tent, and made off with it, dropping it in disgust some little distance away when he realised his mistake.

These, however, were only the earlier efforts of the man-eaters. Later on, as will be seen, nothing flurried or frightened them in the least, and except as food they showed a complete contempt for human beings. Having once marked down a victim, they would allow nothing to deter them from securing him, whether he were protected by a thick fence, or inside a closed tent, or sitting round a brightly burning fire. Shots, shouting and firebrands they alike held in derision.

THE ATTACK ON THE GOODS-WAGON

All this time my own tent was pitched in an open clearing, unprotected by a fence of any kind round it. One night when the medical officer, Dr. Rose, was staying with me, we were awakened about midnight by hearing something tumbling about among the tent ropes, but on going out with a lantern we could discover nothing. Daylight, however, plainly revealed the "pug" marks of a lion, so that on that occasion I fancy one or other of us had a narrow escape. Warned by this experience, I at once arranged to move my quarters, and went to join forces with Dr. Brock, who had just arrived at Tsavo to take medical charge of the district. We shared a hut of palm leaves and boughs, which we had constructed on the eastern side of the river, close to the old caravan route leading to Uganda; and we had it surrounded by a circular boma, or thorn fence, about seventy yards in diameter, well made and thick and high. Our personal servants also lived within the enclosure, and a bright fire was always kept up throughout the night. For the sake of coolness, Brock and I used to sit out under the verandah of this hut in the evenings; but it was rather trying to our nerves to attempt to read or write there, as we never knew when a lion might spring over the boma, and be on us before we were aware. We therefore kept our rifles within easy reach, and cast many an anxious glance out into the inky darkness beyond the circle of the firelight. On one or two occasions, we found in the morning that the lions had come quite close to the fence; but fortunately they never succeeded in getting through.

By this time, too, the camps of the workmen had also been surrounded by thorn fences; nevertheless the lions managed to jump over or to break through some one or other of these, and regularly every few nights a man was carried off, the reports of the disappearance of this or that workman coming in to me with painful frequency. So long, however, as Railhead Camp—with its two or three thousand men, scattered over a wide area—remained at Tsavo, the coolies appeared not to take much notice of the dreadful deaths of their comrades. Each man felt, I suppose, that as the man-eaters had such a large number of victims to choose from, the chances of their selecting him in particular were very small. But when the large camp moved ahead with the railway, matters altered considerably. I was then left with only some few hundred men to complete the permanent works; and as all the remaining workmen were naturally camped together the attentions of the lions became more apparent and made a deeper impression. A regular panic consequently ensued, and it required all my powers of persuasion to induce the men to stay on. In fact, I succeeded in doing so only by allowing them to knock off all regular work until they had built exceptionally thick and high bomas round each camp. Within these enclosures fires were kept burning all night, and it was also the duty of the night-watchman to keep clattering half a dozen empty oil tins suspended from a convenient tree. These he manipulated by means of a long rope, while sitting in the hopes of terrifying away the man-eaters. In spite of all these precautions, however, the lions would not be denied, and men continued to disappear.

When the railhead workmen moved on, their hospital camp was left behind. It stood rather apart from the other camps, in a clearing about three-quarters of a mile from my hut, but was protected by a good thick fence and to all appearance was quite secure. It seemed, however, as if barriers were of no avail against the "demons", for before very long one of them found a weak spot in the boma and broke through. On this occasion the Hospital Assistant had a marvellous escape. Hearing a noise outside, he opened the door of his tent and was horrified to see a great lion standing a few yards away looking at him. The beast made a spring towards him, which gave the Assistant such a fright that he jumped backwards, and in doing so luckily upset a box containing medical stores. This crashed down with such a loud clatter of breaking glass that the lion was startled for the moment and made off to another part of the enclosure. Here, unfortunately, he was more successful, as he jumped on to and broke through a tent in which eight patients were lying. Two of them were badly wounded by his spring, while a third poor wretch was seized and dragged off bodily through the thorn fence. The two wounded coolies were left where they lay; a piece of torn tent having fallen over them; and in this position the doctor and I found them on our arrival soon after dawn next morning. We at once decided to move the hospital closer to the main camp; a fresh site was prepared, a stout hedge built round the enclosure, and all the patients were moved in before nightfall.

As I had heard that lions generally visit recently deserted camps, I decided to sit up all night in the vacated boma in the hope of getting an opportunity of bagging one of them; but in the middle of my lonely vigil I had the mortification of hearing shrieks and cries coming from the direction of the new hospital, telling me only too plainly that our dreaded foes had once more eluded me. Hurrying to the place at daylight I found that one of the lions had jumped over the newly erected fence and had carried off the hospital bhisti (water-carrier), and that several other coolies had been unwilling witnesses of the terrible scene which took place within the circle of light given by the big camp fire. The bhisti, it appears, had been lying on the floor, with his head towards the centre of the tent and his feet nearly touching the side. The lion managed to get its head in below the canvas, seized him by the foot and pulled him out. In desperation the unfortunate water-carrier clutched hold of a heavy box in a vain attempt to prevent himself being carried off, and dragged it with him until he was forced to let go by its being stopped by the side of the tent. He then caught hold of a tent rope, and clung tightly to it until it broke. As soon as the lion managed to get him clear of the tent, he sprang at his throat and after a few vicious shakes the poor bhisti's agonising cries were silenced for ever. The brute then seized him in his mouth, like a huge cat with a mouse, and ran up and down the boma looking for a weak spot to break through. This he presently found and plunged into, dragging his victim with him and leaving shreds of torn cloth and flesh as ghastly evidences of his passage through the thorns. Dr. Brock and I were easily able to follow his track, and soon found the remains about four hundred yards away in the bush. There was the usual horrible sight. Very little was left of the unfortunate bhisti—only the skull, the jaws, a few of the larger bones and a portion of the palm with one or two fingers attached. On one of these was a silver ring, and this, with the teeth (a relic much prized by certain castes), was sent to the man's widow in India.

Again it was decided to move the hospital; and again, before nightfall, the work was completed, including a still stronger and thicker boma. When the patients had been moved, I had a covered goods-wagon placed in a favourable position on a siding which ran close to the site which had just been abandoned, and in this Brock and I arranged to sit up that night. We left a couple of tents still standing within the enclosure, and also tied up a few cattle in it as bait for the lions, who had been seen in no less than three different places in the neighbourhood during the afternoon (April 23). Four miles from Tsavo they had attempted to seize a coolie who was walking along the line. Fortunately, however, he had just time to escape up a tree, where he remained, more dead than alive, until he was rescued by the Traffic Manager, who caught sight of him from a passing train. They next appeared close to Tsavo Station, and a couple of hours later some workmen saw one of the lions stalking Dr. Brock as he was returning about dusk from the hospital.

In accordance with our plan, the doctor and I set out after dinner for the goods-wagon, which was about a mile away from our hut. In the light of subsequent events, we did a very foolish thing in taking up our position so late; nevertheless, we reached our destination in safety, and settled down to our watch about ten o'clock. We had the lower half of the door of the wagon closed, while the upper half was left wide open for observation: and we faced, of course, in the direction of the abandoned boma, which, however, we were unable to see in the inky darkness. For an hour or two everything was quiet, and the deadly silence was becoming very monotonous and oppressive, when suddenly, to our right, a dry twig snapped, and we knew that an animal of some sort was about. Soon afterwards we heard a dull thud, as if some heavy body had jumped over the boma. The cattle, too, became very uneasy, and we could hear them moving about restlessly. Then again came dead silence. At this juncture I proposed to my companion that I should get out of the wagon and lie on the ground close to it, as I could see better in that position should the lion come in our direction with his prey. Brock, however, persuaded me to remain where I was; and a few seconds afterwards I was heartily glad that I had taken his advice, for at that very moment one of the man-eaters—although we did not know it—was quietly stalking us, and was even then almost within springing distance. Orders had been given for the entrance to the boma to be blocked up, and accordingly we were listening in the expectation of hearing the lion force his way out through the bushes with his prey. As a matter of fact, however, the doorway had not been properly closed, and while we were wondering what the lion could be doing inside the boma for so long, he was outside all the time, silently reconnoitring our position.

Presently I fancied I saw something coming very stealthily towards us. I feared however, to trust to my eyes, which by that time were strained by prolonged staring through the darkness, so under my breath I asked Brock whether he saw anything, at the same time covering the dark object as well as I could with my rifle. Brock did not answer; he told me afterwards that he, too, thought he had seen something move, but was afraid to say so lest I should fire and it turn out to be nothing after all. After this there was intense silence again for a second or two, then with a sudden bound a huge body sprang at us. "The lion!" I shouted, and we both fired almost simultaneously—not a moment too soon, for in another second the brute would assuredly have landed inside the wagon. As it was, he must have swerved off in his spring, probably blinded by the flash and frightened by the noise of the double report which was increased a hundredfold by the reverberation of the hollow iron roof of the truck. Had we not been very much on the alert, he would undoubtedly have got one of us, and we realised that we had had a very lucky and very narrow escape. The next morning we found Brock's bullet embedded in the sand close to a footprint; it could not have missed the lion by more than an inch or two. Mine was nowhere to be found.

Thus ended my first direct encounter with one of the man-eaters.

THE REIGN OF TERROR

The lions seemed to have got a bad fright the night Brock and I sat up in wait for them in the goods-wagon, for they kept away from Tsavo and did not molest us in any way for some considerable time—not, in fact, until long after Brock had left me and gone on safari (a caravan journey) to Uganda. In this breathing space which they vouchsafed us, it occurred to me that should they renew their attacks, a trap would perhaps offer the best chance of getting at them, and that if I could construct one in which a couple of coolies might be used as bait without being subjected to any danger, the lions would be quite daring enough to enter it in search of them and thus be caught. I accordingly set to work at once, and in a short time managed to make a sufficiently strong trap out of wooden sleepers, tram-rails, pieces of telegraph wire, and a length of heavy chain. It was divided into two compartments—one for the men and one for the lion. A sliding door at one end admitted the former, and once inside this compartment they were perfectly safe, as between them and the lion, if he entered the other, ran a cross wall of iron rails only three inches apart, and embedded both top and bottom in heavy wooden sleepers. The door which was to admit the lion was, of course, at the opposite end of the structure, but otherwise the whole thing was very much on the principle of the ordinary rat-trap, except that it was not necessary for the lion to seize the bait in order to send the door clattering down. This part of the contrivance was arranged in the following manner. A heavy chain was secured along the top part of the lion's doorway, the ends hanging down to the ground on either side of the opening; and to these were fastened, strongly secured by stout wire, short lengths of rails placed about six inches apart. This made a sort of flexible door which could be packed into a small space when not in use, and which abutted against the top of the doorway when lifted up. The door was held in this position by a lever made of a piece of rail, which in turn was kept in its place by a wire fastened to one end and passing down to a spring concealed in the ground inside the cage. As soon as the lion entered sufficiently far into the trap, he would be bound to tread on the spring; his weight on this would release the wire, and in an instant down would come the door behind him; and he could not push it out in any way, as it fell into a groove between two rails firmly embedded in the ground.

In making this trap, which cost us a lot of work, we were rather at a loss for want of tools to bore holes in the rails for the doorway, so as to enable them to be fastened by the wire to the chain. It occurred to me, however, that a hard-nosed bullet from my .303 would penetrate the iron, and on making the experiment I was glad to find that a hole was made as cleanly as if it had been punched out.

When the trap was ready I pitched a tent over it in order further to deceive the lions, and built an exceedingly strong boma round it. One small entrance was made at the back of the enclosure for the men, which they were to close on going in by pulling a bush after them; and another entrance just in front of the door of the cage was left open for the lions. The wiseacres to whom I showed my invention were generally of the opinion that the man-eaters would be too cunning to walk into my parlour; but, as will be seen later, their predictions proved false. For the first few nights I baited the trap myself, but nothing happened except that I had a very sleepless and uncomfortable time, and was badly bitten by mosquitoes.

As a matter of fact, it was some months before the lions attacked us again, though from time to time we heard of their depredations in other quarters. Not long after our night in the goods-wagon, two men were carried off from railhead, while another was taken from a place called Engomani, about ten miles away. Within a very short time, this latter place was again visited by the brutes, two more men being seized, one of whom was killed and eaten, and the other so badly mauled that he died within a few days. As I have said, however, we at Tsavo enjoyed complete immunity from attack, and the coolies, believing that their dreaded foes had permanently deserted the district, resumed all their usual habits and occupations, and life in the camps returned to its normal routine.

At last we were suddenly startled out of this feeling of security. One dark night the familiar terror-stricken cries and screams awoke the camps, and we knew that the "demons" had returned and had commenced a new list of victims. On this occasion a number of men had been sleeping outside their tents for the sake of coolness, thinking, of course, that the lions had gone for good, when suddenly in the middle of the night one of the brutes was discovered forcing its way through the boma. The alarm was at once given, and sticks, stones and firebrands were hurled in the direction of the intruder. All was of no avail, however, for the lion burst into the midst of the terrified group, seized an unfortunate wretch amid the cries and shrieks of his companions, and dragged him off through the thick thorn fence. He was joined outside by the second lion, and so daring had the two brutes become that they did not trouble to carry their victim any further away, but devoured him within thirty yards of the tent where he had been seized. Although several shots were fired in their direction by the jemadar of the gang to which the coolie belonged, they took no notice of these and did not attempt to move until their horrible meal was finished. The few scattered fragments that remained of the body I would not allow to be buried at once, hoping that the lions would return to the spot the following night; and on the chance of this I took up my station at nightfall in a convenient tree. Nothing occurred to break the monotony of my watch, however, except that I had a visit from a hyena, and the next morning I learned that the lions had attacked another camp about two miles from Tsavo—for by this time the camps were again scattered, as I had works in progress all up and down the line. There the man-eaters had been successful in obtaining a victim, whom, as in the previous instance, they devoured quite close to the camp. How they forced their way through the bomas without making a noise was, and still is, a mystery to me; I should have thought that it was next to impossible for an animal to get through at all. Yet they continually did so, and without a sound being heard.

After this occurrence, I sat up every night for over a week near likely camps, but all in vain. Either the lions saw me and then went elsewhere, or else I was unlucky, for they took man after man from different places without ever once giving me a chance of a shot at them. This constant night watching was most dreary and fatiguing work, but I felt that it was a duty that had to be undertaken, as the men naturally looked to me for protection. In the whole of my life I have never experienced anything more nerve-shaking than to hear the deep roars of these dreadful monsters growing gradually nearer and nearer, and to know that some one or other of us was doomed to be their victim before morning dawned. Once they reached the vicinity of the camps, the roars completely ceased, and we knew that they were stalking for their prey. Shouts would then pass from camp to camp, "Khabar dar, bhaieon, shaitan ata" ("Beware, brothers, the devil is coming"), but the warning cries would prove of no avail, and sooner or later agonising shrieks would break the silence and another man would be missing from roll-call next morning.

I was naturally very disheartened at being foiled in this way night after night, and was soon at my wits' end to know what to do; it seemed as if the lions were really "devils" after all and bore a charmed life. As I have said before, tracking them through the jungle was a hopeless task; but as something had to be done to keep up the men's spirits, I spent many a wry day crawling on my hands and knees through the dense undergrowth of the exasperating wilderness around us. As a matter of fact, if I had come up with the lions on any of these expeditions, it was much more likely that they would have added me to their list of victims than that I should have succeeded in killing either of them, as everything would have been in their favour. About this time, too, I had many helpers, and several officers—civil, naval and military—came to Tsavo from the coast and sat up night after night in order to get a shot at our daring foes. All of us, however, met with the same lack of success, and the lions always seemed capable of avoiding the watchers, while succeeding at the same time in obtaining a victim.

I have a very vivid recollection of one particular night when the brutes seized a man from the railway station and brought him close to my camp to devour. I could plainly hear them crunching the bones, and the sound of their dreadful purring filled the air and rang in my ears for days afterwards. The terrible thing was to feel so helpless; it was useless to attempt to go out, as of course the poor fellow was dead, and in addition it was so pitch dark as to make it impossible to see anything. Some half a dozen workmen, who lived in a small enclosure close to mine, became so terrified on hearing the lions at their meal that they shouted and implored me to allow them to come inside my boma. This I willingly did, but soon afterwards I remembered that one man had been lying ill in their camp, and on making enquiry I found that they had callously left him behind alone. I immediately took some men with me to bring him to my boma, but on entering his tent I saw by the light of the lantern that the poor fellow was beyond need of safety. He had died of shock at being deserted by his companions.

From this time matters gradually became worse and worse. Hitherto, as a rule, only one of the man-eaters had made the attack and had done the foraging, while the other waited outside in the bush; but now they began to change their tactics, entering the bomas together and each seizing a victim. In this way two Swahili porters were killed during the last week of November, one being immediately carried off and devoured. The other was heard moaning for a long time, and when his terrified companions at last summoned up sufficient courage to go to his assistance, they found him stuck fast in the bushes of the boma through which for once the lion had apparently been unable to drag him. He was still alive when I saw him next morning, but so terribly mauled that he died before he could be got to the hospital.

Within a few days of this the two brutes made a most ferocious attack on the largest camp in the section, which for safety's sake was situated within a stone's throw of Tsavo Station and close to a Permanent Way Inspector's iron hut. Suddenly in the dead of night the two man-eaters burst in among the terrified workmen, and even from my boma, some distance away, I could plainly hear the panic-stricken shrieking of the coolies. Then followed cries of "They've taken him; they've taken him," as the brutes carried off their unfortunate victim and began their horrible feast close beside the camp. The Inspector, Mr. Dalgairns, fired over fifty shots in the direction in which he heard the lions, but they were not to be frightened and calmly lay there until their meal was finished. After examining the spot in the morning, we at once set out to follow the brutes, Mr. Dalgairns feeling confident that he had wounded one of them, as there was a trail on the sand like that of the toes of a broken limb. After some careful stalking, we suddenly found ourselves in the vicinity of the lions, and were greeted with ominous growlings. Cautiously advancing and pushing the bushes aside, we saw in the gloom what we at first took to be a lion cub; closer inspection, however, showed it to be the remains of the unfortunate coolie, which the man-eaters had evidently abandoned at our approach. The legs, one arm and half the body had been eaten, and it was the stiff fingers of the other arm trailing along the sand which had left the marks we had taken to be the trail of a wounded lion. By this time the beasts had retired far into the thick jungle where it was impossible to follow them, so we had the remains of the coolie buried and once more returned home disappointed.

Now the bravest men in the world, much less the ordinary Indian coolie, will not stand constant terrors of this sort indefinitely. The whole district was by this time thoroughly panic-stricken, and I was not at all surprised, therefore, to find on my return to camp that same afternoon (December 1) that the men had all struck work and were waiting to speak to me. When I sent for them, they flocked to my boma in a body and stated that they would not remain at Tsavo any longer for anything or anybody; they had come from India on an agreement to work for the government, not to supply food for either lions or "devils." No sooner had they delivered this ultimatum than a regular stampede took place. Some hundreds of them stopped the first passing train by throwing themselves on the rails in front of the engine, and then, swarming on to the trucks and throwing in their possessions anyhow, they fled from the accursed spot.

After this the railway works were completely stopped; and for the next three weeks practically nothing was done but build "lion-proof" huts for those workmen who had had sufficient courage to remain. It was a strange and amusing sight to see these shelters perched on the top of water-tanks, roofs and girders—anywhere for safety—while some even went so far as to dig pits inside their tents, into which they descended at night, covering the top over with heavy logs of wood. Every good-sized tree in the camp had as many beds lashed on to it as its branches would bear—and sometimes more. I remember that one night when the camp was attacked, so many men swarmed on to one particular tree that down it came with a crash, hurling its terror-stricken load of shrieking coolies close to the very lions they were trying to avoid. Fortunately for them, a victim had already been secured, and the brutes were too busy devouring him to pay attention to anything else.

THE DISTRICT OFFICER'S NARROW ESCAPE

Some little time before the flight of the workmen, I had written to Mr. Whitehead, the District Officer, asking him to come up and assist me in my campaign against the lions, and to bring with him any of his askaris (native soldiers) that he could spare. He replied accepting the invitation, and told me to expect him about dinner-time on December 2, which turned out to be the day after the exodus. His train was due at Tsavo about six o'clock in the evening, so I sent my "boy" up to the station to meet him and to help in carrying his baggage to the camp. In a very short time, however, the "boy" rushed back trembling with terror, and informed me that there was no sign of the train or of the railway staff, but that an enormous lion was standing on the station platform. This extraordinary story I did not believe in the least, as by this time the coolies—never remarkable for bravery—were in such a state of fright that if they caught sight of a hyena, of a baboon, or even a dog, in the bush, they were sure to imagine it was a lion; but I found out next day that it was an actual fact, and that both stationmaster and signalman had been obliged to take refuge from one of the man-eaters by locking themselves in the station building.

I waited some little time for Mr. Whitehead, but eventually, as he did not put in an appearance, I concluded that he must have postponed his journey until the next day, and so had my dinner in my customary solitary state. During the meal I heard a couple of shots, but paid no attention to them, as rifles were constantly being fired off in the neighbourhood of the camp. Later in the evening, I went out as usual to watch for our elusive foes, and took up my position in a crib made of sleepers which I had built on a big girder close to a camp which I thought was likely to be attacked. Soon after settling down at my post, I was surprised to hear the man-eaters growling and purring and crunching up bones about seventy yards from the crib. I could not understand what they had found to eat, as I had heard no commotion in the camps, and I knew by bitter experience that every meal the brutes obtained from us was announced by shrieks and uproar. The only conclusion I could come to was that they had pounced upon some poor unsuspecting native traveller. After a time I was able to make out their eyes glowing in the darkness, and I took as careful aim as was possible in the circumstances and fired; but the only notice they paid to the shot was to carry off whatever they were devouring and to retire quietly over a slight rise, which prevented me from seeing them. There they finished their meal at their ease.

As soon as it was daylight, I got out of my crib and went towards the place where I had last heard them. On the way, whom should I meet but my missing guest, Mr. Whitehead, looking very pale and ill, and generally dishevelled.

"Where on earth have you come from?" I exclaimed. "Why didn't you turn up to dinner last night?"

"A nice reception you give a fellow when you invite him to dinner," was his only reply.

"Why, what's up?" I asked.

"That infernal lion of yours nearly did for me last night," said White-head.

"Nonsense, you must have dreamed it!" I cried in astonishment.

For answer he turned round and showed me his back. "That's not much of a dream, is it?" he asked.

His clothing was rent by one huge tear from the nape of the neck downwards, and on the flesh there were four great claw marks, showing red and angry through the torn cloth. Without further parley, I hurried him off to my tent, and bathed and dressed his wounds; and when I had made him considerably more comfortable, I got from him the whole story of the events of the night.

It appeared that his train was very late, so that it was quite dark when he arrived at Tsavo Station, from which the track to my camp lay through a small cutting. He was accompanied by Abdullah, his sergeant of askaris, who walked close behind him carrying a lighted lamp. All went well until they were about half-way through the gloomy cutting, when one of the lions suddenly jumped down upon them from the high bank, knocking Whitehead over like a ninepin, and tearing his back in the manner I had seen. Fortunately, however, he had his carbine with him, and instantly fired. The flash and the loud report must have dazed the lion for a second or two, enabling Whitehead to disengage himself; but the next instant the brute pounced like lightning on the unfortunate Abdullah, with whom he at once made off. All that the poor fellow could say was: "Eh, Bwana, simba" ("Oh, Master, a lion"). As the lion was dragging him over the bank, Whitehead fired again, but without effect, and the brute quickly disappeared into the darkness with his prey. It was, of course, this unfortunate man whom I had heard the lions devouring during the night. Whitehead himself had a marvellous escape; his wounds were happily not very deep, and caused him little or no inconvenience afterwards.

On the same day, December 3, the forces arrayed against the lions were further strengthened. Mr. Farquhar, the Superintendent of Police, arrived from the coast with a score of sepoys to assist in hunting down the man-eaters, whose fame had by this time spread far and wide, and the most elaborate precautions were taken, his men being posted on the most convenient trees near every camp. Several other officials had also come up on leave to join in the chase, and each of these guarded a likely spot in the same way, Mr. Whitehead sharing my post inside the crib on the girder. Further, in spite of some chaff, my lion trap was put in thorough working order, and two of the sepoys were installed as bait.

Our preparations were quite complete by nightfall, and we all took up our appointed positions. Nothing happened until about nine o'clock, when to my great satisfaction the intense stillness was suddenly broken by the noise of the door of the trap clattering down. "At last," I thought, "one at least of the brutes is done for." But the sequel was an ignominious one.

The bait-sepoys had a lamp burning inside their part of the cage, and were each armed with a Martini rifle, with plenty of ammunition. They had also been given strict orders to shoot at once if a lion should enter the trap. Instead of doing so, however, they were so terrified when he rushed in and began to lash himself madly against the bars of the cage, that they completely lost their heads and were actually too unnerved to fire. Not for some minutes—not, indeed, until Mr. Farquhar, whose post was close by, shouted at them and cheered them on—did they at all recover themselves. Then when at last they did begin to fire, they fired with a vengeance—anywhere, anyhow. Whitehead and I were at right angles to the direction in which they should have shot, and yet their bullets came whizzing all round us. Altogether they fired over a score of shots, and in the end succeeded only in blowing away one of the bars of the door, thus allowing our prize to make good his escape. How they failed to kill him several times over is, and always will be, a complete mystery to me, as they could have put the muzzles of their rifles absolutely touching his body. There was, indeed, some blood scattered about the trap, but it was small consolation to know that the brute, whose capture and death seemed so certain, had only been slightly wounded.

Still we were not unduly dejected, and when morning came, a hunt was at once arranged. Accordingly we spent the greater part of the day on our hands and knees following the lions through the dense thickets of thorny jungle, but though we heard their growls from time to time, we never succeeded in actually coming up with them. Of the whole party, only Farquhar managed to catch a momentary glimpse of one as it bounded over a bush. Two days more were spent in the same manner, and with equal unsuccess; and then Farquhar and his sepoys were obliged to return to the coast. Mr. Whitehead also departed for his district, and once again I was left alone with the man-eaters.

THE DEATH OF THE FIRST MAN-EATER

A day or two after the departure of my allies, as I was leaving my boma soon after dawn on December 9, I saw a Swahili running excitedly towards me, shouting out "Simba! Simba!" ("Lion! Lion!"), and every now and again looking behind him as he ran. On questioning him I found that the lions had tried to snatch a man from the camp by the river, but being foiled in this had seized and killed one of the donkeys, and were at that moment busy devouring it not far off. Now was my chance.

I rushed for the heavy rifle which Farquhar had kindly left with me for use in case an opportunity such as this should arise, and, led by the Swahili, I started most carefully to stalk the lions, who, I devoutly hoped, were confining their attention strictly to their meal. I was getting on splendidly, and could just make out the outline of one of them through the dense bush, when unfortunately my guide snapped a rotten branch. The wily beast heard the noise, growled his defiance, and disappeared in a moment into a patch of even thicker jungle close by. In desperation at the thought of his escaping me once again, I crept hurriedly back to the camp, summoned the available workmen and told them to bring all the tom-toms, tin cans and other noisy instruments of any kind that could be found. As quickly as possible I posted them in a half-circle round the thicket, and gave the head jemadar instructions to start a simultaneous beating of the tom-toms and cans as soon as he judged that I had had time to get round to the other side. I then crept round by myself and soon found a good position and one which the lion was most likely to retreat past, as it was in the middle of a broad animal path leading straight from the place where he was concealed. I lay down behind a small ant hill, and waited expectantly. Very soon I heard a tremendous din being raised by the advancing line of coolies, and almost immediately, to my intense joy, out into the open path stepped a huge maneless lion. It was the first occasion during all these trying months upon which I had had a fair chance at one of these brutes, and my satisfaction at the prospect of bagging him was unbounded.

Slowly he advanced along the path, stopping every few seconds to look round. I was only partially concealed from view, and if his attention had not been so fully occupied by the noise behind him, he must have observed me. As he was oblivious to my presence, however, I let him approach to within about fifteen yards of me, and then covered him with my rifle. The moment I moved to do this, he caught sight of me, and seemed much astonished at my sudden appearance, for he stuck his forefeet into the ground, threw himself back on his haunches and growled savagely. As I covered his brain with my rifle, I felt that at last I had him absolutely at my mercy, but . . . never trust an untried weapon! I pulled the trigger, and to my horror heard the dull snap that tells of a misfire.

Worse was to follow. I was so taken aback and disconcerted by this untoward accident that I entirely forgot to fire the left barrel, and lowered the rifle from my shoulder with the intention of reloading—if I should be given time. Fortunately for me, the lion was so distracted by the terrific din and uproar of the coolies behind him that instead of springing on me, as might have been expected, he bounded aside into the jungle again. By this time I had collected my wits, and just as he jumped I let him have the left barrel. An answering angry growl told me that he had been hit; but nevertheless he succeeded once more in getting clear away, for although I tracked him for some little distance, I eventually lost his trail in a rocky patch of ground.

Bitterly did I anathematise the hour in which I had relied on a borrowed weapon, and in my disappointment and vexation I abused owner, maker, and rifle with fine impartiality. On extracting the unexploded cartridge, I found that the needle had not struck home, the cap being only slightly dented; so that the whole fault did indeed lie with the rifle, which I later returned to Farquhar with polite compliments. Seriously, however, my continued ill-luck was most exasperating; and the result was that the Indians were more than ever confirmed in their belief that the lions were really evil spirits, proof against mortal weapons. Certainly, they did seem to bear charmed lives.

After this dismal failure there was, of course, nothing to do but to return to camp. Before doing so, however, I proceeded to view the dead donkey, which I found to have been only slightly devoured at the quarters. It is a curious fact that lions always begin at the tail of their prey and eat upwards towards the head. As their meal had thus been interrupted evidently at the very beginning, I felt pretty sure that one or other of the brutes would return to the carcase at nightfall. Accordingly, as there was no tree of any kind close at hand, I had a staging erected some ten feet away from the body. This machan was about twelve feet high and was composed of four poles stuck into the ground and inclined toward each other at the top, where a plank was lashed to serve as a seat. Further, as the nights were still pitch dark, I had the donkey's carcase secured by strong wires to a neighbouring stump, so that the lions might not be able to drag it away before I could get a shot at them.

At sundown, therefore, I took up my position on my airy perch, and much to the disgust of my gun-bearer, Mahina, I decided to go alone. I would gladly have taken him with me, indeed, but he had a bad cough, and I was afraid lest he should make any involuntary noise or movement which might spoil all. Darkness fell almost immediately, and everything became extraordinarily still. The silence of an African jungle on a dark night needs to be experienced to be realised; it is most impressive, especially when one is absolutely alone and isolated from ones fellow creatures, as I was then. The solitude and stillness, and the purpose of my vigil, all had their effect on me, and from a condition of strained expectancy I gradually fell into a dreamy mood which harmonised well with my surroundings. Suddenly I was startled out of my reverie by the snapping of a twig; and, straining my ears for a further sound,

I fancied I could hear the rustling of a large body forcing its way through the bush. "The man-eater," I thought to myself; "surely to-night my luck will change and I shall bag one of the brutes." Profound silence again succeeded; I sat on my eyrie like a statue, every nerve tense with excitement. Very soon, however, all doubts as to the presence of the lion was dispelled. A deep long-drawn sigh—sure sign of hunger—came up from the bushes, and the rustling commenced again as he cautiously advanced. In a moment or two a sudden stop, followed by an angry growl, told me that my presence had been noticed; and I began to fear that disappointment awaited me once more.

But no; matters quickly took an unexpected turn. The hunter became the hunted; and instead of either making off or coming for the bait prepared for him, the lion began stealthily to stalk me! For about two hours he horrified me by slowly creeping round and round my crazy structure, gradually edging his way nearer and nearer. Every moment I expected him to rush it; and the staging had not been constructed with an eye to such a possibility. If one of the rather flimsy poles should break, or if the lion could spring the twelve feet which separated me from the ground . . . the thought was scarcely a pleasant one. I began to feel distinctly "creepy," and heartily repented my folly in having placed myself in such a dangerous position. I kept perfectly still, however, hardly daring even to blink my eyes: but the long continued strain was telling on my nerves, and my feelings may be better imagined than described when about midnight suddenly something came flop and struck me on the back of the head. For a moment I was so terrified that I nearly fell off the plank, as I thought that the lion had sprung on me from behind. Regaining my senses in a second or two, I realised that I had been hit by nothing more formidable than an owl, which had doubtless mistaken me for the branch of a tree—not a very alarming thing to happen in ordinary circumstances, I admit, but coming at the time it did, it almost paralysed me. The involuntary start which I could not help giving was immediately answered by a sinister growl from below.

After this I again kept as still as I could, though absolutely trembling with excitement; and in a short while I heard the lion begin to creep stealthily towards me. I could barely make out his form as he crouched among the whitish undergrowth; but I saw enough for my purpose and before he could come any nearer, I took careful aim and pulled the trigger. The sound of the shot was at once followed by a most terrific roar, and then I could hear him leaping about in all directions. I was no longer able to see him, however, as his first bound had taken him into the thick bush; but to make assurance doubly sure, I kept blazing away in the direction in which I heard him plunging about. At length came a series of mighty groans, gradually subsiding into deep sighs, and finally ceasing altogether; and I felt convinced that one of the "devils" who had so long harried us would trouble us no more.

As soon as I ceased firing, a tumult of inquiring voices was borne across the dark jungle from the men in camp about a quarter of a mile away. I shouted back that I was safe and sound, and that one of the lions was dead: whereupon such a mighty cheer went up from all the camps as must have astonished the denizens of the jungle for miles around. Shortly I saw scores of lights twinkling through the bushes: every man in camp turned out, and with tom-toms beating and horns blowing came running to the scene. They surrounded my eyrie, and to my amazement prostrated themselves on the ground before me, saluting me with cries of "Mabarak! Mabarak!" which I believe means "blessed one" or "saviour." All the same, I refused to allow any search to be made that night for the body of the lion, in case his companion might be close by; besides, it was possible that he might be still alive, and capable of making a last spring. Accordingly we all returned in triumph to the camp, where great rejoicings were kept up for the remainder of the night, the Swahili and other African natives celebrating the occasion by an especially wild and savage dance.

For my part, I anxiously awaited the dawn; and even before it was thoroughly light I was on my way to the eventful spot, as I could not completely persuade myself that even yet the "devil" might not have eluded me in some uncanny and mysterious way. Happily my fears proved groundless, and I was relieved to find that my luck—after playing me so many exasperating tricks—had really turned at last. I had scarcely traced the blood for more than a few paces when, on rounding a bush, I was startled to see a huge lion right in front of me, seemingly alive and crouching for a spring. On looking closer, however, I satisfied myself that he was really and truly stone-dead, whereupon my followers crowded round, laughed and danced and shouted with joy like children, and bore me in triumph shoulder-high round the dead body. These thanksgiving ceremonies being over, I examined the body and found that two bullets had taken effect—one close behind the left shoulder, evidently penetrating the heart, and the other in the off hind leg. The prize was indeed one to be proud of; his length from tip of nose to tip of tail was nine feet eight inches, he stood three feet nine inches high, and it took eight men to carry him back to camp. The only blemish was that the skin was much scored by the boma thorns through which he had so often forced his way in carrying off his victims.

The news of the death of one of the notorious man-eaters soon spread far and wide over the country: telegrams of congratulations came pouring in, and scores of people flocked from up and down the railway to see the skin for themselves.

THE DEATH OF THE SECOND MAN-EATER

It must not be imagined that with the death of this lion our troubles at Tsavo were at an end; his companion was still at large, and very soon began to make us unpleasantly aware of the fact. Only a few nights elapsed before he made an attempt to get at the Permanent Way Inspector, climbing up the steps of his bungalow and prowling round the verandah. The Inspector, hearing the noise and thinking it was a drunken coolie, shouted angrily "Go away!" but, fortunately for him, did not attempt to come out or to open the door. Thus disappointed in his attempt to obtain a meal of human flesh, the lion seized a couple of the Inspector's goats and devoured them there and then.

On hearing of this occurrence, I determined to sit up the next night near the Inspector's bungalow. Fortunately there was a vacant iron shanty close at hand, with a convenient loophole in it for firing from; and outside this I placed three full-grown goats as bait, tying them to a half-length of rail, weighing about 250 lbs. The night passed uneventfully until just before daybreak, when at last the lion turned up, pounced on one of the goats and made off with it, at the same time dragging away the others, rail and all. I fired several shots in his direction, but it was pitch dark and quite impossible to see anything, so I only succeeded in hitting one of the goats. I often longed for a flashlight on such occasions.

Next morning I started off in pursuit and was joined by some others from the camp. I found that the trail of the goats and rail was easily followed, and we soon came up, about a quarter of a mile away, to where the lion was still busy at his meal. He was concealed in some thick bush and growled angrily on hearing our approach; finally, as we got closer, he suddenly made a charge, rushing through the bushes at a great pace. In an instant, every man of the party scrambled hastily up the nearest tree, with the exception of one of my assistants, Mr. Winkler, who stood steadily by me throughout. The brute, however, did not press his charge home: and on throwing stones into the bushes where we had last seen him, we guessed by the silence that he had slunk off. We therefore advanced cautiously, and on getting up to the place discovered that he had indeed escaped us, leaving two of the goats scarcely touched.

Thinking that in all probability the lion would return as usual to finish his meal, I had a very strong scaffolding put up a few feet away from the dead goats, and took up my position on it before dark. On this occasion I brought my gun-bearer, Mahina, to take a turn at watching, as I was by this time worn out for want of sleep, having spent so many nights on the look-out. I was just dozing off comfortably when suddenly I felt my arm seized, and on looking up saw Mahina pointing in the direction of the goats. "Sher!" ("Lion!") was all he whispered. I grasped my double smooth-bore, which I had charged with slug, and waited patiently. In a few moments I was rewarded, for as I watched the spot where I expected the lion to appear, there was a rustling among the bushes and I saw him stealthily emerge into the open and pass almost directly beneath us. I fired both barrels practically together into his shoulder, and to my joy could see him go down under the force of the blow.

Quickly I reached for the magazine rifle, but before I could use it, he was out of sight among the bushes, and I had to fire after him quite at random. Nevertheless I was confident of getting him in the morning, and accordingly set out as soon as it was light. For over a mile there was no difficulty in following the blood trail, and as he had rested several times I felt sure that he had been badly wounded. In the end, however, my hunt proved fruitless, for after a time the traces of blood ceased and the surface of the ground became rocky, so that I was no longer able to follow the spoor.

About this time Sir Guilford Molesworth, K. C. I. E., late Consulting Engineer to the Government of India for State Railways, passed through Tsavo on a tour of inspection on behalf of the Foreign Office. After examining the bridge and other works and expressing his satisfaction, he took a number of photographs, one or two of which he has kindly allowed me to reproduce in this book. He thoroughly sympathised with us in all the trials we had endured from the man-eaters, and was delighted that one at least was dead. When he asked me if I expected to get the second lion soon, I well remember

The Uganda Railway

his half-doubting smile as I rather too confidently asserted that I hoped to bag him also in the course of a few days.

As it happened, there was no sign of our enemy for about ten days after this, and we began to hope that he had died of his wounds in the bush. All the same we still took every precaution at night, and it was fortunate that we did so, as otherwise at least one more victim would have been added to the list. For on the night of December 27, I was suddenly aroused by terrified shouts from my trolley men, who slept in a tree close outside my boma to the effect that a lion was trying to get at them. It would have been madness to have gone out, as the moon was hidden by dense clouds and it was absolutely impossible to see anything more than a yard in front of one; so all I could do was to fire off a few rounds just to frighten the brute away. This apparently had the desired effect, for the men were not further molested that night; but the man-eater had evidently prowled about for some time, for we found in the morning that he had gone right into every one of their tents, and round the tree was a regular ring of his footmarks.

The following evening I took up my position in this same tree, in the hope that he would make another attempt. The night began badly, as while climbing up to my perch I very nearly put my hand on a venomous snake which was lying coiled round one of the branches. As may be imagined, I came down again very quickly, but one of my men managed to despatch it with a long pole. Fortunately the night was clear and cloudless, and the moon made every thing almost as bright as day. I kept watch until about 2 a.m., when I roused Mahina to take his turn. For about an hour I slept peacefully with my back to the tree, and then woke suddenly with an uncanny feeling that something was wrong. Mahina, however, was on the alert, and had seen nothing; and although I looked carefully round us on all sides, I too could discover nothing unusual. Only half satisfied, I was about to lie back again, when I fancied I saw something move a little way off among the low bushes. On gazing intently at the spot for a few seconds, I found I was not mistaken. It was the man-eater, cautiously stalking us.

The ground was fairly open round our tree, with only a small bush every here and there; and from our position it was a most fascinating sight to watch this great brute stealing stealthily round us, taking advantage of every bit of cover as he came. His skill showed that he was an old hand at the terrible game of man-hunting; so I determined to run no undue risk of losing him this time. I accordingly waited until he got quite close—about twenty yards away—and then fired my .303 at his chest. I heard the bullet strike him, but unfortunately it had no knockdown effect, for with a fierce growl he turned and made off with great long bounds. Before he disappeared from sight, however, I managed to have three more shots at him from the magazine rifle, and another growl told me that the last of these had also taken effect.

We awaited daylight with impatience, and at the first glimmer of dawn we set out to hunt him down. I took a native tracker with me, so that I was free to keep a good look-out, while Mahina followed immediately behind with a Martini carbine. Splashes of blood being plentiful, we were able to get along quickly; and we had not proceeded more than a quarter of a mile through the jungle when suddenly a fierce warning growl was heard right in front of us. Looking cautiously through the bushes, I could see the man-eater glaring out in our direction, and showing his tusks in an angry snarl. I at once took careful aim and fired. Instantly he sprang out and made a most determined charge down on us. I fired again and knocked him over; but in a second he was up once more and coming for me as fast as he could in his crippled condition. A third shot had no apparent effect, so I put out my hand for the Martini, hoping to stop him with it. To my dismay, however, it was not there. The terror of the sudden charge had proved too much for Mahina, and both he and the carbine were by this time well on their way up a tree. In the circumstances there was nothing to do but follow suit, which I did without loss of time; and but for the fact that one of my shots had broken a hind leg, the brute would most certainly have had me. Even as it was. I had barely time to swing myself up out of his reach before he arrived at the foot of the tree.

When the lion found he was too late, he started to limp back to the thicket; but by this time I had seized the carbine from Mahina, and the first shot I fired from it seemed to give him his quietus, for he fell over and lay motionless. Rather foolishly, I at once scrambled down from the tree and walked up towards him. To my surprise and no little alarm he jumped up and attempted another charge. This time, however, a Martini bullet in the chest and another in the head finished him for good and all; he dropped in his tracks not five yards away from me, and died gamely, biting savagely at a branch which had fallen to the ground.

By this time all the workmen in camp, attracted by the sound of the firing, had arrived on the scene, and so great was their resentment against the brute who had killed such numbers of their comrades that it was only with the greatest difficulty that I could restrain them from tearing the dead body to pieces. Eventually, amid the wild rejoicings of the natives and coolies, I had the lion carried to my boma, which was close at hand. On examination we found no less than six bullet holes in the body, and embedded only a little way in the flesh of the back was the slug which I had fired into him from the scaffolding about ten days previously. He measured nine feet six inches from tip of nose to tip of tail, and stood three feet eleven and a half inches high; but, as in the case of his companion, the skin was disfigured by being deeply scored all over by the boma thorns.

The news of the death of the second "devil" soon spread far and wide over the country, and natives actually travelled from up and down the line to have a look at my trophies and at the "devil-killer," as they called me. Best of all, the coolies who had absconded came flocking back to Tsavo, and much to my relief work was resumed and we were never again troubled by man-eaters. It was amusing, indeed, to notice the change which took place in the attitude of the workmen towards me after I had killed the two lions. Instead of wishing to murder me, as they once did, they could not now do enough for me, and as a token of their gratitude they presented me with a beautiful silver bowl, as well as with a long poem written in Hindustani describing all our trials and my ultimate victory. As the poem relates our troubles in somewhat quaint and biblical language, I have given a translation of it in the appendix. The bowl I shall always consider my most highly prized and hardest won trophy. The inscription on it reads as follows:—

Sir,—We, your Overseer, Timekeepers, Mistaris and Workmen, present you with this bowl as a token of our gratitude to you for your bravery in killing two man-eating lions at great risk to your own life, thereby saving us from the fate of being devoured by these terrible monsters who nightly broke into our tents and took our fellow-workers from our side. In presenting you with this bowl, we all add our prayers for your long life, happiness and prosperity. We shall ever remain, Sir, Your grateful servants,

Baboo Purshotam Hurjee Purmar, Overseer and Clerk of the Works, on behalf of your Workmen.

Dated at Tsavo, January 30, 1899.

Before I leave the subject of "The Man-Eaters of Tsavo," it may be of interest to mention that these two lions possess the distinction, probably unique among wild animals, of having been specifically referred to in the House of Lords by the Prime Minister of the day. Speaking of the difficulties which had been encountered in the construction of the Uganda Railway, the late Lord Salisbury said:—

"The whole of the works were put a stop to for three weeks because a party of man-eating lions appeared in the locality and conceived a most unfortunate taste for our porters. At last the labourers entirely declined to go on unless they were guarded by an iron entrenchment. Of course it is difficult to work a railway under these conditions, and until we found an enthusiastic sportsman to get rid of these lions, our enterprise was seriously hindered."

Also, *The Spectator* of March 3, 1900, had an article entitled "The Lions that Stopped the Railway," from which the following extracts are taken:—

"The parallel to the story of the lions which stopped the rebuilding of Samaria must occur to everyone, and if the Samaritans had quarter as good cause for their fears as had the railway coolies, their wish to propitiate the local deities is easily understood. If the whole body of lion anecdote, from the days of the Assyrian Kings till the last year of the nineteenth century, were collated and brought together, it would not equal in tragedy or atrocity, in savageness or in sheer insolent contempt for man, armed or unarmed, white or black, the story of these two beasts. . . .

"To what a distance the whole story carries us back, and how impossible it becomes to account for the survival of primitive man against this kind of foe! For fire—which has hitherto been regarded as his main safeguard against the carnivora—these cared nothing. It is curious that the Tsavo lions were not killed by poison, for strychnine is easily used, and with effect.* Poison may have been used early in the history of man, for its powers are employed with strange skill by the men in the tropical forest, both in American and West Central Africa. But there is no evidence that the old inhabitants of Europe, or if Assyria or Asia Minor, ever killed lions or wolves by this means. They looked to the King or chief, or some champion, to kill these monsters for them. It was not the sport but the duty of Kings, and was in itself a title to be a ruler of men. Theseus, who cleared the roads of beasts and robbers; Hercules, the lion killer; St. George, the dragon-slayer, and all the rest of their class owed to this their everlasting fame. From the story of the Tsavo River we can appreciate their services to man even at this distance of time. When the jungle twinkled with hundreds of lamps, as the shout went on from camp to camp that the first lion was dead, as the hurrying crowds fell prostrate in the midnight forest, laying their heads on his feet, and the Africans danced savage and ceremonial dances of thanksgiving, Mr. Patterson must have realised in no common way what it was to have been a hero and deliverer in the days when man was not yet undisputed lord of the creation, and might pass at any moment under the savage dominion of the beasts."

(*I may mention that poison was tried, but without effect. The poisoned carcases of transport animals which had died from the bite of the tsetse fly were placed in likely spots, but the wily man-eaters would not touch them, and much preferred live men to dead donkeys.)

Well had the two man-eaters earned all this fame; they had devoured between them no less than twenty-eight Indian coolies, in addition to scores of unfortunate African natives of whom no official record was kept.

CHAPTER 7

DE SHOOTINEST GENT'MAN

By Nash Buckingham

Supper was a delicious memory. In the matter of a certain goose stew, Aunt Molly had fairly outdone herself. And we, in turn, had jolly well done her out of practically all the goose. It may not come amiss to explain frankly and aboveboard the entire transaction with reference to said goose. Its breast had been deftly detached, lightly grilled and sliced into ordinary "mouth-size" portions. The remainder of the dismembered bird, back, limbs and all parts of the first part thereunto pertaining were put into an iron pot. Keeping company with the martyred fowl, in due proportion of culinary wizardry, were sundry bell peppers, two cans of mock turtle soup, diced roast pork, scrambled ham rinds, peas, potatoes, some corn and dried garden okra, shredded onions and pretty much anything and everything that wasn't tied down or that Molly had lying loose around her kitchen. This stew, served right royally, and attended by outriders of "cracklin' bread," was flanked by a man-at-arms in the form of a saucily flavored brown gravy. I recall a dish of broiled teal and some country puddin' with ginger pour-over, but merely mention these in passing.

So the Judge and I, in rare good humor (I forgot to add that there had been a dusty bottle of the Judge's famous port), as becomes sportsmen blessed with a perfect day's imperfect duck shooting, had discussed each individual

bird brought to bag, with reasons, pro and con, why an undeniably large quo-
ta had escaped uninjured. We bordered upon that indecisive moment when
bedtime should be imminent, were it not for the delightful trouble of getting
started in that direction. As I recollect it, ruminating upon our sumptuous
repast, the Judge had just countered upon my remark that I had never gotten
enough hot turkey hash and beaten biscuits, by stating decisively that his
craving for smothered quail remained inviolate, when the door opened softly
and in slid "Ho'ace"! He had come, following a custom of many years, to take
final breakfast instructions before packing the embers in "Steamboat Bill,"
the stove, and dousing our glim.

Seeing upon the center table, t'wixt the Judge and me, a bottle and the
unmistakable ingredients and tools of the former's ironclad rule for a hunter's
nightcap, Ho'ace paused in embarrassed hesitation and seated himself quickly
upon an empty shell case. His attitude was a cross between that of a timid gazelle's scenting danger and a wary hunter's sighting game and effacing himself
gently from the landscape.

Long experience in the imperative issue of securing an invitation to "get
his'n" had taught Ho'ace that it were ever best to appear humbly disinterested and

thoroughly foreign to the subject until negotiations, if need be even much later, were opened with him directly or indirectly. With old-time members he steered along the above lines. But with newer ones or their uninitiated guests, he believed in quicker campaigning, or, conditions warranting, higher pressure sales methods. The Judge, reaching for the sugar bowl, mixed his sweetening water with adroit twirl and careful scrutiny as to texture; fastening upon Ho'ace meanwhile a melting look of liquid mercy. In a twinkling, however, his humor changed and the darky found himself in the glare of a forbidding menace, creditable in his palmiest days to the late Mister Chief Justice Jeffries himself.

"Ho'ace," demanded the Judge, tilting into his now ready receptacle a gurgling, man-size libation, "who is the best shot—the best duck-shot— you have ever paddled on this lake—barring—of course—a-h-e-m-m— myself?" Surveying himself with the coyness of a juvenile, the Judge stirred his now beading toddy dreamily and awaited the encore. Ho'ace squirmed a bit as the closing words of the Judge's query struck home with appalling menace upon his ears. He plucked nervously at his battered headpiece. His eyes, exhibiting a vast expanse of white, roamed pictured walls and smoke-dimmed ceiling in furtive, reflective, helpless quandary. Then speaking slowly and gradually warming to his subject, he fashioned the following alibi.

"Jedge, y' know, suh, us all has ouh good an' ouh bad days wid de ducks. Yes, my Lawdy, us sho' do. Dey's times whin de ducks flies all ovah ev'ything an' ev'ybody, an' still us kain't none o' us hit nuthin'—lak me an' you wuz dis mawnin'." At this juncture the Judge interrupted, reminding Ho'ace that he meant when the Judge—and not the Judge and Ho'ace—was shooting.

"An' den deys times whin h'it look lak dey ain't no shot too hard nur nary a duck too far not t'be kilt. But Mister Buckin'ham yonder—Mister Nash— he brung down de shootin'est gent'man what took all de cake. H'it's lots o' d' members here whut's darin' shooters, but dat fren' o' Mister Nash's—uum- mppphhh—don't never talk t' me 'bout him whur de ducks kin hear. 'Cause dey'll leave de laik ef dey hears he's even comin' dis way.

"Dat gent'man rode me jes' lak I wuz' er saddle, an' he done had on rooster spurs. Mister Nash he brung him on down here an' say, 'Ho'ace,' he say, 'here's a gent'man frum Englan', 'he say, 'Mister Money—Mister Harol' Money—an' say I wants you t' paddle him tomorrow an' see dat he gits er gran' shoot—unnerstan'?' I say, 'Yaas, suh, Mister Nash,' I say, 'dat I'll sho'ly do, suh. Mister Money gwi' hav' er fine picnic ef I has t' see dat he do my sef—but kin he shoot, suh?'

"Mister Nash, he say, 'Uh—why—uh—yaas, Ho'ace, Mister Money he's—uh—ve'y fair shot—'bout lak Mister Immitt Joyner or Mister Hal Howard.' I say t' mysef, I say, 'Uuummmpphhh—huuummmppphhh— well—he'ah now—ef dats d' case, me an' Mister Money gwi' do some shoo- tin' in d' mawnin.'

"Mister Money he talk so kin'er queer an' brief like, dat I hadda pay clos't inspection t' whut he all de time asayin'. But nex' mawnin', whin me an' him goes out in de bote, I seen he had a gre't big ol' happy bottle o' Brooklyn Handicap in dat shell box so I say t' m'sef, I say, 'W-e-l-l-l—me an' Mister Money gwi' got erlong someway, us is.'

"I paddles him on up de laik an' he say t' me, say, 'Hawrice—uh—hav yo'—er—got anny wager,' he say, 'or proposition t' mek t' me, as regards," he say, 't' shootin' dem dar eloosive wil'fowls?' he say.

"I kinder studies a minit, 'cause, lak I done say, he talk so brief. Den I says, 'I guess you is right 'bout dat, suh.'

"He say, 'Does you follow me, Hawrice, or is I alone?' he say.

"I says, 'Naw, suh, Mister, I'm right wid you in dis bote.'

" 'You has no proposition t' mek wid me den?' he say.

"S' I, 'Naw, suh, Boss, I leaves all dat wid you, suh, trustin' t' yo' gin'ro- siry, suh.'

" 'Ve'y good, Hawrice,' he say, 'I sees you doan grasp de principul. Now I will mek you de proposition,' he say. I jes' kep' on paddlin'. He say, 'Ev'y time I miss er duck you gits er dram frum dis hu'ah bottle—ev'y time I kills er duck—I gits de drink—which is h'it—come—come—speak up, my man.'

"I didn' b'lieve I done heard Mister Money rightly, an' I say, 'Uh—Mister Money,' I say, 'suh, does you mean dat I kin d' chice whedder you misses or kills ev'y time an' gits er drink?'

"He say, 'Dat's my defi',' he say.

"I says, 'Well, den—w-e-l-l—den—ef dat's de case, I gwi' choose ev'y time yo' misses, suh.' Den I say t'm'sef, I say, 'Ho'acc, right hu'ah whar you gotta be keerful, 'ginst you fall outa d' bote an' git fired frum d' lodge; 'cause ef'n you gits er drink ev'y time dis gent'man misses an' he shoot lak Mister Hal Howard, you an' him sho' gwi' drink er worl' o' liquah—er worl' o' liquah.'

"I pushes on up nurly to de Han'werker stan', an' I peeks in back by da li'l pocket whut shallers off'n de laik, an' sees some sev'ul blackjacks—four on 'em—settin' in dar. Dey done seen us, too. An' up come dey haids. I spy 'em twis'in', an' turnin'—gittin' raidy t' pull dey freight frum dar. I says, 'Mister Money,' I says, 'yawnder sets some ducks—look out now, suh, 'cause dey gwi' try t' rush on out pas' us whin dey come outa dat pocket.' Den I think, 'W-e-l-l-l, hu'ah whar I knocks d' gol' fillin' outa d' mouf o' Mister Money's bottle o' Brooklyn Handicap!'

"I raised de lid o' d' shell box an' dar laid dat ol' bottle—still dar. I say, 'Uuummmppphhh—hummmph.' Jus' 'bout dat time up goes dem black-haids an' outa dar dey come—dey did—flyin' low t' d' watah—an' sorta raisin' lak—y' knows how dey does h'it, Jedge?'

"Mister Money he jus' pick up dat fas' feedin' gun—t'war er pump—not one o' dese hu'ah new afromatics—an' whin he did, I done reach f' d' bottle, 'cause I jes' natcherly know'd dat my time had done come. Mister Money he swings down on dem bullies. Ker-py—ker-py-powie-powie—splamp-splamp-splamp—ker-splash—Lawdy mussy—gent'-mans—fo' times, right in d' same place, h'it sounded lak—an' d' las' duck fell ker-flop almos' in ouh bote.

"I done let go d' bottle, an' Mister Money say—mighty cool lak—say, 'Hawrice, say, kin'ly to examine dat las' chap clos'ly,' he say, 'an' obsurve,' he say, 'ef'n he ain' shot thru de eye.'

"I rakes in dat blackjack, an' sho' nuff—bofe eyes done shot plum out—yaas, suh, bofe on 'em right on out. Mister Money say, 'I wuz—er—slightly afraid,' he say, 'dat I had unknowin'ly struck dat fella er trifle too far t' win'ward,' he say. 'A ve'y fair start, Hawrice,' he say. 'You'd bettah place me in my station, so we may continue on wid'out interruption,' he say.

" 'Yaas, suh,' I say. 'I'm on my way right dar now, suh, 'an I say t' m'sef, I say, 'Mek haste, Man, an' put dis gent'man in his bline an' giv' him er proper chanc't to miss er duck. I didn' hones'ly b'lieve but whut killin' all four o' dem other ducks so peart lak wuz er sorter accident. So I put him on de Han' werker bline. He seen I kep' de main shell bucket an' d' liquah, but he never said nuthin'. I put out d' m 'coys an' den creep back wid d' bote into d' willows t' watch.

"Pretty soon, hu'ah come er big ole drake flyin' mighty high. Ouh ole hen bird she holler t' him, an' d' drake he sorter twis' his haid an' look down. 'Warn't figurin' nuthin' but whut Mister Money gwi' let dat drake circle an' come 'mongst d' m 'coys—but—aw—aw! All uv er sudden he jus' raise up sharp lak an'—kerzowie! Dat ole drake jus' throw his haid on his back an' ride on down—looked t' me lak he fell er mile—an' whin he hit he thow'd watah fo' feet. Mister Money he nuvver said er word—jus' sot dar!

"Hu'ah come another drake—way off t' d' lef'—up over back o' me. He turn eroun'—quick lak—he did an'—kerzowie—he cut him on down, too. Dat drake fall way back in d' willows an' cose I hadda wade after 'im.

"Whilst I wuz gone, Mister Money shoot twice. An' whin I come stumblin' back, dar laid two mo' ducks wid dey feets in de air. Befo' I hav' time t' git in de bote again he done knock down er hen away off in d' elbow brush.

"I say, 'Mister Money, suh, I hav' behin' some farknockin' guns in my time an' I'se er willin' worker, shoe—but ef you doan, please suh, kill dem ducks closer lak, you gwi' kill yo' willin' supporter Ho'ace in de mud.' He say, 'Da's all right 'bout dat,' he say. 'Go git d' bird—he kain't git er-way 'cause h'its dead ez er wedge.'

"Whin I crawls back t' d' bote dat las' time—it done got mighty col'. Dar us set—me in one en' ashiverin' an' dat ole big bottle wid de gol' haid in de far en'. Might jus' ez well bin ten miles so far ez my chances had done gone.

"Five mo' ducks come in—three singles an' er pair o' sprigs. An' Mister Money he chewed 'em all up lak good eatin'. One time, tho' he had t' shoot one o' them high-flyin' sprigs twice, an' I done got halfway in de bote reachin' fer dat bottle—but de las' shot got 'im. Aftah while, Mister Money say—'Hawrice,' he say, 'how is you hittin' off—my man?'

" 'Mister Money' I say, 'I'se pow'ful col', suh, an' ef you wants er 'unable, no 'count paddler t' tell you d' truth, suh, I b'lieves I done made er pow'ful po' bet.' He say 'Poss'bly so, Hawrice, poss'bly so.' But dat 'poss'bly' didn' git me nuthin'.

"Jedge, y' Honor, you know dat gent'man sot dar an' kill ev'ry duck come in, an' had his limit long befo' de eight-o'clock train runned. I done gone t' watchin' an' de las' duck whut come by wuz one o' dem lightnin'-express teals. Hu'ah he come—er greenwing drake—look lak' somebody done blowed er buckshot pas' us. I riz' up an' hollered, 'Fly fas', ole teal, do yo' bes'—caus' Ho'ace needs er drink.' But Mister Money jus' jumped up an' thow'd him forty feet—skippin' 'long d' watah. I say, 'Hol' on, Mister Money, hol' on—you done kilt d' limit.'

" 'Oh,' he say, 'I hav'—hav' I?'

"I say, 'Yaas, suh, an' you ain't bin long 'bout h'it—neither.

"He say, 'What are you doin' gittin' so col' then?'

"I say, 'I spec' findin' out dat I hav' done made er bad bet had er lot t' do wid d' air.'

"An' dar laid dat Brooklyn Handicap all dat time—he nuvver touched none—an' me neither. I paddles him on back to de house, an' he comes er stalkin' on in hu'ah, he did—lookin' kinda mad lak—never said nuthin' 'bout no drink. Finally he say, 'Hawrice,' he say, 'git me a bucket o' col' watah.' I say t' m'sef, I say, 'W-e-l-l-l, das mo' lak h'it—ef he wants er bucket o' watah. Boy—you gwi' see some real drinkin' now.'

"Whin I come in wid d' pail, Mister Money took offin all his clothes an' step out onto d' side po'ch an' say, 'Th'ow dat watah ovah me, Hawrice. I am lit'rully compel,' he say, 't' have my col' tub ev'y mawnin'.' M-a-n-n-n-n! I sho' tow'd dat ice col' watah onto him wid all my heart an' soul. But he jus' gasp an' hollah, an' jump up an' down an' slap hisse'f. Den he had me rub him red wid er big rough towel. I sho' rubbed him, too. Come on in d' clubroom hu'ah, he did, an' mek hisse'f comfort'ble in dat big ol' rockin' chair yonder—an' went t' readin'. I brought in his shell bucket an' begin cleanin' his gun. But I seen him kinder smilin' t' hisse'f. Atta while, he says 'Hawrice,' he say, 'you hav' done los' yo' bet?'

"I kinder hang my haid lak, an' 'low, 'Yaas, suh, Mister Money, I don' said farewell t' d' liquah!'

"He say, 'Yo' admits den dat you hav' done los' fair an' square—an' dat yo' realizes h'it?'

" 'Yaas, suh!'

"He say, 'Yo' judgmint,' he say, 'wuz ve'y fair, considerin',' he say, 'de great law uv' av'ridge—but circumstance,' he say, 'has done render de ult'mate outcome subjec' t' d' mighty whims o' chance?'

"I say, 'Yaas, suh,' ve'y mournful lak.

"He say, 'In so far as realizin' on anything 'ceptin' de mercy o' d' Cote— say—you is absolutely nonest—eh, my man?'

"I say, 'Yaas, suh, barrin' yo' mercy, suh.'

"Den he think er moment, an' say, 'Verrree—verree—good!'

"Den he 'low, 'Sence you acknowledges d' cawn, an' admits dat you hav' done got grabbed,' he say, 'step up,' he say, 'an' git you a tumbler—po' yo'sef er drink—po' er big one, too.'

"I never stopped f' nuthin' den—jes' runned an' got me a glass outa de kitchen. Ole Molly, she say, 'Whur you goin' so fas'?' I say, 'Doan stop me now ole 'ooman—I got business—p'ticler business—an' I sho' poh'd me er big bait o' liquah—er whole sloo' o' liquah. Mister Money say, 'Hawrice—de size o' yo' po'tion,' he say, 'is primus facious ev'dence,' he say, 'dat you gwi' spout er toast in honor,' he say, 'o' d' occasion.'

"I say, 'Mister Money, suh,' I say, 'all I got t' say, suh, is dat you is de kingpin, champeen duck shotter so far as I hav' done bin' in dis life—an' ve'y prob'ly as far as I'se likely t' keep on goin', too.' He sorter smile t' hisse'f!

" 'Now, suh, please, suh, tell me dis—is you ever missed er duck—anywhar'—anytime—anyhow—suh?'

"He say 'Really, Hawrice,' he say, 'you embarrasses me,' he say, 'so hav' another snifter—there is mo', considerably mo',' he say, 'in yo' system what demands utt'rance,' he say.

"I done poh'd me another slug o' Brooklyn Handicap an' say, 'Mister Money,' I say, 'does you expec' t' ever miss another duck ez long ez you lives, suh?'

"He say, 'Hawrice,' he say, 'you embarrasses me,' he say, 'beyon' words— you overwhelms me,' he say. 'Git t' hell outa hu'ah befo' you gits us bofe drunk.'"

CHAPTER 8
THINKING LIKE A MOUNTAIN
By Aldo Leopold

A deep chesty bawl echoes from rimrock to rimrock, rolls down the mountain, and fades into the far blackness of the night. It is an outburst of wild defiant sorrow, and of contempt for all the adversities of the world.

Every living thing (and perhaps many a dead one as well) pays heed to that call. To the deer it is a reminder of the way of all flesh, to the pine a forecast of midnight scuffles and of blood upon the snow, to the coyote a promise of gleanings to come, to the cowman a threat of red ink at the bank, to the hunter a challenge of fang against bullet. Yet behind these obvious and immediate hopes and fears there lies a deeper meaning, known only to the mountain itself. Only the mountain has lived long enough to listen objective-ly to the howl of a wolf.

Those unable to decipher the hidden meaning know nevertheless that it is there, for it is felt in all wolf country, and distinguishes that country from all other land. It tingles in the spine of all who hear wolves by night, or who scan their tracks by day. Even without sight or sound of wolf, it is implicit in a hundred small events: the midnight whinny of a pack horse, the rattle of rolling rocks, the bound of a fleeing deer, the way shadows lie under the spruces. Only the ineducable tyro can fail to sense the presence or absence of wolves, or the fact that mountains have a secret opinion about them.

My own conviction on this score dates from the day I saw a wolf die. We were eating lunch on a high rimrock, at the foot of which a turbulent river

elbowed its way. We saw what we thought was a doe fording the torrent, her breast awash in white water. When she climbed the bank toward us and shook out her tail, we realized our error: it was a wolf. A half-dozen others, evidently grown pups, sprang from the willows and all joined in a welcoming melee of wagging tails and playful maulings. What was literally a pile of wolves writhed and tumbled in the center of an open flat at the foot of our rimrock.

In those days we had never heard of passing up a chance to kill a wolf. In a second we were pumping lead into the pack, but with more excitement than accuracy: how to aim a steep downhill shot is always confusing. When our rifles were empty, the old wolf was down, and a pup was dragging a leg into impassable slide-rocks.

We reached the old wolf in time to watch a fierce green fire dying in her eyes. I realized then, and have known ever since, that there was something new to me in those eyes—something known only to her and to the mountain. I was young then, and full of trigger-itch; I thought that because fewer wolves meant more deer, that no wolves would mean hunters' paradise. But after seeing the green fire die, I sensed that neither the wolf nor the mountain agreed with such a view.

Since then I have lived to see state after state extirpate its wolves. I have watched the face of many a newly wolfless mountain, and seen the south-facing slopes wrinkle with a maze of new deer trails. I have seen every edible bush and seedling browsed, first to anaemic desuetude, and then to death. I have seen every edible tree defoliated to the height of a saddlehorn. Such a mountain looks as if someone had given God a new pruning shears, and forbidden Him all other exercise. In the end the starved bones of the hoped-for deer herd, dead of its own too-much, bleach with the bones of the dead sage, or molder under the high-lined junipers.

I now suspect that just as a deer herd lives in mortal fear of its wolves, so does a mountain live in mortal fear of its deer. And perhaps with better cause, for while a buck pulled down by wolves can be replaced in two or three years, a range pulled down by too many deer may fail of replacement in as many decades.

So also with cows. The cowman who cleans his range of wolves does not realize that he is taking over the wolf's job of trimming the herd to fit the range. He has not learned to think like a mountain. Hence we have dust-bowls, and rivers washing the future into the sea.

River valley in the Yukon mountains

SECTION TWO
UPLAND BIRDS

CHAPTER 9

THE SUNDOWN COVEY

By Lamar Underwood

"Plate 76" of *Birds of America* by John James Audubon

Nobody ever used that name, really. But it was the covey of bobwhite quail that we always looked for almost with longing, as we turned our hunt homeward in the afternoon. By the time we came to that last stretch of ragged corn and soybean fields where this covey lived, the pines and moss-draped oaks would be looming darkly in the face of the dying sun. The other events of the afternoon never seemed to matter then. Tired pointer dogs bore ahead with new drive; we would watch carefully as they checked out each birdy objective, sure that we were headed for a significant encounter before we reached the small lane that led to the Georgia farmhouse. I always chose to think of those birds as "the sundown covey," although my grandfather or uncle usually would say something like "Let's look in on that bunch at the end of the lane." And then, more times than not, the evening stillness would be broken by my elder's announcement, "Yonder they are!" and we would move toward the dogs on point—small stark-white figures that always seemed to be chiseled out of the shadowy backdrop against the evening swamp.

There's always something special about hunting a covey of quail that you know like an old friend. One covey's pattern of movements between fields and swampy sanctuaries can be an intriguing and baffling problem. Another may be remarkably easy to find, and yet always manage to rocket away through such a thick tangle that you've mentally colored them gone, even before your finger touches the trigger. Another might usually present a good covey shot, while the singles tear away to . . . the backside of the moon, as far as you've been able to tell. My best hunts on more distant but greener pastures somehow have never seemed as inwardly satisfying as a day when a good dog and I can spend some time on familiar problems like these. Give me a covey I know, one that has tricked me, baffled me, eluded me—and by doing so brought me back to its corner of the woods for years.

In this sense, the covey we always hunted at sundown was even more special. As the nearest bunch of birds to the house, it was the most familiar. Here, trembling puppies got onto their first points. A lad learned that two quick shots into the brownish blur of the covey rise would put nothing into his stiff new hunting coat. A man returning from a war saw the birds running quick-footed across the lane and knew that he really was home again. The generations rolled on through times of kerosene lamps and cheap cotton to Ed Sullivan and soil-bank subsidies. And that same covey of bobwhites that had always seemed a part of the landscape still whistled in the long summer afternoons and hurtled across dead cornstalks that rattled in the winter breezes.

The hunters who looked for that covey and others in the fields nearby disciplined themselves never to shoot a covey below six birds. That number left plenty of seed for replenishment, so that every fall the coveys would again number fifteen to thirty birds, depending on how they had fared against predators.

Eventually, all that acreage moved out of our family. My visits to those coveys became less frequent as I necessarily turned toward education and then fields of commerce that were far away. But even during some marvelous quail-hunting days in other places, I often longed for return hunts to those intriguing coveys of the past. Would the swamp covey by the old pond still be up to their usual trick of flying into the field in the afternoon? Where would the singles from the peafield covey go now? Would the sundown covey still be there?

Finally, not long ago, the opportunity came for me to knock about a bit down in the home county. Several hunts with friends seemed as mere preludes to the long-awaited day when I got a chance to slip away alone to the old home grounds.

A soft rain had fallen during the night, but when I parked the truck by a thicket of pines just after sunrise, a stiff breeze had started tearing the overcast apart, and patches of blue were showing through the dullness. Shrugging into my bird vest, I ignored the shufflings and impatient whines that sounded from the dog box and stood a moment looking across a long soybean field that stretched toward a distant line of pines. I was mentally planning a route that would take me in a big circle to a dozen or so familiar coveys, then bring me to the sundown covey in the late evening. I unlatched the dog box, and the pointer, Mack, exploded from the truck and went through a routine of nervous preliminaries. I did the same, checking my bulging coat for shells, lunch and coffee. Then I clicked the double shut and stepped into the sedge alongside the field, calling: "All right, Mack. Look around!"

The pointer loped away in that deceptive, ground-eating gait that was his way of going. At age four, he had not exactly developed into the close worker I had been wanting. His predecessors who had run these fields in decades before were big-going speedsters suited to those times. Controlled burning and wide-roaming livestock kept the woodlands open then. Now most of the forests were so choked with brush and vines that wide-working dogs brought a legacy of frustration. Mack was easy to handle but tended to bend out too far from the gun unless checked back frequently. I really hated

hearing myself say "Hunt close!" so often, but I hated even worse those ago-
nizing slogging searches when he went on point in some dark corner of the
swamp a quarter-mile from where I thought he'd been working.

The sun was bright on the sedge and pines now, and the air winy-crisp
after the rain. Mack was a bouncing flash of white as he worked through
the sedge and low pines. Once he started over the fence into the field, but I
called him back. I wanted him to keep working down the edge. While the
bean field seemed a tempting place to catch a breakfasting bevy, the cover
bordering it offered much better chances—at least three to one, according to
the quail-hunting education I had received here as a youngster. I could still
imagine the sound of my grandfather's voice as he preached:

"Never mind all them picturebook covey rises in those magazines you
read. It's only now and then you'll catch these old coveys in the open. Birds
once had to range wide and root for their keep. Now all the work's done for
'em. Combines and cornpickers leave so much feed scattered in the field the
birds can feed in a few minutes, then leg it back into the cover. That's where
you want to work. First, if they haven't gone to feed, you're likely to find
'em. If they've walked into the field, the dog'll trail 'em out. If they've already
been into the field and fed, you'll still find 'em. Only time you'll miss is when
they've flown into the field and are still there."

I had seen this simple philosophy pay increasing dividends as the years
wore on. As the cover became thicker and the coveys smarter, the clear covey
shot had become a rare, treasured experience. To spend a lot of time working
through the fields was to be a dreamer of the highest order.

Still in the cover, we rounded the end of the small field and headed up
the other side. I was beginning to feel the bite of the day's first disappointment; Mack had picked up no scent at all. Where were they? This covey had
always been easy to find. Maybe they had been shot out, I thought. Maybe
the whole place has been shot out.

I decided to play out a hunch. I pulled down a rusty strand of fence and
stepped out into the field. Mack leaped the wire and raced away at full gallop.
Far downfield he turned into the wind and suddenly froze in one of the most

dramatic points I've ever seen. I knew he was right on top of those birds, his body curved tautly, his tail arching. "Oh ho!" I said aloud. "So you beggars did fly to the field."

My strides lengthened and became hurried. I snapped the gun open and checked the shells in an unnecessary gesture of nervousness. Normally steady hands seemed to tremble a little and felt very thick and uncertain. My heart-beat was a thunderous throb at the base of my throat.

My tangled nerves and wire-taut reflexes scarcely felt the nudge of a thought that said, "Relax. You've done this before." The case of shakes I undergo every time I step up to a point makes it difficult to attach any importance to that idea. Covey-rise jitters are known to have only one cure: action.

On my next step, the earth seemed to explode. The air was suddenly filled with blurry bits and pieces of speeding fragments, all boring toward the pines that loomed ahead. I found myself looking at one particular whirring form, and when the stock smacked against my face, the gun bucked angrily. The brown missile was unimpressed. He faded into the swamp, along with a skyful of surviving kinsmen. My loosely poked second shot failed to drop a tail-ender.

Mighty sorry gathering up of partridges, I thought, using the expression that was my uncle's favorite on the occasions when we struck out on a covey rise. "Sorry, boy," I called to Mack, who was busy vacuuming the grass in a futile search for downed birds.

My elders would have thought that bevy's maneuver of flying out to the field was the lowest trick in the book. But now the practice had become so typical among smart southern Bobs that it was hardly worth lamenting.

I called Mack away from his unrewarding retrieve and headed after those singles. The woods ahead looked clear enough for some choice shooting if I could keep Mack close.

Thirty minutes later I emerged from those woods a frustrated, angry man. My estimate that the birds had landed in the grassy, open pinelands was about two hundred yards wrong. Instead they had sailed on into one

of the thickest, darkest sweet-gum swamps I've ever cursed a bird dog in. It took Mack all of fifteen seconds to get lost, and when I found him on point after ten minutes of searching I proceeded to put the first barrel into a gum tree and the second into a screen of titi bushes. Then the heebie-geebies really took over as I walked over two separate singles that jumped unannounced. Finally, Mack pointed again, but as I fought through the tearing clutches of briers and vines to get to him, I bumped another single, which I shot at without a glimmer of hope. That action caused Mack to take matters into his own hands and send the bird he was pointing vaulting away through the trees. Then followed a lot of unnecessary yelling, and we headed for the clear.

I should have known better. Single-bird hunting in that part of Georgia had become a sad business. Now I was discovering that my old hunting grounds were in the same shape as the rest of the county. If you were going to mess with singles, you had to wait for the right type of open woods. Most were just too thick to see a dog, much less a six-ounce bird. The day's shooting was certainly not going to follow the patterns of the past when it came to singles. I would have to wait until I got a bevy scattered in a better place.

We cut away from the field into a section of low moss-draped oak trees. Mack ranged ahead, working smartly. My frustrations of the first covey slipped away as I began considering the coming encounter with the next set of old friends. This covey, if they were still in business, would be composed of dark swamp birds that lived in the edge of the creek swamp but used this oak ridge to feed on acorns during early mornings and late afternoons. They were extremely hard to catch in the open, sometimes running for hundreds of yards in front of a dog on point. But what a sight they always made as they hurtled up among the moss-draped oaks on the lucky occasions when we did get them pinned nicely.

This oak ridge was fairly open, so I let Mack move on out a little bit. When he cut through one thickish cluster of trees and did not come out right away, I knew he had 'em.

Incredible I thought. The first two coveys are still here, and we've worked 'em both. Then the words turned into brass in my mouth as I eased up to the dog and past him. The thunderous rise I had been expecting failed to occur. I let Mack move on ahead to relocate. Catlike, he crept through the low grass for a few yards, then froze again. I moved out in front once more, and still nothing happened.

Then, suddenly I heard them. Several yards out front the dry leaves rustled under the flow of quick-moving feet. The covey was up to its old trick of legging it for the sanctuary of the swamp.

I hurried forward, crashing through the briers. Just ahead, the low cover gave way to a wall of sweetgum and cypress that marked the beginning of the swamp. Too late! I caught the sound of wings whirring. The birds had made the edge and were roaring off through the trees. They seemed to get up in groups of two and three. I caught an occasional glimpse of dim blurs through the screen of limbs and snapped a shot at one. Leaves and sticks showered down as Mack raced forward. Seconds later he emerged from the brush carrying a plump rooster bobwhite.

Had you seen me grinning over that bird, you might have thought I hadn't scored in five years. But the shot seemed mighty satisfying under the conditions. A few moments like this could make the day a lot more glorious than a coatful of birds ever could.

Now we followed an old lane that led down across the swamp and out beside a tremendous cornfield surrounded by pine and gallberry flats. I expected to find a couple of coveys here—and did, too, as the morning wore on in a succession of encounters with my old friends. A heart-warming double from a bevy Mack pinned along a fence row was followed by a succession of bewildering misses when we followed the singles into an open gallberry flat where I should have been able to score. Then we had the fun of unraveling a particularly difficult relocation problem when Mack picked up some hot scent in the corn but could not trail out to the birds. The edge of the field sloped down a grassy flat to an old pond with pine timber on the far side. I just knew those birds had flown across that pond to the woods to hole up for the day. When I took Mack over he made a beautiful point, standing just inside the woods. I wish I could always dope out a covey like that.

We spent the middle of the day stretched out on the grass on the pond dam. The sandwiches and coffee couldn't have tasted better. The sun was warm, and crows and doves flew against the blue sky. I thought about old hunts and old friends and couldn't have felt better.

In the afternoon we had a couple of interesting pieces of action, but failed to find some of my old neighbor coveys at home. My thoughts kept reaching ahead to the late-afternoon time when I would near the old now-deserted house by the lane and see the sundown covey again. Surely they would still be there. After all, we had been finding most of the old coveys. Who says you can't go home again? Who's afraid of you, Tom Wolfe?

The sun was dipping toward the pines and a sharp chill had come on when I skirted the last field and entered a stretch of open pine woods where I was counting on finding the covey of birds that I had carried in my mind all my life. Before I had gone fifty yards I came on something that shocked me as though I'd walked up on a ten-foot rattlesnake. A newly cut stake had been driven in the ground, and a red ribbon tied to the top of it. Farther on there was another, then another.

I had known that the new Savannah-Atlanta-Super-High-Speed-Interstate-Get-You-There-Quick-Highway was to pass through this general area. But surely, a couple of miles away. Not here. Not right here.

Gradually, my disbelief turned into anger. I felt like heading for the car right then and getting the hell out of there. Then suddenly three-shots boomed in the woods some distance ahead.

Well, it was apparent that the sundown covey was still around. But an intruder had found them. I decided to go on up and talk to whoever it was. Actually, he probably had as much right to be here as I did now. I couldn't believe he was a regular hunter on this land, though. The coveys I had been finding all day were too populous with birds to be gunned heavily.

I walked slowly through the pines for a few minutes without spotting the other hunter. Then his gun thudded again, this time from farther down in the swamp. He's after the singles now, I thought. I called in Mack and waited there opposite the swamp. The other fellow would have to come out this way.

During the next few minutes two more separate shots sounded. The sun sank lower, and the breeze blew harder in the pines. Finally, I heard the bushes shaking and a man came out of the cover. When Mack started barking he spotted me and headed my way. As he came up I saw that he was young, carried an automatic and wore no hunting coat. He had some quail by the legs in his left hand.

"Looks like you did some good," I said.

"Yea, I got six."

"Where's your dog?" I asked.

"Oh, I don't have a dog. I spotted a covey crossing the road down there by the lane. I had the gun in the truck, so I went after 'em. Got three when I flushed 'em and three more down in the branch. Tiny little covey, though. I

don't think there were more than six when I first flushed 'em. I imagine people been framin' into this bunch all the time." My heart sank when he said
that. I didn't know what to say. He paused a minute, looking at Mack. "That's
a nice dog. He any good?"

"Fair," I said. "Maybe you shouldn't have done that."

"What?"

"Shoot a small covey on down that way."

"Don't mean nothing. There's always a covey of birds along here. Every
year. But there won't be for long. Interstate's coming through."

"Yea," I said slowly. "I see it is."

"Well, I gotta run. That's sure a nice-looking dog, Mister. See you
around."

I watched him walk away. Then I leaned back against a pine, listening to
the swamp noises. The wings of a pair of roost-bound ducks whispered overhead. An owl tuned up down in the swamp. Somehow I kept thinking that
I would hear some birds calling each other back into a covey. Perhaps two or
three had slipped away unseen from the roadside.

The night pressed down. Trembling in the cold, I started for the truck.
Orion wheeled overhead. I started thinking about some new places I wanted
to try. But never again did I hear that flutelike call that had sounded for me
from that swamp so many times before.

CHAPTER 10

FIRST GROUSE

By William G. Tapply

Children," my father liked to say, "should be seen and not heard."

It was something I tried hard to be good at. I made a special point of being seen, because I didn't want to be overlooked. So when my father rose before dawn on those Saturday mornings in October and November, I got up, too. I helped lug the gear up from the cellar and set it out on the back porch—the leg o' mutton shotgun case, my father's big duffel bag, the wicker lunch basket, and the canvas bag that held boxes of shells, topographic maps, the dog's belled collar, cans of horsemeat, and rags pungent with Hoppe's.

In the kitchen, my father worked over the black skillet where the bacon sizzled and spat. When his partner arrived, I sat with the men at the cramped table watching the suburban sky brighten over the back yard. My father's partner called himself Grampa Grouse. My father called him Grampa, and I was expected to, also. Grampa Grouse was white-haired, rosy-cheeked, and jolly, always bubbling with enthusiasm—my vision of Santa Claus—and he loved to tell extravagant stories about partridge and the dogs and men who hunted them.

I ate with the men, and the dogs waited under the table. Grampa Grouse slipped crusts of toast and strips of bacon to them, and when the men pushed back their chairs and lit their pipes, the dogs' tails began to thump against the floor, and then they uncurled themselves and scratched and skidded across the linoleum to the back door and began to whine and bump their noses against it.

That, in turn, signaled the men to get up from the table. "The dogs need to bust their boilers," Grampa Grouse would say, and he'd let them into the back yard. My father would kiss my mother and clap my shoulder. And then the two men would leave.

On Sunday night I would meet them at Grampa Grouse's wagon when it pulled into the driveway. I'd help my father lug in the gear and the dead birds, and then I'd watch while he cleaned them at the kitchen sink. My job was to swab out the barrels of my father's shotgun and rub it down with an oily rag. I performed this important job with care. I knew my father would peer through the barrels and look for fingerprints on the metal, and I understood that cleaning a shotgun properly was one step toward shooting it.

I didn't really mind being left behind. My day would come. I knew that.

I imagined it would be a dramatic moment, like getting married or having my first drink of whiskey. There would be a speech about the serious nature of firearms and adult responsibility and the honored ceremonies of grouse hunting, and how being seen and not heard was important for men as well as boys.

When it actually happened, though, the moment could have almost slipped past without being noticed. One Friday evening in the October after I turned eleven, my father looked up from his newspaper and said, "Want to come with us tomorrow?"

I rode in the back seat for the two-hour drive into New Hampshire. My father and Grampa Grouse talked about business and politics and foreign policy, about men and bird dogs who had died, subjects not selected for my interest, but not censored because I was in the back seat, either. They included me, I understood, by not excluding me.

I was not allowed to carry a gun on this my first grouse hunt, of course. "Walk directly behind me," my father instructed me while we laced on our boots at the first cover. "Stay close to me, and keep your eyes and ears open. When a bird flushes, fall flat to the ground. If you can't do that, you'll have to stay in the car."

Grouse covers, I quickly learned, were thick, hostile places, nothing like the Aden Lassell Ripley watercolors that hung in my father's den. Grouse covers were hilly, rocky, brushy, muddy hellholes where hunters had to wade through juniper clumps and claw through briar patches and clamber over blowdown. I struggled to keep up with my father. Sometimes saplings snapped back against my face and made my eyes water.

Once my feet got tangled and I fell. Before I could scramble to my feet, my father stopped and looked back at me. "You've got to keep up," he said.

"I tripped," I said. "It's hard walking."

"You can go back to the car if you want."

"I'm okay."

The first time a grouse flushed, I watched my father's gun snap up and shoot into the thick autumn foliage. The gun seemed to react on its own, independent of the man who carried it. I never saw the bird. I only heard the sudden, explosive whirr.

"Well?" called Grampa Grouse from somewhere off to the right.

"Nope," called my father. "Dog busted him."

Then he turned and looked at me. I was standing there right behind him. "I told you to fall to the ground when a bird gets up," he said.

"I heard the noise," I said. "I didn't know . . ."

"That was a grouse. That's the noise they make when they flush. You've got to go to the ground."

"Okay," I said. "I understand."

I learned that grouse hunting involved miles of hard walking, a great deal of yelling at the dogs, frequent shooting, and not much killing.

The day was warm and I soon grew tired. The part I liked best was returning to Grampa's wagon after each cover. There the men would pour coffee for me from a big steel Thermos. The coffee was cut with milk and sweetened with sugar. I had never tasted coffee before that day. It wasn't whiskey, but drinking coffee for the first time nevertheless seemed important to me.

Many grouse flushed that morning, and I quickly learned to fall to the ground at the sound. When my father finally shot one, he turned and said, "Did you see that?"

"Of course not," I said. "I was lying on the ground."

He smiled.

We ate lunch by a brook in the woods. Thick corned beef-and-cheese sandwiches between slices of bread my mother had baked. Big wedges of

applesauce cake, my mother's secret recipe. More sweet coffee. I grew drowsy. My legs ached.

After a while, Grampa Grouse unfolded himself, stood up, and stretched. "Better get a move on," he said. "Don't want to get all bogged down."

It grew cloudy and cooler in the afternoon. A soft rain began to sift down from the gray sky, and the woods were silent except for the tinkle of the dogs' bells and the occasional whistles that my father exchanged with Grampa Grouse. My pants soaked up rainwater from the brush. I found myself stumbling. I hoped it would be over soon. I plodded along behind my father, my eyes on the ground so I wouldn't trip and fall again.

We were moving through an old apple orchard. It grew thick with juniper and thornapple and popple and alder. A blanket of small, hard Baldwin apples carpeted the ground under the trees. They cracked under my boots. The woods smelled sweet with their ripe aroma.

Suddenly my father stopped. "Look!" he hissed.

I peered along his pointing arm and saw the big bird perched on the lowest limb of a gaunt old apple tree. One of the dogs stood directly underneath, looking up. The grouse craned its neck, peering down at the dog.

My father pressed his shotgun into my hands. "Shoot him," he said.

I had fired my father's shotgun just once in my life. I'd shot it at a rusty old oil drum. The oil drum had disintegrated. My father had said, "Good shot," but I understood it had nothing to do with marksmanship. This had been a lesson about the power of shotguns.

I pressed the gun against my shoulder, aimed it at the grouse in the apple tree, and tugged at the trigger. Nothing happened.

"The safety," my father whispered. "Quick."

I remembered. I thumbed off the safety, set the bird over the barrels, and pulled the trigger. The gun sounded louder than I remembered from shooting at the oil drum. The grouse fell from the tree.

"Hey!" my father said. "You got him. Good shot."

The dog came trotting in with the dead grouse in his mouth. My father took it from the dog, stroked the bird's feathers, then handed it to me. "Your first grouse," he said. "Congratulations."

I carried the grouse by its feet through the rest of the cover. When we got back to Grampa Grouse's wagon, my father took a picture of me. Grampa punched my shoulder and called me Nimrod.

The men tried to act as if my first grouse was a big triumph, but I understood that hitting a sitting grouse with a shotgun was no great feat. No different from shooting an oil drum, really. Something any boy could do. I also understood, because I'd been paying attention that day, that the men shot only at flying grouse.

Being seen but not heard, of course, I did not share this understanding with my father and Grampa Grouse.

After that day, I accompanied my father almost every autumn weekend, and when I turned thirteen, my father gave me my own shotgun, a single-barreled Savage 20-gauge with a thumb safety.

Being seen and not heard, I had come to realize, enabled me to learn a great deal. I absorbed what the men said—from the back seat and in grouse covers and while eating lunch alongside brooks and in hotel dining rooms. I watched what the dogs did and the paths my father took through the woods, and I noticed the kinds of places where grouse hid.

Now, carrying my own shotgun and walking my own routes through covers, I found I had a good instinct for grouse. My father and I and Grampa Grouse worked as a team, pinching birds between us so that one or the other of us would get a good shot.

There were a lot of grouse in the New England woods in those days, and I had my share of chances. My father had told me that having a single-shot gun would make me a better marksman, but it didn't work out that way. I had quick reflexes, and soon my Savage was coming to my shoulder and my thumb was flicking off the safety and I was pulling the trigger without any conscious thought. I shot often. I took crossing shots and straightaway shots and odd-angled shots at flying grouse. I learned to shoot through the leaves where I thought a grouse might be headed, and sometimes I shot at the sound of the flush when all I saw was a quick blur.

I never once hit a flying grouse.

"Keep shooting," my father counseled. "You can't hit what you don't shoot at. It'll happen. The good old law of averages, right?"

A couple of times I broke my private vow and shot a grouse out of a tree or off a stone wall. I did it out of anger and frustration at my own incompetence, and even when my father congratulated me on bagging a bird, I found that it gave me no satisfaction whatsoever. Men, I knew, did not shoot sitting grouse.

So for the entire season of my thirteenth year and most of the next one, too, I kept my wingshooting streak alive. I shot often and missed every time.

When we hunted with other men, neither my father nor I mentioned my perfect record, the fact that I had never once downed a flying grouse. Since everybody missed grouse far more often than they hit them, nobody except my father knew my secret.

I understood that shooting grouse out of the air was not really the main point of grouse hunting. I liked figuring out where a grouse might be, sneaking up on it, planning how I'd get a shot when it flushed, or if I didn't, one of the other men would. I liked watching the dogs work. I liked the New England woods in the fall, the way the melting frost glistened on the goldenrod early in the morning and the way Baldwin apples smelled when the ground was blanketed with them. I liked riding in the back seat with the dogs, listening to the men talk, being seen and not heard.

But I had never shot a flying grouse. That single fact separated me from the men. Shooting a few from trees or stone walls didn't count. Boys did that, but not men.

On the final weekend of that year's grouse season, my father and I traveled to a new area. We hunted with three old friends of his, men I had never met.

These men included me in their conversations and treated me like a man. They had not known me when I plodded through grouse covers in my father's footsteps. They had not witnessed my first grouse, shot out of a tree.

They didn't know that I had never shot a grouse on the wing. I spoke when spoken to, and otherwise continued to be seen and not heard.

We found very few grouse on Saturday. Two of the men missed hasty shots. I never saw a feather, never even had a chance to shoot and miss.

Sunday, the last day of the season, was one of those dark, bitter, late-November New England days. Winter was in the air. Heavy clouds hung over the leafless woods, and now and then a few hard little kernels of snow spit down from the sky. We hunted hard all morning and never flushed a grouse. At lunch the men talked about calling it a season and getting an early start for home.

But one of them said he had a secret cover we ought to try first, and the others agreed, although I noticed their lack of enthusiasm.

The birdy part of the cover lay at the end of a long tote road that twisted down a hill through a mixture of pine and poplar. The men and I trudged along with our shotguns at our sides while the dogs, who seemed to have lost their enthusiasm, too, snuffled along ahead of us.

Suddenly the man in front stopped and raised his hand. "We got a point," he whispered.

I looked, and under an apple tree at the foot of the hill, I saw the dog stretched out.

"There she is!" hissed the man a moment later, and I saw her, too—a grouse pecking fallen apples about fifteen feet from the dog's nose.

We stood there in the path for a minute, just watching, the dog staunch on point, the grouse oblivious, pecking apples, taking a step, bending to take another peck.

Then one of the men touched my shoulder and said: "You take her."

I caught my father's eye. He nodded. So I stepped forward, gripping my Savage single-shot at port arms, and approached the place where the dog was still on point.

The grouse had wandered into the thick undergrowth, and for a minute I couldn't see her. Then I did. She had stopped and twisted her neck around to look directly at me. I stood there, staring back into her intelligent, glittery eyes.

From behind me, one of the men said, "Go ahead. Shoot her. Quick, before she flies."

I raised my gun to my shoulder and aimed at the bird. The grouse kept peering at me.

Then I lowered my gun. I couldn't do it. Shooting this grouse on the ground would prove nothing, and I felt that I had something I needed to prove.

Boys, I thought, shoot grouse on the ground. Men only shoot them when they're flying.

I'd miss, of course. I always did. So what? Better to miss like a man than kill a grouse like a boy.

Then the grouse ducked her head, scuttled deeper into the brush, and disappeared from sight. I stepped forward, paused, took another step.

The grouse exploded, practically from under my feet. She rose, then suddenly angled toward the left. I have no memory of my gun coming up, my thumb flicking off the safety, my finger pulling the trigger.

But I heard the muffled thump of the bird hitting the ground and the quick flurry of wingbeats, and then I heard the men behind me shouting.

A moment later the dog brought the grouse to me. I took her in my hand, smoothed her feathers, tucked her into the pocket in the back of my vest, and walked back to where the men were standing. I was surprised that I felt no particular elation.

"Good shot," said one of the men. "Nice goin'," said another, and I caught the tone I'd hoped for in their voices: It had been a good shot, not a spectacular one, they were saying. It was a shot that grouse hunters often miss but sometimes make, and I had done well.

There was no exaggerated celebration, as there might have been had they known that I had never before shot a grouse out of the air, and that was exactly the way I wanted it.

I glanced at my father, begging him with my eyes not to reveal my secret. My father nodded once, then turned to the other men. "So," he said, "is the rest of this cover worth hunting?"

CHAPTER 11

SPILLER COUNTRY

By William G. Tapply

Three or four times a year I take my old friend's shotgun from my gun
cabinet, break it apart, check it for rust, and give it a good cleaning. It's a Parker 20, VH grade, a nice gun—beautiful, in fact—and
perhaps modestly valuable. It looks like it's been hunted hard, and it has. Its
bluing is worn shiny around the breech and at the ends of the barrels, there
are dents in the stock, and the recoil pad is beginning to crumble. I've never
bothered to have it appraised. It's not for sale, so why bother, although men
who know its provenance have offered me what I'm sure is ten times what a
shrewd gunsmith would pay.

I fit it together, snap it to my shoulder, trace the hard flight of a grouse cutting across the wall of my den, and remember all the birds it's shot—and all those I've missed with it. Then I sit back, lay the little Parker on my lap, close my eyes, and indulge myself in a moment of nostalgia—for the days when I tromped the uplands with Burt Spiller, and for the days when ruffed grouse prospered in Spiller country.

According to my father's meticulous journals, I hunted with Burton L. Spiller for the first time on November 10, 1951. Well, I didn't actually hunt in those days. I was eleven, too young to carry a gun in the woods. Instead, I followed at my father's heels all day—through briar and alder and mud, up hill and over stone wall and around blowdown. I didn't mind. Grouse hunting in those days was exciting enough even if you couldn't shoot.

One English setter, two men, and one boy flushed 23 separate grouse that November day in Burt's string of southern New Hampshire covers. Burt, who was sixty-five, walked the field edges and shot one of them with his sleek little Parker. My father dropped three.

Dad's journals suggest that was an average day back then.

In the 1955 season we became a regular threesome. At nine every Saturday morning, Dad and I pulled up in front of Burt's white frame house in East Rochester. A leg o' mutton gun case, black lunch pail, and pair of well-oiled boots were already lined up on the porch, and when Dad tooted the horn, Burt came out, waved, and lugged his gear to the car. "Hi," he always grinned. "I've been expecting you. It looks like a wonderful day."

Burton L. Spiller was born on December 21, 1886, the right time—in Portland, Maine, the right place.

The nineteenth-century Maine farmers had opened the land. They moved rocks to clear pastureland and piled them along the edges to make Frost's "good fences." They planted apples—Baldwins and Gravensteins, Northern Spies and Russets and Pippins. Second-growth birch and popple and alder and hemlock pushed in when the farms were abandoned. Just about the time young Burt was old enough to carry a shotgun into the woods, classic grouse cover was everywhere. No wonder Burt Spiller became a partridge hunter.

He blasted his first grouse off the ground with his father's 10-gauge duck gun when he was seven. "Many, many times I have stood as I stood then," he wrote in "His Majesty, the Grouse," his first published story, "but there has never been another grouse—or another thrill like that one. The kick is still there, as I presume it still is in the old 10-gauge, but—well—we are a little harder around the heart and shoulders than we were then."

A year later the Spillers moved down the seacoast to the little hamlet of Wells, and young Burt's lifelong love affair with the ruffed grouse was sealed. "Other boys of my acquaintance might content themselves with slaying elephants and lions and other inconsequential members of the animal kingdom," he wrote, "but I wanted none of that??? . . . . Nothing but the lordly pa'tridge would satisfy me."

Eventually Burt bartered his bicycle and his watch for a 16-gauge double and "began to kill grouse regularly on the wing. I used the word 'regularly' advisedly," he wrote, "for the regularity was truly astounding. I shot a bird and killed it. Then I shot at forty nine more and missed ingloriously. Then I killed another."

When he was a young man, he teamed up briefly with a pair of market hunters, an experience that steeped him in grouse lore and sharpened his wingshooting eye. But eventually he recognized "the difference between a sportsman and that reprehensible thing I was becoming. . . . [so] I bought a bird dog and became a sportsman."

In 1911 Burton Spiller married and settled in East Rochester, New Hampshire, where he lived out the rest of his life. He was a blacksmith and a welder, and during the Great War he built submarines at the Portsmouth Naval Shipyard. He raised and bred prize-winning gladioli. He carved violins and made hunting knives. He hunted—not just grouse and woodcock, but ducks and deer, too—and he fished for brook trout and landlocked salmon.

And although he was pretty much self-educated, he began to write, working nights on his old Oliver typewriter. He sold "His Majesty, the Grouse" to Field & Stream in 1931. It was the first of 53 Spiller stories that magazine would print. The last was "Grouse Oddities," in 1967, when Burt was 81.

Between 1935 and 1938 the Derrydale Press published a Spiller book a year—all numbered, deluxe editions limited to 950 copies. First came the classic GROUSE FEATHERS, then THOROUGHBRED and FIRE-LIGHT and MORE GROUSE FEATHERS. All have been reprinted one time or another. Those original Derrydales are treasures.

Around that time, someone dubbed Burt "the poet laureate of the ruffed grouse." The name stuck, as it should have.

In 1962 DRUMMER IN THE WOODS, a collection of previous-ly-published grouse stories (mostly from *Field & Stream*), appeared. Burt also wrote a boy's adventure yarn called NORTHLAND CASTAWAYS, and in 1974, the year after he died, FISHIN' AROUND, a collection of his low-key fishing stories, appeared.

I guess at one time or another while the two of us were eating my moth-er's applesauce cake by a New Hampshire brook or bouncing over a dirt road between covers or trudging side-by-side down an overgrown tote road, Burt told me most of his stories. Whenever I reread a couple of them, as I do every time I take out the old Parker, I can hear Burt's soft voice, see the twinkle in his eye, and feel his finger poking my arm for emphasis.

In 1955, when I began hunting regularly with him, Burt was already 69 years old. He was a small, wiry, soft-spoken man, old enough to be my father's father. I called him "Mr. Spiller," as I'd been taught. But on the first morning of our first hunt he put his hand on my shoulder and said, "Burt, please. Call me Burt. When a grouse gets up, you can't go yelling 'Mark! Mr. Spiller' now, can you?"

I never heard him raise his voice, curse even mildly, or criticize or poke fun at any man or dog. He was a devout church-going family man who did not hunt on Sundays, even though it was legal in New Hampshire, or drink alcohol, but he was neither pious nor self-righteous.

A good joke, for Burt, was a joke on himself. His favorite stories were about the grouse that outsmarted him and the times he got lost in the woods.

He wore an old-fashioned hearing aid, the kind that plugged into his ear with wires running to the battery in his pocket. "I can hear pretty well," he told me cheerfully, "but sometimes I have trouble picking up the direction." It had to have been a terrible handicap for a grouse hunter, and it probably accounted for the fact that even in those years when partridge were bountiful in his covers, many a day passed when Burt never fired his gun.

When he saw a bird, though, his swing was as silky as I guessed it had been fifty years earlier. Once he and I were trudging side-by-side up the old Tripwire woodsroad on our way back to the car. Our guns dangled at our sides, and we were talking and admiring the way the October sunlight filtered through the golden foliage of the beeches that bordered the roadway and arched overhead. Dad and the dog were working their way along parallel with us somewhere far off to the left.

Suddenly Dad yelled, "Mark! Your way!"

A moment later a grouse crashed through the leaves and rocketed across the narrow road in front of us. It didn't make it. Burt's Parker spoke once, and the bird cartwheeled to the ground.

It was a spectacular shot.

Burt picked up the stone-dead partridge and stroked its neck feathers. Then he looked up at me. He shook his head and smiled apologetically. "Sorry," he said. "I should have let you take him."

He knew, of course, that the odds of my shooting that grouse were exactly the same as his own when he'd been my age: about one in fifty. But that was Burt.

I was young and eager, and I tended to measure the success of a day's hunting by the heft of my game pocket. I learned how to hit flying grouse the old fashioned way—by shooting often and relying on the law of averages—and as much as I missed, and as much as I expected to miss, I still tended to kick stumps and grumble and sulk when it kept happening.

Burt used to tell me, "Just keep shootin'. You can't hit anything if you don't shoot. And always remember: Every time you hit a flying grouse is a good shot."

I noticed that he never grumbled or sulked when he missed, although, to be accurate, he didn't seem to miss very often. Even on those days when birds were scarce, and it rained, and the dog behaved poorly, and nobody got any shots, Burt always had fun. Afterwards, when we dropped him off at his house, he always smiled and said the same thing: "A wonderful hunt. See you next week."

Gradually I learned to say the same thing at the end of every day—"A wonderful hunt"—and mean it. Burt taught me that.

He was moving a lot slower in 1964, and although he still wore the old hearing aid, he didn't seem to pick up sounds as well. Burt was 78 that year. But he still greeted us the same way when we picked him up in the morning: "Hi. I've been expecting you. It looks like a wonderful day."

On the second weekend of the season after we laced on our boots at our Bullring cover for the day's first hunt, Burt said, "Uh, Bill? Can I heft your gun?"

I handed him my cheap Savage single-shot.

He threw it to his shoulder. "Comes up nice," he said. "Mind if I try it?"

"Sure," I said, though I couldn't understand why he'd want to.

"Here," he said. "You better take mine." He handed me his slick little Parker.

I carried Burt's gun through the Bullring, and he carried mine. I recall missing a couple of woodcock with it. Burt, straggling along the fringes of the cover, had no shots.

At our next stop, Burt picked up the Savage. "Never got to fire it back there," he said. "Mind if I try again?"

And so Burt lugged my gun around that day while I carried his Parker, and Dad's journal reports that I ended up shooting a woodcock, while Burt never dirtied the barrel of that Savage.

When we dropped him off, he said, "Why don't you hang onto that gun if you want to."

"Well, sure," I stammered. "I mean, I'd love to."

He smiled and waved. "A wonderful hunt, wasn't it?"

The next week when we stopped for Burt, it was my Savage that stood on his porch alongside his lunch pail and boots, and he carried it all day while I toted the Parker. And nothing was ever again said about it. We had swapped guns, and Burt had managed to accomplish it his own way, without ceremony. He never even gave me the chance to properly thank him.

I know for certain that Burton Spiller shot only one more grouse in his life, and it happened a couple of weeks after we'd exchanged guns. He was following a field edge while Dad and I were slogging through the thick stuff, and a bird flushed wild and headed in Burt's direction. Dad screamed, "Mark! Burt!" and I could hear the frustration in his voice, knowing that Burt probably couldn't hear him and wouldn't hear or see the bird.

But a moment later, from far off to our right, came a single shot.

We hooked over to the field and emerged behind Burt. He was trudging slowly up the slope, my gun over his right shoulder and a grouse hanging by its legs from his left hand.

Burt Spiller shot his last partridge with my gun.

The following Saturday—October 31, 1964—sometime in the morning, Burt fell. He never complained—didn't even tell us when it happened—but by the middle of the afternoon he had to call it quits.

He was still hurting the next week and the week after, and then the season was over.

Burt Spiller had hunted grouse for the last time.

During the next decade, Dad and I visited him periodically. He always had a smile and wanted to hear about the hunting. He continued to write stories and raise gladioli right up to his death on May 26, 1973.

A few months later, the old Savage came back to me with Burt's instruction: "For Bill's son."

Dad and I continued to hunt Spiller country for the next several seasons. Then one October we found a power line had cut the heart out of Schoolhouse. The next winter, Bullring became a highway cloverleaf and a Stop & Shop parking lot took the upper end of Tap's Corner. A couple of years later, the dirt road to The Old Hotel got paved over, and pastel-colored ranch houses sprouted up along both sides.

Burt's covers, those that remained, changed, too. Mankiller and Tripwire just didn't look birdy anymore. The hillsides that had once sprouted thick with juniper and birch whips and head-high alders grew into mature pine-and-hardwood forests, and after a while we stopped hunting Spiller country altogether.

Anyway, it would never be the same. It always seemed as if we'd forgotten the most important stop of all—at the white frame house in the village of East Rochester, where Burt would come to his door on a Saturday morning, grin and wave, lug his gear to the car, and say, "Hi. I've been expecting you. It looks like a wonderful day."

CHAPTER 12

TARGETING THE THUNDER MAKER

By Robert F. Jones

Some upland wingshots I know spend their spring months engaged in such lesser outdoor activities as trout fishing, turkey hunting, running white-water rivers, gardening or even (for shame!) playing golf. Not I. From mid-April to early May you'll find me at dawn prowling the vernal woods of southwestern Vermont or walking the adjacent dirt roads, rain or shine, listening for the sound of distant thunder. Spring, after all, is the prime drumming season for ruffed grouse.

As the late Gordon Gullion—who knew more about *Bonasa umbellus* than any other researcher of the 20th Century—wrote in *Grouse of the North Shore*, "Fishermen working a favorite trout stream in the spring often hear the drummer's roll from nearby hillsides. Canoeists drifting down a river on a midsummer afternoon may hear an occasional drum from the bordering woodlands. In the fall, hunters waiting quietly for a wary white-tail frequently hear the distant drumming of the male ruffed grouse. Mid-winter drumming is infrequent, but occurs from time to time. It is not often heard, but the unmistakable marks [of the drummer's wings] can be found on snow-covered logs in January and February." Yet the peak of drumming activity comes "as the snow melts in the spring and the breeding season approaches."

I'm not out there listening to drummers for the sheer, heartwarming, aesthetic experience of it. To my ear, a drumming grouse is nowhere near as mellifluous as a "singing" woodcock or a gobbling wild turkey. And just being out at dawn during April in Vermont can make for a wet, muddy, bone-chilling morning. Even if the sky is clear and the sun has some strength to it that only provokes the black flies to chow down more greedily. But for the dedicated grouse hunter, these excursions are worth the discomfort. If you know where a cock grouse is drumming in springtime, you know he'll be in the same general vicinity five or six months later, come bird season. And if his drumming has managed to secure him a mate or two, there'll be plenty of naive young grouse wandering the woods as well.

The spring woods just wouldn't be the same without the thunderous drumming of ruffed grouse.

Though spring drumming serves as an advertisement for hen grouse to "come and get it," the most important purpose of sounding the thunder is to warn all other male grouse within hearing to keep clear of the drummer's turf. This is usually a chunk of woods about eight or 10 acres in area. As Gullion notes, "In contiguous, good ruffed grouse habitat, drumming males are often spaced quite evenly, about 148 to 159 yards apart. . . . "I've never found them that close together, but if your spring scouting expeditions are profitable and local habitat is good, you may hear as many as three or four drummers sounding off almost simultaneously. Under the right conditions—a cold, windless, slightly misty morning—a drummer can be heard as far as a half-mile away, though a quarter-mile is more often the case in the dense woods ruffs prefer. Heavy spruce or fir cover muffles the sound even further.

During the spring drumming season, cock grouse sound off for five to eight seconds per drum roll, and the riffs are almost always spaced four minutes apart.

Gullion writes, "The drumming sound is made by the bird leaning back on his tail and striking his wings against the air violently enough to create a momentary vacuum, much as lighting does when it flashes through the sky.... Contrary to some of the tales one hears, the male grouse does not beat on a log with his wings, nor does he peck the log to drum."

Though the classic drumming scene, beloved of 19th Century artists, pictures a cock grouse standing tall on a massive, hollow, moss-covered blowdown in thick, primeval woods, it turns out that today's grouse don't even need logs to drum on. Gullion, during his 33 years of study (1958 to 1991) in the Cloquet Forest of northeastern Minnesota, found them playing Gene

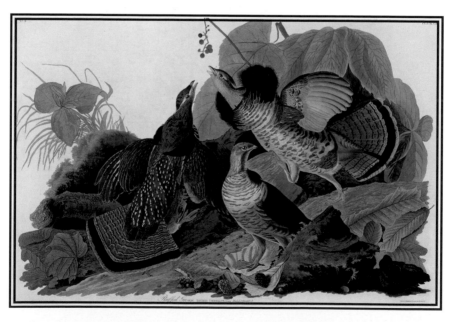

"Ruffed Grouse" by John J. Audubon, circa 1861. Courtesy of the online collection of the Brooklyn Museum

Krupa on boulders, woodpiles, exposed road culverts, the roots of trees, mounds of bare dirt "and even the snowbanks along roadways." Here in interior New England I often find them drumming atop old stone walls where former pastures have reverted to aspen groves. The frayed, molted wing feathers on or near the walls confirm that these are indeed drumming sites.

There's often a kind of ventriloquial quality to a grouse's drumbeat. This is especially true in the steep, hilly, wooded country that characterizes most good New England grouse coverts. What's more, ruffs sometimes change position while drumming on their log or stone wall or boulder, turning a complete 180 between drum rolls. This can throw off the listener's sense of the drummer's location by as much as 30 to 45 degrees. Still, if you wait patiently for perhaps a half-hour—say seven or eight solos, quietly changing position from time to time—you can usually zero in on the drumming site. Approaching it is another matter.

Gullion found that at Cloquet "good drumming sites are quite predator-proof." This clumsy, two-legged predator can second that conclusion. During my first bird season in Vermont I spent many a grouseless morning trying to sneak up on and bushwhack a drummer that had the nerve to sound off not a hundred yards from my house. For some reason this bird was drumming as if it were springtime—which they'll do. I once heard a ruff, maybe this same one, drumming his wings off at midnight on New Year's Eve, under a full moon that turned the snowy meadow behind my house into a reflecting shield that almost made me wince. He kept it up until moonset, at 5 a.m.

My "house grouse" was brazen, to say the least. This was in the early years of my great black Lab Luke, and the grouse drove both of us nuts. Time after time we tried to flush the thunder-maker, pussyfooting up on his drumming site like a couple of scalp-hunting Apaches, but whenever we got to the knoll where he worked his tympanic magic, he was gone. We never heard him flush. He just walked off into the woods as silent as a ghost. Ten or 20 minutes later we would hear him sound off again from one of his subsidiary drumming logs. His primary log, a wind-toppled white pine, was anchored by a big ball of roots and dirt. Gullion calls this a "guard object," and male

Cloquet forest, Minnesota

grouse are "partial" to such blowdowns. "On this sort of site," he says, "the bird will usually select a drumming stage on the trunk about three to five feet from the root mass [which] provides protection against predation for as much as an eighth to a quarter of the horizon." Luke and I always seemed to approach the bird from the wrong quarter. When we finally wised up, we tried to outflank the bird, coming in from a different direction that took us through heavy young aspen whips and up a steep hill. By the time we got up there, of course, he was always long gone.

"In spite of the drumming [which alerts predators] and the amount of time that a male grouse may spend on his log," Gullion says, "he is probably more secure there than at any other time in his life. We have never seen evidence of predation at a log that was in really good cover." Tell me about it.

Of course, man is only a minor predator on the ruffed grouse. Bobcats, lynx, foxes and coyotes are far more successful at procuring a pa'tridge supper. But the raptors do even better. Great horned owls, gray owls, barred owls and goshawks cut a wide swath through grouse populations, particularly during snowless winters. If the snow is deep enough, grouse can burrow into a drift to spend the night, but in an open winter they must roost in the trees, making them easy pickings for night-hunting owls. And during daylight hours, most of which grouse spend feeding, often popping buds and catkins from various trees (primarily aspen), they are vulnerable to attack by goshawks. Indeed, Gullion remarks, "goshawk" could very well be a contraction of the words "grouse hawk," so successful are these big blue-gray accipiters at snagging ruffs.

You would therefore think that a male grouse would be a damned fool to announce his presence from his drumming log and stay there for more than an hour a day. But drumming logs are chosen carefully. They're usually surrounded by a thick growth of brush or saplings. "This should extend at least three feet above the level of the log," Gullion writes, "and more often 15 or 20 feet. At preferred sites the density of hardwood saplings is usually in the range of 3,000 to 7,000 stems per acre." Mighty thick stuff. Brush surrounding drumming sites is even denser—close to 10,000 stems per acre. "This vertical cover," Gullion continues, "should have a fairly even distribution around the drumming [log] to provide optimum protection for the male. The drumming male also needs a clear escape route from the log, a path where there are few branches or stems to impede rapid movement by a fleeing bird."

No wonder Luke and I could never flush the house grouse. But trying to do so produced some good shooting despite our frustrations. The knoll where the drumming log lay looked down on a piece of wet ground that harbored plenty of woodcock. A half-dozen times during our stalks we flushed young grouse-of-the-year feeding in the vicinity, and I managed to scratch down two or three of them. So all was not in vain.

The following spring I managed to catch a glimpse of my nemesis. More than a glimpse. I left Luke at home one morning and crawled on my hands and knees up to the knoll. It was just getting light, and the ground was so damp that no leaves or twigs crackled as I stalked closer and closer to the thunder-maker. He was drumming every four minutes—hot, hectic flurries like a chain saw starting—and I timed my movements to coincide with his riffs. He was really fired up now, so into it that he'd lost his fear of man. Gullion on a number of occasions got so close to drumming grouse that "they would step onto an opened hand and allow themselves to be lifted above the ground, but they would not allow another hand to be brought close to them; they would not tolerate being restrained in any manner. . . . On several occasions when the moon was full, using a headlamp, I have sneaked close enough to touch drummers on their logs."

Well, I have yet to "count coup" on a drumming grouse. But on that spring morning I finally saw one in action. From 10 yards away, lying flat on my belly in the wet leaf mold, I watched him tilt his fanned tail back, erect his ruff and sound off with a blur of wings—bup, bup, bup, vrooooom! I watched him drum for nearly a half-hour. Finally he spotted me, dropped backward off his log and high-tailed it—God knows where.

The following fall I left him alone and hunted other coverts.

SECTION THREE
TURKEY HUNTING

CHAPTER 13

THE TWENTY-FIVE-POUND GOBBLER

By Archibald Rutledge

I suppose that there are other things which make a hunter uneasy, but of one thing I am very sure: that is to locate and to begin to stalk a deer or a turkey, only to find that another hunter is doing precisely the same thing at the same time. The feeling I had was worse than uneasy. It is, in fact, as inaccurate as if a man should say, after listening to a comrade swearing roundly, "Bill is expressing himself uneasily."

To be frank, I was jealous; and all the more so because I knew that Dade Saunders was just as good a turkey-hunter as I am—and maybe a good deal better. At any rate, both of us got after the same whopping gobbler. We knew this turkey and we knew each other; and I am positive that the wise old bird knew both of us far better than we knew him.

But we hunters have ways of improving our acquaintance with creatures that are over-wild and shy. Both Dade and I saw him, I suppose, a dozen times: and twice Dade shot at him. I had never fired at him, for I did not want to cripple, but to kill; and he never came within a hundred yards of me. Yet I felt that the gobbler ought to be mine; and for the simple reason that Dade Saunders was a shameless poacher and a hunter-out-of-season.

I have in mind the day when I came upon him in the pine-lands in mid-July, when he had in his wagon five bucks in the velvet, all killed that morning. Now, this isn't a fiction story; this is fact. And after I have told you of those bucks, I think you'll want me to beat Dade to the great American bird.

This wild turkey had the oddest range that you could imagine. You hear of turkeys ranging "original forests," "timbered wilds," and the like. Make up your mind that if wild turkeys have a chance they are going to come near civilization. The closer they are to man, the farther they are away from their other enemies. Near civilization they at least have (but for the likes of Dade Saunders) the protection of the law. But in the wilds what protection do they have from wildcats, from eagles, from weasels (I am thinking of young turkeys as well as old), and from all their other predatory persecutors?

Well, as I say, time and again I have known wild turkeys to come, and to seem to enjoy coming, close to houses. I have stood on the porch of my plantation home and have watched a wild flock feeding under the great live-oaks there. I have repeatedly flushed wild turkeys in an autumn cornfield. I have shot them in rice stubble.

Of course they do not come for sentiment. They are after grain. And if there is any better wild game than a rice-field wild turkey, stuffed with peanuts, circled with browned sweet potatoes, and fragrant with a rich gravy that plantation cooks know how to make, I'll follow you to it.

The gobbler I was after was a haunter of the edges of civilization. He didn't seem to like the wild woods. I think he got hungry there. But on the

margins of fields that had been planted he could get all he wanted to eat of the things he most enjoyed. He particularly liked the edges of cultivated fields that bordered either on the pinewoods or else on the marshy rice-lands.

One day I spent three hours in the gaunt chimney of a burned rice-mill, watching this gobbler feeding on such edges. Although I was sure that sooner or later he would pass the mouth of the chimney, giving me a chance for a shot, he kept just that distance between us that makes a gun a vain thing in a man's hands. But though he did not give me my chance, he let me watch him all I pleased. This I did through certain dusty crevices between the bricks of the old chimney.

If I had been taking a post-graduate course in caution, this wise old bird would have been my teacher. Whatever he happened to be doing, his eyes and his ears were wide with vigilance. I saw him first standing beside a fallen pine log on the brow of a little hill where peanuts had been planted. I made the shelter of the chimney before he recognized me. But he must have seen the move I made.

I have hunted turkeys long enough to be thoroughly rid of the idea that a human being can make a motion that a wild turkey cannot see. One of my woodsman friends said to me, "Why, a gobbler can see anything. He can see a jaybird turn a somersault on the verge of the horizon." He was right.

Watching from my cover I saw this gobbler scratching for peanuts. He was very deliberate about this. Often he would draw back one huge handful (or footful) of viney soil, only to leave it there while he looked and listened. I have seen a turkey do the same thing while scratching in leaves. Now, a buck while feeding will alternately keep his head up and down; but a turkey gobbler keeps his down very little. That bright black eye of his, set in that sharp bluish head, is keeping its vision on every object on the landscape.

My gobbler (I called him mine from the first time I saw him) found many peanuts, and he relished them. From that feast he walked over into a patch of autumn-dried crabgrass. The long pendulous heads of this grass, full of seeds, he stripped skilfully. When satisfied with this food, he dusted himself beside an old stump. It was interesting to watch this; and while he was doing it I wondered if it was not my chance to leave the chimney, make a detour, and come up behind the stump. But of course just as I decided to do this, he got up, shook a small cloud of dust from his feathers, stepped off into the open, and there began to preen himself.

A short while thereafter he went down to a marshy edge, there finding a warm sandy hole on the sunny side of a briar patch, where he continued his dusting and loafing. I believe that he knew the stump, which shut off his view of what was behind it, was no place to choose for a midday rest.

All this time I waited patiently; interested, to be sure, but I would have been vastly more so if the lordly old fellow had turned my way. This I expected him to do when he got tired of loafing. Instead, he deliberately walked into the tall ranks of the marsh, which extended riverward for half a mile. At that I hurried forward, hoping to flush him on the margin; but he had vanished for that day. But though he had escaped me, the sight of him had made me keen to follow him until he expressed a willingness to accompany me home.

Just as I was turning away from the marsh I heard a turkey call from the shelter of a big live-oak beside the old chimney. I knew that it was Dade Saunders, and that he was after my gobbler. I walked over to where he was making his box-call plead. He expressed no surprise on seeing me. We greeted each other as two hunters, who are not over-friendly, greet when they find themselves after the same game.

"I seen his tracks," said Dade. "I believe he limps in the one foot since I shot him last Sunday will be a week."

"He must be a big bird," I said; "you were lucky to have a shot."

Dade's eyes grew hungrily bright.

"He's the biggest in these woods, and I'll git him yet. You jest watch me."

"I suppose you will, Dade. You are the best turkey-hunter of these parts."

I hoped to make him overconfident; and praise is a great corrupter of mankind. It is not unlikely to make a hunter miss a shot. I remember that a friend of mine once said laughingly: "If a man tells me I am a good shot, I will miss my next chance, as sure as guns; but if he cusses me and tells me I'm not worth a darn, then watch me shoot!"

Dade and I parted for the time. I went off toward the marsh, whistling an old song. I wanted to have the gobbler put a little more distance between himself and the poacher. Besides, I felt that it was right of me to do this: for while I was on my own land, my visitor was trespassing. I hung around in the scrub—oak thickets for a while; but no gun spoke out, I knew that the old gobbler's intelligence plus my whistling game had "foiled the relentless" Dade. It was a week later that the three of us met again.

Not far from the peanut field there is a plantation corner. Now, most plantation corners are graveyards; that is, cemeteries of the old days, where slaves were buried. Occasionally now Negroes are buried there, but pathways have to be cut through the jungle-like growths to enable the cortege to enter.

Such a place is a wilderness for sure. Here grow towering pines, mournful and moss-draped. Here are hollies, canopied with jasmine-vines; here are thickets of myrtle, sweet gum, and young pines. If a covey of quail goes into such a place, you might as well whistle your dog off and go after another lot of birds.

Here deer love to come in the summer, where they can hide from the heat and the gauze-winged flies. Here in the winter is a haunt for woodcock, a good range (for great live-oaks drop their sweet acorns) for wild turkeys, and a harbor for foxes. In those great pines and oaks turkeys love to roost. It was on the borders of just such a corner that I roosted the splendid gobbler.

It was a glowing December sunset. I had left the house an hour before to stroll the plantation roads, counting (as I always do) the number of deer and turkey tracks that had recently been made in the soft damp sand. Coming near the dense corner, I sat against the bole of a monster pine. I love to be a mere watcher in woodlands as well as a hunter.

About two hundred yards away there was a little sunny hill, grown to scrub-oaks. They stood sparsely; that enabled me to see well what I now saw. Into my vision, with the rays of the sinking sun gleaming softly on the bronze of his neck and shoulders, the great gobbler stepped with superb beauty. Though he deigned to scratch once or twice in the leaves, and peck indifferently at what he thus uncovered, I knew he was bent on roosting; for not only was it nearly his bedtime, but he seemed to be examining with critical judgment every tall tree in his neighborhood.

He remained in my sight ten minutes; then he stepped into a patch of gallberries. I sat where I was. I tried my best to be as silent and as motionless as the bodies lying in the ancient graves behind me. The big fellow kept me on the anxious bench for five minutes. Then he shot his great bulk into the air, beating his ponderous way into the huge pine that seemed to sentry that whole wild tract of woodland.

I marked him when he came to his limb. He sailed up to it and alighted with much scraping of bark with his No. 10 shoes. There was my gobbler poised against the warm red sky of that winter twilight. It was hard to take my sight from him; but I did so in order to get my bearings in relation to his position. His flight had brought him nearer to me than he had been on the ground. But he was still far out of gun-range.

There was no use for me to look into the graveyard, for a man cannot see a foot into such a place. I glanced down the dim pinewood road. A moving object along its edge attracted my attention. It skulked. It seemed to flit like a ghostly thing from pine to pine. But, though I was near a cemetery, I knew I was looking at no "haunt." It was Dade Saunders.

He had roosted the gobbler, and he was trying to get up to him. Moreover, he was at least fifty yards closer to him than I was. I felt like shouting to him to get off my land; but then a better thought came. I pulled out my turkey call.

The first note was good, as was intended. But after that there came some heart-stilling squeaks and shrills. In the dusk I noted two things; I saw Dade make a furious gesture, and at almost the same instant the old gobbler launched out from the pine, winging a lordly way far across the graveyard thicket. I walked down slowly and peeringly to meet Dade.

"Your call's broke," he announced.

"What makes you think so?" I asked.

"Sounds awful funny to me," he said; "more than likely it might scare a turkey. Seen him lately?" he asked.

"You are better at seeing that old bird than I am, Dade."

Thus I put him off; and shortly thereafter we parted. He was sure that I had not seen the gobbler; and that suited me all right.

Then came the day of days. I was up at dawn, and when certain red lights between the stems of the pines announced daybreak, I was at the far southern end of the plantation, on a road on either side of which were good turkey woods. I just had a notion that my gobbler might be found there, as he had of late taken to roosting in a tupelo swamp near the river, and adjacent to these woodlands.

Where some lumbermen had cut away the big timber, sawing the huge short-leaf pines close to the ground, I took my stand (or my seat) on one of these big stumps. Before me was a tangle of undergrowth; but it was not very thick or high. It gave me the screen I wanted; but if my turkey came out through it, I could see to shoot.

It was just before sunrise that I began to call. It was a little early in the year (then the end of February) to lure a solitary gobbler by a call; but otherwise the chance looked good. And I am vain enough to say that my willow box was not broken that morning. Yet it was not I but two Cooper's hawks that got the old wily rascal excited.

They were circling high and crying shrilly over a certain stretch of deep woodland; and the gobbler, undoubtedly irritated by the sounds, or at least not to be outdone by two mere marauders on a domain which he felt to be his own, would gobble fiercely every time one of the hawks would cry. The hawks had their eye on a building site; wherefore their excited maneuvering and shrilling continued; and as long as they kept up their screaming, so long did the wild gobbler answer in rivalry or provoked superiority, until his wattles must have been fiery red and near to bursting.

I had an idea that the hawks were directing some of their crying at the turkey, in which case the performance was a genuine scolding match of the wilderness. And before it was over, several gray squirrels had added to the already raucous debate their impatient coughing barks. This business lasted nearly an hour, until the sun had begun to make the thickets "smoke off" their shining burden of morning dew.

I had let up on my calling for awhile; but when the hawks had at last been silenced by the distance, I began once more to plead. Had I had a gobbler-call, the now enraged turkey would have come to me as straight as a surveyor runs a line. But I did my best with the one I had. I had answered by one short gobble, then by silence.

I laid down my call on the stump and took up my gun. It was in such a position that I could shoot quickly without much further motion. It is a genuine feat to shoot a turkey on the ground after he has made you out. I felt that a great moment was coming.

But you know how hunter's luck sometimes turns. Just as I thought it was about time for him to be in the pine thicket ahead of me, when, indeed, I thought I had heard his heavy but cautious step, from across the road, where lay the companion tract of turkey-woods to the one I was in, came a delicately pleading call from a hen turkey. The thing was irresistible to the gobbler; but I knew it to be Dade Saunders. What should I do?

At such a time a man has to use all the headwork he has. And in hunting I had long since learned that that often means not to do a darn thing but to sit tight. All I did was to put my gun to my face. If the gobbler was going to Dade, he might pass me. I had started him coming; if Dade kept him going, he might run within hailing distance. Dade was farther back in the woods than I was. I waited.

No step was heard. No twig was snapped. But suddenly, fifty yards ahead of me, the great bird emerged from the thicket of pines. For an instant the sun gleamed on his royal plumage. My gun was on him, but the glint of the sun along the barrel dazzled me. I stayed my finger on the trigger. At that instant he made me out. What he did was smart. He made himself so small that I believed it to be a second turkey. Then he ran crouching through the vines and huckleberry bushes.

Four times I thought I had my gun on him, but his dodging was that of an expert. He was getting away; moreover, he was making straight for Dade. There was a small gap in the bushes sixty yards from me, off to my left. He had not yet crossed that. I threw my gun in the opening. In a moment he flashed into it, running like a racehorse. I let him have it. And I saw him go down.

Five minutes later, when I had hung him on a scrub-oak, and was admiring the entire beauty of him, a knowing, cat-like step sounded behind me.

"Well, sir," said Dade, a generous admiration for the beauty of the great bird overcoming other less kindly emotions, "so you beat me to him."

There was nothing for me to do but to agree. I then asked Dade to walk home with me so that we might weigh him. He carried the scales well down at the 25-pound mark. An extraordinary feature of his manly equipment was the presence of three separate beards, one beneath the other, no two connected. And his spurs were respectable rapiers.

"Dade," I said, "what am I gong to do with this gobbler? I am alone here on the plantation."

The pineland poacher did not solve my problem for me.

"I tell you," said I, trying to forget the matter of the five velveted bucks, "some of the boys from down the river are going to come up on Sunday to see how he tastes. Will you join us?"

You know Dade Saunders' answer; for when a hunter refuses an invitation to help eat a wild turkey, he can be sold to a circus.

CHAPTER 14

THE TURKEY CURE

By Sydney Lea

B Y NOW, NEARLY EVERY TIME I walked down to let my pointers out, I flushed the broad-wing hen who nests in the same white pine each spring. She's always been a sort of genie of renewal, and the life force in me surges to regard her tail in flight, the severity of its black and white bands somehow metaphorizing the distinction between seasons. Dark winter, bright spring.

This year, thanks to last autumn's bountiful mast, the chipmunk and red squirrel populations seem to have grown threefold, a great thing for a hawk, of course, and for all the other predators—fox, coyote, fisher, and so on—whose energy has thrilled me from boyhood. And yet this time around, such tokens of regeneration, and others—loosing of freshets, budding out of broadleafs, sweet ruckus of peepers, patrol of kingfishers—none of these quickened me as before. My tendency to foist poetic readings onto nature, however irresistible, struck me as more than ever inaccurate in its willfulness.

Perhaps the suicide, a year back, kept me down like this, as it had all through the winter. The beautiful boy, my oldest son's bosom friend, had fallen into a contemporary trap, the one called crack, and ended in a California closet, a cheap belt for a noose. But if that horror proved a central motive for my long depression, I might have chosen from a myriad: the obscene death by cancer, say, of my father-in-law, too weak at the last even to cough for himself. A brilliant, handsome, volatile man, he'd stuck to being a journalism professor, loathing the job for the final decade, waiting out retirement age, at which he was diagnosed all but instantly. No time for his many writing intentions, none for the book-length thing on that Canadian copper mine, the history, sociology, mythology, of its region, which he'd never visit after all.

Or I could batten on my mother's life-threatening aortal operation, from which she recovered, but which forecast the closing of a crucial cycle: she who'd borne would leave me. Years before the surgery, I'd had an odd vision, whether in sleep or awake I still can't say. Standing on the cobbly stoop of my Maine hunting camp, I looked upward and beheld the heavens' vault sealing itself like a womb after birth, so that it couldn't recur, the dream of reentry that all through life any child will crave when otherwise comfortless.

Closed out. The world blank as a sheet of paper, as the sheet unmarked by my wife's father. In which blank realm my role would be to evaluate students' poems and fictions, not to write any more of these myself, not to write anything at all. Rather, I'd continue to fetch and carry my kids, but would be no proper father, down in the mouth all day and night; no proper husband, either, to the woman too good for me by half, who deserved worship, probably, but at the least some friendship. My agenda? Do dishes. Cook so-so meals by the hundred. Watch the years mount: the yellow leaves of spring apparently stained overnight to those other yellows of autumn; the hare gone white from brown in a blink; warbler ceding to snowbird. Watch my body slump. Fifty would be sixty would be seventy. Tomorrow.

Attending all this, a changed prospect on the hunt. I'd long considered myself, particularly, one of the better grouse men I knew, but by virtue of a chainsaw accident that radically cut my leg and my woods time in the preceding fall and by virtue of a rock-bottom bird population in the past few years, the tasty little monuments to success lay more and more seldom in the freezer. It was also hard to make a young dog under these circumstances, and a made dog has forever been an even more important sort of monument.

In short, I was beginning to surmise that my skills in this formerly sacramental portion of existence were dying, like men and women all around me. If there'd been a time when I was one to whom—as a student of the great Aldo Leopold marveled about him—"the game just seemed to come," that time was fled.

The blank—and the random. Absences and murderous presences. Death as multifold, a gang of thugs who killed by hanging or by instilling mortal illness, who invited the potentially lethal scalpel. Death, whose many incursions seemed perfectly analogized by the awful croppings-up of so-called development in my hunting grounds. Such grounds, or so in my vanity I'd for decades imagined, belonged to me. To me and my dogs. Me and my prey. Me and my friends, so many of them either perished now or diminished or otherwise moved on, out of my ken.

The first morning of Vermont's turkey season, I had practically to horse-whip myself out of bed, sensing my failure before the fact, anticipating my fatigue, which would set in by noon and put me behind in my journeyman jobs. I'd have held such tiredness in contempt, of course, in naive youth, when a duck blind at dawn segued into seven hours afield behind a pair of gun dogs and then into an evening's carousing till the small hours.

The hardwoods did look beautiful at the top of the first ridge, their leaves pastel, their every storey melodious with migrants. The abandoned twitch roads were so thickly clotted by bluets as still to seem snow-covered. Black duck and mallard croaked in the spring pools. Wake-robin already showed in wet gullies.

There was also a lovesick barred owl chanting not far off. No turkey answered that owl's call, however, nor my own imitation of it. For a month, there'd been sign all over the four good ridges I meant to roam that opening morning: I'd seen a gobbling jake within a hundred yards of my house; I'd heard other gobblers on the west side of the pond that bisects my property. But on that day, no response. None, that is, save the owl's. Defying its reputation for wisdom, the bird luffed in over my head, perched a spell in a

sick butternut, went out disenchanted. And so, given the late drift of my spirits, it was easy, too easy, to construct crude allegory: the world had ceased answering me . . . or had come to answer in inappropriate ways.

I trudged home well before the law said I had to.

Work and parenthood conspired to keep me off those ridges for another ten days. Or so I told myself. In fact, I felt the depressive's gratitude for such impediment, which freed me to moan with self-pity over being thus deprived but left me with no obligation to take up the thing I was deprived of. The best of two bad worlds.

And yet at length I did feel some sort of obligation once more to mount the hills. A better self (inside this worse) had retained some of an old and glorious hope, in however ghostly a guise. And the better self had its reasons: immediately on reaching the granite dune that caps the first ridge, I was greeted with a gobble. The call must instantly have obscured my melancholies, since I don't remember their weight in the ensuing hour. I do remember surveying the terrain around me, simultaneously judging with my damnably poor, gunshot ears the location of the tom. I would need to drop to his elevation if I hoped to call him in.

Well, I knew the country if anyone did. I turned directly away from the gobble, which now came with a heartening frequency, doglegged to a twitch road that ran under a knoll to the west, and then crept back, the knoll covering me till the road petered out by the white oak stand in which I guessed my turkey strutted. The guess was pretty close: he was on the woods' far margin, some two hundred yards from where I quickly set up, my back to a lichened slab, my right foot pointed in his direction, the Browning on my cocked left knee, the veil slipped over my face.

I decided for a start to try no more than a soft, whimpering chirp. It was early, the sky not yet even pearlescent. The turkey yammering right back at me (or so I thought), I whiffed an ozonic scent that I needn't describe to any hunter of wary game; my heart beat in a full, shirt-stretching cadence, and—despite the chill of a northcountry dawn—sweat drops formed on my cheekbones. I slightly lessened the crook of my left leg, to see if it would hold more still in a different position. It did.

Everything perfect. And yet, rather than coming my way, the tom kept working south, meanwhile moving up an elevation. I was patient. I didn't over-call or hasten to relocate. Minutes passed, the bird's cackle fading by degrees, before I made myself take stock of the land again. At last I stood, then circled back to the east, for I knew another hill-hidden trail, the beat of deer and occasional moose, that would provide quiet and easy travel and would put me back on top, about parallel, I believed, with where the turkey now sang.

Again and again I established myself at what appeared ideal places. Again and again I heard the quarry's noise dim, always to the south. So in fact, and in honesty: there were moments when my mopery returned; everything, I told myself, was right about this chase . . . except that I didn't have the requisite skills to end it the way I meant to end it. But I rallied from these instants of despair: I had enough experience to realize that were the problem only in my calling, this tom would long since have spooked, long since have quit gobbling.

In time I judged the problem lay in the bird's already having a hen, and likely more than one. If I were to get a look at him, then, it would be by way not of deception but of ambush. Unable to turn him, I'd need to head him off.

Most of the ridges on my property run more or less north and south, but one is perpendicular to these. It occurred to me that—turkeys so often describing a circle in their morning rambles—this torn and his coterie night well come to that odd ridge out, turning east along it to regain the highest ridge of all, the one where they'd probably roosted. If that bet proved right, the bird would have to travel an almost knife-thin granite strip some hundred yards above the south end of the pond. A good lie for me, then.

The turkey cries suddenly seemed to be moving more quickly, which meant I must get to that strip in a hurry. I dogtrotted to the edge of the ridge, then all but skied down, so abundant were the oak nuts on that flank despite the ardor of the winter deer herd and of spring's rodents. Now and then I felt slight, brief burnings above my left kneecap: adhesions popping under the ugly scar from my Labor Day accident. But this discomfort left me unalarmed: my mind set on being where I needed to be, I even believed (I still think rightly) that the breach of those adhesions would do me nothing but good, would help turn me loose. And in fact, hitting the bottomland, I broke into a run that felt less awkward and leaden than it had for months. A single hooded merganser, sojourning on his way to the Ungava, made to fly as I coursed by, but then elected simply to dip underwater till I was past. I might thus see him again on our pond, little clown, a notion that filled me with strange delight.

Glancing back, I noticed that the morning mist over the water had somehow and abruptly become general, the world gone soft-edged in fog. The top of the scarp I'd just tumbled down had vanished, along with all but the lowest others, into cloud. A mix of that wetness and the sweat of exertion fogged my glasses, which would have to be clear by the time the tom—please, God!—came into view. So I yanked them off and held them in my hand like a baton as I raced onward.

My breath came with surprising ease. "Not bad for an old guy," I whispered to myself, feeling my cheek muscles tauten in a grin. Well behind me, I heard my bitch Sue let out a single, houndlike howl from her kennel, nothing in it to alarm a gobbler. Indeed, I thought I heard the gobbler answer to that wail, and persuaded myself that the answer came from exactly the right quarter, not far west of where I meant soon to arrive. I envisioned the bird as I ran: he'd be coming out of the hornbeam grove just now, stepping into the high hemlocks, his snood turgid and scarlet, his tail clenching and unfurling, his hens fossicking all about.

And before long, he'd reach that granite pathway.

The fog was everywhere now, but it showed itself in weird little pilasters, as if each had wandered off the pondwater and were walking the land in a company of its familiars—thin, benign ghosts.

You'll imagine me single-minded, as I imagined myself. But in recall, there seems to have been so much to notice: by the pond's standpipe, a clump of shoots that in a month or so would bend with the weight of wild iris; above, daylight's first vulture, which hadn't been there and now suddenly was, languidly sliding the updrafts by the ridge I was bound for; a few stubborn gray frogs yet droning at each other, bank to bank; the woods' smell, like chamois.

My boots left prints in the bluets. Again I thought of snow as I studied the earth rolling under me. At last, hearing the turkey rattle the air in that hemlock grove, I started to climb; by now, the illusion of infinite stamina was unraveling: my legs ached, and my breaths were like sobs. Yet I went on, hiking now, to be sure, not running. So much—a world, it seemed—depended on the next few minutes.

The gobbler could not have been more than a few hundred yards away when I reached the top of the ridge. There I discovered, as if placed by providence itself, a tub-sized depression in the granite apron. I scooched into it, then sprawled prone: there was even a cleft in the rock, like the archer's slit in a medieval turret, through which I could see 180 degrees, and through which, fate willing, I'd be able to shoot.

The turkey remained as persistent in his call as he'd been since first I heard it, and he was, no doubt about it, headed my way. I slipped my eyeglasses back on, pulled down the veil, then cursed mutely: once more the ambient fog and my own sweat clouded the lenses so that I could see nothing.

A blank.

I reached up under the veil with my gloved right hand, rubbing a small circle on either side. Within seconds these circles clouded again. The bird's gobble was louder by now than my thoughts. I drew the glasses to the tip of my nose and squinted over them, but I was too blind that way. The cruelty of my circumstance seemed incredible.

And then a cold breeze kicked up. Some may doubt me, may think this all sounds too scripted. I cannot prove a thing, for I was the lone human in that place; I merely know what I know, and I know that such a wind arrived, can all but feel it again as I carry on here.

My vision went clear . . . and the gobbler quit calling.

Long, long minutes yawned. I imagined the tom, with those eyes that beggar comparison, to have seen through the rock-cleft where I lay, to have seen me fuss with my misted lenses, to have scooted off with his hen or his harem, not to reappear. My gloom, however, had evidently and patiently been awaiting its chance to reappear; it stole, as always, first into my gut, from where it would soon make its climb—more deliberate than my own one at dawn—into such parts of me as harbor the spirit. I lay there helpless.

There seem to be (who knows why?) bountiful moments in one's life that one doesn't have to deserve. That foggy morning well behind me now, I think back on a bright boy's terrible self-murder, and how badly I responded on hearing of it; I think of the brusqueness with which I greeted my wife's un-countable acts and words of kindness to me; of how dully I observed the innocence of my smaller children, the decency of my older; of the unacknowl-edged splendors of the earth and air and water among which I'd long dwelled; of my fine physical fortune, which I have taken too often for granted.

The depression I'd felt for the protracted interlude leading up to that hunt now seems to have been so easy, so self-indulgent!

Tall as a man, a bird walked forth, stirring the mist with his bulk, si-lent—behind him, slightly smaller, an apparently endless procession of hen turkeys. I saw them all through the chink in my granite enclosure. My gun barrel rested on a spur of rock, parallel to the pungent, pine-spilled ground.

The tom had grown cautious, as a tom will uncannily, unaccountably, do in such moments. Yet he continued to pick his way toward me, lifting and gingerly replacing each foot, almost in the manner of a heron.

The turkey at last intersected with the lane my shot would take, his beard thrust forward like a bowsprit, lucent with silver dew. He stretched his neck and cocked his head northward. I squeezed the trigger, and he collapsed.

I thumbed back the safety and jerked to my feet, rushing to the spot. As I ran, I found myself expecting no sign of a bird—expecting to awaken, that is, from a dream whose untruth would leave me weeping on that shoulder of stone.

But there the bird did lie, in all his gorgeous giantism. An impossibility, but there indeed he lay. I put the shotgun aside, leaned over, grasping a horny shin with each hand. At my touch the gobbler came back to life, his great wings pistons, his whole frame pumping to reach the catastrophic cliff face just beyond us, down which he would surely hurl himself, never to be found. I held tight to him, my heels hopelessly digging for purchase in the granite. It was like trying to arrest the motion of some machine gone weirdly autonomous.

I now look back upon that desperate wrestle as a necessarily absurd, and comic, chapter in all this. What must I have looked like? A man of two hundred pounds and more being drawn by the will of a wild thing, even in death, toward unseemly conclusion.

But at length I prevailed.

They are hard things to explain to a non-hunter, let alone to an anti-hunter—the recognitions that came to me on that morning. I recognized, say, that the whole ritual had realized itself on my land; indeed, the kill transpired at a distance of no more than three hundred yards from the warm house in which I live.

I live, too, in a country so rich that the thousands of its citizens who have no houses—never mind land—constitute a national disgrace.

Perhaps I'm less a hunter than once I was; but on that spangled ledge it struck me that I did have some skills left anyhow. Maybe my fiftyish body was, as I earlier put it, slumping; but I had gotten to my vantage largely on the run. Nine months earlier, I'd sawn my left quadricep to the bone: two inches lower lay the kneecap; four inches rightward lay the femoral artery; I'd gotten off with three days in a hospital bed, four weeks of crutches, a spectacular and story-laden cicatrice the only residue of the whole ordeal.

I was so well married and so well childed that then as now I could find no adequate words to express my good fortune. But subsuming all these omens of my rare welfare, all these recognitions, is what I can only call a spiritual truth. I will abuse it, as I have done before, as any pilgrim must, but there it was.

Is.

My mother, like Breck the suicide, like Amico the cancer victim, must die, soon or late. As must I. As must every last one of us. And yet for a moment and much more a truth shone clear: Be receptive and you will receive.

I felt, I feel, a great gratitude to a certain wild turkey. Again the anti-hunter winces, no doubt. And yet, walking down that steep ridge, the luminous body slung over my shoulder in all its heft, I recalled, as I do now, the perfection of that bird's coming to me. I had done something right, and my prey had therefore obliged me. What had, been random was for a spell at least coherent.

It was not, however, a bird alone that came to me. The very world, however slight my worthiness for such a miracle, had come as well.

SECTION FOUR
DEER HUNTING

CHAPTER 15

TRAIL'S END

By Sig Olsen

I t was early morning in the northern wilderness, one of those rare breath-less mornings that come only in November, and though it was not yet light enough to see, the birds were stirring. A covey of partridge whirred up from their cozy burrows in the snow and lit in the top of a white birch, where they feasted noisily upon the frozen brown buds. The rolling tattoo of a downy woodpecker, also looking for his breakfast, reverberated again and again through the timber.

They were not the only ones astir however, for far down the trail leading from the Tamarack Swamp to Kennedy Lake browsed a big buck. He worked his way leisurely along, stopping now and then to scratch away the fresh snow and nibble daintily the still tender green things underneath. A large buck he was, even as deer run, and as smooth and sleek as good feeding could make him. His horns, almost too large, were queerly shaped, for instead of being rounded as in other deer, they were broad and palmate, the horns of a true swamp buck.

The eastern skyline was just beginning to tint with lavender as he reached the summit of the ridge overlooking the lake. He stopped for his usual morning survey of the landscape below him. For some reason, ever since his spike-buck days, he had always stopped there to look the country over before working down to water. He did not know that for countless generations before him, in the days when the pine timber stood tall and gloomy round the shores of the lake, other swamp bucks had also stopped, to scent the wind and listen, before going down to drink.

As he stood on the crest of the ridge, his gaze took in the long reaches of dark blue water far below him; the ice rimmed shores with long white windfalls reaching like frozen fingers out into the shallows, and the mottled green and gray of the brush covered slopes. His attention was finally centered on a little log cabin tucked away on the opposite shore in a clump of second growth spruce and balsam. Straight above it rose a thin wreath of pale blue smoke, almost as blue as the clear morning air. The metallic chuck, chuck of an axe ringing on a dry log came clearly across the water, and a breath of air brought to him strange odors that somehow filled him with a vague misgiving.

He was fascinated by the cabin and could not take his gaze from it. On other mornings, it had seemed as much a part of the shoreline as the trees themselves, but now it was different. A flood of almost forgotten memories surged back to him, of days long ago, when similar odors and sounds had brought with them a danger far greater than that of any natural enemy. He rubbed the top of a low hazel bush and stamped his forefeet nervously, undecided what to do. Then, in a flash, the full realization came to him. He understood the meaning of it all. This was the season of the year when man was no longer his friend, and it was not safe to be seen in the logging roads or in the open clearings near the log houses. He sniffed the air keenly a moment longer, to be sure, then snorted loudly as if to warn all the wilderness folk of their danger, and bounded back up the trail the way he had come.

Not until he had regained the heavy protecting timber of the Tamarack Swamp, north of Kennedy Lake did he feel safe. What he had seen made him once again the wary old buck who had lived by his cunning and strength through many a hunting season. Although he was safe for the time being, he was too experienced not to know that before many days had passed, the Tamarack Swamp would no longer be a haven of refuge.

As he worked deeper into the heavy moss hung timber, he stopped frequently to look into the shadows. The trail here was knee-deep in moss and criss-crossed by a labyrinth of narrow rabbit runways. Soon his search was rewarded, for a sleek yearling doe met him at a place where two trails crossed. After nosing each other tenderly, by way of recognition, they began feeding together on the tender shoots of blueberries and still green tufts of swamp grass underneath the protecting blanket of snow.

All that morning they fed leisurely and when the sun was high in the heavens, they worked cautiously over to the edge of the swamp. Here was a warm sunny opening hedged in by huge windfalls grown over with a dense tangle of blackberry vines. They often came here for their afternoon sunning, as the ice-encrusted ovals in the snow attested. Leaping a big windfall that guarded the entrance to the opening, they carefully examined the ground, then picked their beds close together. There they rested contentedly with the warm sun shining upon them, little thinking that soon their peace would be broken.

The snow had fallen early that autumn and good feed had been scarce everywhere, except in the depths of the Tamarack Swamp, where the protecting timber had sheltered the grass and small green things. The plague had killed off most of the rabbits, and the few which survived were already forced to feed upon the bark of the poplar. The heavy crust, forming suddenly the night after the first heavy snow, had imprisoned countless partridge and grouse in their tunnels. As a result, small game was scarce and the wolves were lean and gaunt, although it was yet hardly winter. The stark famine months ahead gave

Tamarack Swamp

promise of nothing but starvation and death, and the weird discordant music of the wolf pack had sounded almost every night since the last full moon.

The swamp buck and his doe had not as yet felt the pinch of hunger, but instinct told them to keep close to the shelter of the Tamarack Swamp, so except for the morning strolls of the buck to the shore of Kennedy Lake, they had seldom ventured far from the timber. They had often heard the wolf pack, but always so far away that there was little danger as long as they stayed under cover.

Several days had passed since the buck had been to the shore of Kennedy Lake. As yet the silence of the swamp had been unbroken except for the crunching of their own hoofs through the icy crust on the trails, and the buck was beginning to wonder if there was really anything to fear. Then one day, as they were again leisurely working their way over to the sunning place in the clearing, they were startled by the strange noises far toward the east end of the swamp. They stopped, every nerve on edge. At times they could hear them quite plainly, then again they would be so faint as to be almost indistinguishable from the other sounds of the forest.

Kennedy Lake

The two deer were not much concerned at first. After satisfying themselves that there was no real danger, they started again down the trail toward the clearing. They could still hear the noises occasionally, but could not tell whether they were coming closer or going further away.

Then just as they neared the edge of the swamp, the sound of heavy footsteps seemed suddenly to grow louder and more distinct. Once more they stopped and stood with heads high, ears pricked up, listening intently. This time they were thoroughly alarmed. Closer and closer came the racket. Now they could hear distinctly the crunching of snow and the crackling of twigs, and then the whole east end of the timber seemed to be fairly alive with tumult, and the air reeked with danger.

The buck ran in a circle, sniffing keenly. The same scent that had come to him from the cabin, now rankled heavily in the air, and he knew the time had come to leave the shelter of the Tamarack Swamp. He hesitated, however, not knowing which way to turn. Back and forth he ran, stopping now and then to paw the ground, or to blow the air through his nostrils with the sharp whistling noise that all deer use when in danger.

A branch cracked sharply close at hand, and the scent came doubly strong from the east. With a wild snort the buck wheeled and led the way toward the western end of the swamp followed closely by the doe. Their only hope lay in reaching a heavy belt of green hemlock timber which they knew was separated from the western end of the Tamarack Swamp by a broad stretch of barren, burned-over slashing. As they neared the edge of the swamp they stopped, dreading to leave its protection. From where they stood they could see the dark wall of timber half a mile away. A brushy gully ran diagonally toward it across the open slashing, offering some protection, but the hills on either side were as stark and bare as an open field.

Again came the crack and crunch, now so close that the very air burned with danger. It was time to go. They bounded out of the timber, their white flags waving defiance, and were soon in the brush gully, going like the wind. Just as they sailed over a windfall, the buck caught a glimpse of something moving on a big black pine stump on top of the ridge to their right. Then the quiet was shattered by a succession of rending crashes and strange singing and whining sounds filled the air above them.

Again and again came the crashes. Suddenly the little doe stopped dead in her tracks. She gave a frightened baa-aa-a of pain and terror as the blood burst in a stream from a jagged wound in her throat. The buck stopped and ran back to where she stood, head down and swaying unsteadily. He watched her a moment, then, growing nervous, started down the trail again. The doe tried bravely to follow, but fell half way across a windfall too high for her to clear. Again the buck stopped and watched her anxiously. The snow by the windfall was soon stained bright red with blood, and the head of the little doe sank lower and lower in spite of her brave efforts to hold it up.

Hurriedly the buck looked about him. Several black figures were coming rapidly down the ridge. He nosed his doe gently, but this time she did not move. Raising his head he looked toward the approaching figures. Danger was close, but he could not leave his mate.

A spurt of smoke came from one of the figures, followed by another crash. This time the buck felt a blow so sharp that it made him stumble.

Staggering to his feet, he plunged blindly down the gully. His flag was down, the sure sign of a wounded deer. Again and again came the crashes and the air above him whined and sang as the leaden pellets searched for their mark. The bark flew from a birch tree close by, spattering him with fragments. In spite of his wound, he ran swiftly and was soon out of range in the protecting green timber. He knew that he would not be tracked for at least an hour, as his pursuers would wait for him to lie down and stiffen.

He was bleeding badly from a long red scar cutting across his flank, and his back trail was sprinkled with tiny red dots. Where he stopped to rest and listen, little puddles of blood would form that quickly turned bluish black in the snow. For two hours he ran steadily, and then was so weakened by loss of blood that at last he was forced to lie down.

After a short rest, he staggered to his feet, stiffened badly. The bed he had melted in the snow was stained dark red from his bleeding flank. The cold, however, had contracted the wound and had stopped the bleeding a little. He limped painfully down the trail, not caring much which direction it led. Every step was torture. Once when crossing a small gully, he stumbled and fell on his wounded leg. It rested him to lie there, and it was all he could do to force himself on.

While crossing a ridge, the wind bore the man scent strongly to him, and he knew that now he was being trailed. Once, he heard the brush crack behind him, and was so startled that the wound was jerked open and the bleeding started afresh. He watched his back trail nervously, expecting to see his pursuer at any moment and hear again the rending crash that would mean death.

He grew steadily weaker and knew that unless night came soon, he would be overtaken. He had to rest more often now, and when he did move it was to stagger aimlessly down the trail, stumbling on roots and stubs. It was much easier now to walk around the windfalls than to try to jump over as he had always done before.

The shadows were growing longer and longer, and in the hollows it was already getting dusk. If he could last until nightfall he would be safe. But the man scent was getting still stronger, and he realized at last that speed alone could not save him. Strategy was the only course. If his pursuer could be thrown off the trail, only long enough to delay him half an hour, darkness would be upon the wilderness and he could rest.

So waiting until the trail ran down onto a steep ravine filled with brush and windfalls, the buck suddenly turned and walked back on his own trail as far as he dared. It was the old trick of back tracking that deer have used for ages to elude their pursuers. Then stopping suddenly, he jumped as far to the side as his strength would permit, landing with all four feet tightly bunched together in the very center of a scrubby hazel bush. From there, he worked his way slowly into a patch of scrub spruce and lay down exhausted under an old windfall. Weakened as he was from loss of blood and from the throbbing pain in his flank, it was all he could do to keep his eyes riveted on his back trail, and his ears strained for the rustling and crunching that he feared would come, unless darkness came first.

It seemed that he had barely lain down, when without warning, the brush cracked sharply, and not 100 yards away appeared a black figure. The buck was petrified with terror. His ruse had failed. He shrank as far down as he could in the grass under the windfall and his eyes almost burst from their sockets. Frantically he thought of leaving his hiding place, but knew that would only invite death. The figure came closer and closer, bending low over the trail and peering keenly into the spruce thicket ahead. In the fading light the buck was well hidden by the windfall, but the blood spattered trail led straight to his hiding place. Discovery seemed certain.

The figure picked its way still nearer. It was now within 30 feet of the windfall. The buck watched, hardly daring to breathe. Then, in order to get a better view into the thicket, the hunter started to climb a snow covered stump close by. Suddenly, losing his balance, he slipped and plunged backwards into the snow. The buck saw his chance. Gathering all his remaining strength, he dashed out of his cover and was soon hidden in the thick growth of spruce.

It was almost dark now and he knew that as far as the hunter was concerned, he was safe. Circling slowly around, he soon found a sheltered hiding place in a dense clump of spruce where he could rest and allow his wound to heal.

Night came swiftly, bringing with it protection and peace. The stars came out one by one, and a full November moon climbed into the sky, flooding the snowy wilderness with its radiance.

Several hours had passed since the buck had lain down to rest in the spruce thicket. The moon was now riding high in the heavens and in the open

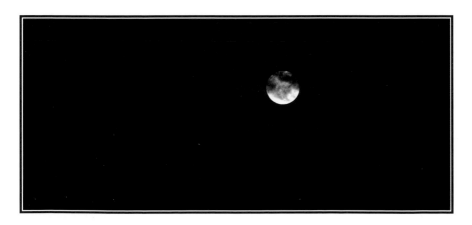

places it was almost as light as day. Although well hidden, he dozed fitfully, waking at times with a start, thinking that again he was being trailed. He would then lie and listen, with nerves strained to the breaking point, for any sounds of the wild that might mean danger. An owl hooted over in a clump of timber, and the new forming ice on the shores of Kennedy Lake, half a mile away, rumbled ominously. Then he heard a long quavering call, so faint and far away that it almost blended with the whispering of the wind. The coarse hair on his shoulders bristled as he recognized the hunting call of the age-old enemy of his kind. It was answered again and again. The wolf pack was gathering, and for the first time in his life, the buck knew fear. In the shelter of the Tamarack Swamp there had been little danger, and even if he had been driven to the open, his strength and speed would have carried him far from harm. Now, sorely wounded and far from shelter, he would have hardly a fighting chance should the pack pick up his trail.

They were now running in full cry, having struck a trail in the direction of the big swamp far to the west. To the buck, the weird music was as a song of death. Circling and circling, for a time they seemed to draw no nearer. As yet he was not sure whether it was his own blood bespattered trail that they were unraveling, or that of some other one of his kind. Then, suddenly, the cries grew in fierceness and volume and sounded much closer than before. He listened spellbound as he finally realized the truth it was his own trail they were following. The fiendish chorus grew steadily louder and more venomous, and now had a new note of triumph in it that boded ill for whatever came in its way.

He could wait no longer and sprang to his feet. To his dismay, he was so stiffened and sore, that he could hardly take a step. Forcing himself on, he hobbled painfully through the poplar brush and clumps of timber in the direction of the lake. Small windfalls made him stumble, and having to walk around hummocks and hollows made progress slow and difficult. How he longed for his old strength and endurance. About two-thirds of the distance to the lake had been covered and already occasional glimpses of water appeared between the openings.

Suddenly the cries of the pack burst out in redoubled fury behind him, and the buck knew they had found his warm blood-stained bed. Plunging blindly on, he used every ounce of strength and energy that he had left, for now the end was only a matter of minutes. The water was his only hope, for by reaching that he would at least escape being torn to shreds by the teeth of the pack. He could hear them coming swiftly down the ridge behind him and every strange shadow he mistook for one of the gliding forms of his pursuers. They were now so close that he could hear their snarls and yapping. Then a movement caught his eye in the checkered moonlight. A long gray shape had slipped out of the darkness and was easily keeping pace with him. Another form crept in silently on the other side and both ran like phantoms with no apparent effort. He was terror stricken, but kept on desperately. Other ghost-like shapes filtered in from the timber, but still they did not close. The water was just ahead. They would wait till he broke from the brush that lined the shore. With a crash, he burst through the last fringe of alders and charged forward. As he did so, a huge gray form shot out of the shadows and launched itself at his throat. He saw the movement in time and caught the full force of the blow on his horns. A wild toss and the snarling shape splashed into the ice rimmed shallows. At the same instant the two that had been running along side closed, one for his throat and the other for his hamstrings. The first he hit a stunning blow with his sharp front hoof, but as he did so the teeth of the other fastened on the tendon of his hind leg. A frantic leap loosened his hold and the buck half plunged and half slid over the ice into the waters of Kennedy Lake. Then the rest of the pack tore down to the beach with a deafening babble of snarls and howls, expecting to find their quarry down or at bay. When they realized that they had been outwitted, their anger was hideous and the air was rent with howls and yaps.

The cold water seemed to put new life into the buck and each stroke was stronger than the one before. Nevertheless, it was a long hard swim, and before he was half way across the benumbing cold had begun to tell. He fought on stubbornly, his breath coming in short, choking sobs and finally, after what seemed ages, touched the hard sandy bottom of the other shore.

Dragging himself painfully out, he lay down exhausted in the snow. All sense of feeling had left his tortured body, but the steady lap, lap of the waves against the tinkling shore ice soothed him into sleep.

When he awoke, the sun was high in the heavens. For a long time he lay as in a stupor, too weak and sorely stiffened to move. Then with a mighty effort he struggled to his feet, and stood motionless, bracing himself unsteadily. Slowly his strength returned and leaving his bed, he picked his way carefully along the beach, until he struck the trail, down which he had so often come to drink. He followed it to the summit of the ridge overlooking the lake.

The dark blue waters sparkled in the sun, and the rolling spruce covered ridges were green as they had always been. Nothing had really changed, yet never again would it be the same. He was a stranger in the land of his birth, a lonely fugitive where once he had roamed at will, his only choice to leave forever the ancient range of his breed. For a time he wavered torn between his emotions, then finally turned to go. Suddenly an overwhelming desire possessed him, to visit again the place where last he had seen his mate. He worked slowly down the trail to the old Tamarack Swamp and did not stop until he came to the old meeting place deep in the shadows where the two trails crossed. For a long time he did not move, then turned and headed into the north to a new wilderness far from the old, a land as yet untouched, the range of the Moose and Caribou.

CHAPTER 16

THE RACK

By Jay Cassell

"I found his antler, Dad," the throaty voice of my 6-year-old son, James, crackled over the telephone. "I saw it in the woods when Mom was driving me home from school, right near where we went hunting! Are you coming home tonight?"

When I told him that my flight wouldn't get in until 11:00, and that I wouldn't be home until midnight, there was a disappointed silence over the phone. Then, "Well, okay, but don't look at it until morning, so I can show you. Promise?"

I promised. We had a deal. I told him I'd see him soon, then asked to talk with his mother.

"Love you, Dad."

"Love you too, James."

Unbelievable. My son had found the shed antler of the buck I had hunted, unsuccessfully, all season. The big 10-pointer I had seen the day before deer season, the one with the wide spread and thick beams. He had seen me that day, having winded me as I pussyfooted through some thickets for a closer look. I think he somehow knew that he was safe, that he was far enough away from me.

I had scouted the 140-acre farm and adjoining woods near my home in suburban New York, the farm that I had gotten permission to hunt after five years of asking. "You can hunt this year," Dan the caretaker had said to me during the summer, when I asked my annual question. "I kicked those other guys off the property. They were in here with ATVs and Jeeps, bringing two and three friends every day they hunted, without even asking. Lot of nerve, I thought. Got sick of 'em, so I kicked 'em off. Now I'll let you hunt, and your buddy John, three other guys, and that's all. I want some local people on here that I know and trust."

When Dan had told me that, I couldn't believe it. But there it was, so I took advantage of it. Starting in September, I began to scout the farm. I had seen bucks on the property in previous years while driving by, but now I got a firsthand look. There was sign virtually everywhere: rubs, scrapes, droppings in the hillside hayfields, in the mixed hardwoods, in the thick hemlock stands towering over the rest of the woods. I found what were obviously rubs left by a big deer. In a copse of hemlocks near the edge of the property, bordering an Audubon nature preserve, were scrapes and, nearby, about five or six beech saplings absolutely ripped apart by antlers.

With James's help, I set up my tree stand overlooking a heavily used trail that seemed to be a perfect escape route out of the hemlocks. James and I also found an old permanent tree stand, which he and I repaired with a few 2x4s and nails. This would officially be "his" tree stand—or tree house, as he called it.

Opening day couldn't come fast enough. James and I talked about it constantly. Even though he's only 6, and can't really hunt yet, he couldn't wait for deer season. He knows what deer tracks and droppings look like; can tell how scrapes and rubs are made; can even identify where deer have passed in the leaf-covered forest floor. My plan was to hunt the first few days of the season by myself while James was in school, and then take him on a weekend. If luck was with me, maybe I'd take the big buck and could then concentrate on filling my doe tag with my son's help.

Opening day came and went, with no trophy 10-pointer in sight, or any other bucks, for that matter. A lot of other days came and went too, most of them cold, windy and rainy. Three weeks into the two-month-long season, on a balmy Sunday in the 50s, James and I packed our camo backpacks with candy bars and juice boxes, binoculars and grunt calls, and at 2:00 P.M. off we went, on our first day of hunting together. When we reached the spot where I always park my car, on a hillside field, I dabbed some camo paint onto James's face, which he thought was cool. Then we started hiking up the field and into the woods, toward the hemlocks.

We saw one whitetail disappear over a knob as we hiked into James's stand. I didn't really care, though. This was the first time I was taking my son

hunting! It would be the first of many, I hoped. I wouldn't force it on him, just introduce him to the sport, and keep my fingers crossed.

At James's stand, we sat down and had a couple of candy bars. "Can I blow on the deer call now, Dad?" I said yes, and he proceeded to honk away on the thing like a trumpet player.

"Do it quietly," I advised. "And remember, always whisper, don't talk loudly. And don't move around so much!"

What with James honking on the call and fidgeting—checking out my bow, looking around, pointing to the hawk soaring overhead, crumpling up his candy bar wrapper and stuffing it into his pocket—I was sure no self-respecting deer would come within a mile of us. None did, not to my son's stand, or to mine, or to the rocks where we later sat, overlooking a trail and those ripped-up beech saplings, until darkness finally settled over the woods. But that was okay.

Hiking out of the woods, we met my friend John coming from his tree stand.

"I saw that 10-pointer today," he began, giving James a poke in the ribs with his finger.

"Where?"

"Up near those hemlocks, the same area you and I have been hunting. We were probably 100 yards away from each other."

"Well, what happened?" Part of me was saying, Great, he got the buck! The other part of me was saying, Pleeeease tell me you didn't shoot him. John looked at me sheepishly.

"I was watching that trail, and I saw a doe headed my way, right where I always put my climbing tree stand. Then, right behind her, I saw a buck—you know that 6-pointer we've seen over by the lake? Well, I started to draw back on him—he was only 30 yards away—but then I saw some movement to my left. It was HIM! Cutting through the hemlocks. That 6-pointer and doe got out of there fast, and the 10-pointer got to within 10 yards of my stand, stopped broadside to me, and then looked up straight at me!"

"Did you shoot? Did you shoot?"

"I couldn't. I was shaking too much. I mean, I could even hear the arrow rattling against the rest. Eventually, he just took off down the trial. Man, he was something. Must weigh 200 pounds!"

Later, driving the short ride home, James said, "Hey, Dad. How come John didn't shoot that deer?"

"Shooting a deer is a lot harder than many people think. Even if everything else is right, sometimes you can get so nervous that you just can't shoot, no matter how much you want to. John's time will come, though. He works at it."

I didn't see the buck until two days after Christmas. Hunting by myself, I left my normal tree stand and circled around to the backside of the hemlocks. At 4:00 P.M., I was wedged between some boulders that overlook a well-used trail. It was 20°F, getting dark, and I was cold and shivering uncontrollably. But I kept hearing a rustling behind me. Another squirrel. But it wasn't. Suddenly, 60 yards through the trees, I could see a big deer headed my way. It was moving with a purpose. It stopped at what appeared to be a scrape, and I could see a huge symmetrical rack dip down as the buck stuck his nose to the ground. Then he stood up, urinated into the scrape, turned, and headed back into the hemlocks. If he had kept coming down the trail, I would have had a clean 15-yard shot. It wasn't meant to be.

That was my season. I didn't see that 10-pointer again, and I missed my only shot of the year, a 35-yarder at a forkhorn that sailed high. Such is deer hunting.

So now I was returning home from my trip. I walked in the door at midnight, quickly read through some mail on the counter, soon slipped into bed. My wife rolled over and whispered, "Don't forget to wake up James before you go to work. He really wants to show you that rack."

The alarm went off at 6:30, and I got up to take a shower.

"Psst, Dad, is that you?" came a sleepy voice from my son's room.

"Yes, buddy, how are you?"

"Wait here, Dad!"

Before I could say another word, he jumped out of bed, put on his over-sized bear-paw slippers, and went padding down the stairs to the basement. When he returned, he had the biggest grin on his face that I've ever seen.

"Look, Dad!"

And there it was, half of the 10-pointer's rack. A long, thick main beam, four long, heavy points, the back one eight inches. Amazing. And that buck will be there next year.

"Dad, can I put it on my wall?"

"Of course."

"And can we go look for the other half of his antlers tomorrow, because tomorrow's Saturday, and I don't have school, and you once told me that their antlers usually fall off pretty close together. Please?"

"Sure, James. If you're good in school today."

The deal was made. We never found the other half of the shed, though. It snowed, and we couldn't really look. Mice probably ate the other half.

But you know what? I think maybe my future hunting companion was born this past season.

SECTION FIVE
AFRICA AND ASIA

CHAPTER 17

KARAMOJO

By W. D. M. Bell

I. Into the Unknown

My earliest recollection of myself is that of a child whose sole ambition in life was to hunt. At a very early age I conceived the idea of hunting the American bison. With this end in view I gathered together a few oddments, such as the barrels of a double-barreled pistol, a clasp knife, a few bits of string and all the money—chiefly pennies—that I could lay hands on. This bison-hunting expedition was prematurely cut short at the Port of Glasgow by the critical state of its finances, for after buying a pork pie for two pence its treasury was found to be almost empty. This was a sad blow, and it was while thinking it over on a doorstep that a kindly policeman instituted proceedings which resulted in the lost and crestfallen child being restored to his family. But the growth of years and the acquirement of the art of reading—by which I discovered that bison no longer existed in America—my ambition became fixed on becoming an elephant hunter. The reading of Gordon Cumming's books on Africa finished the business. An elephant hunter I determined to become; this idea never left me. Finally, after all kinds of vicissitudes I arrived in Africa and heard of a wonderful new and unexplored country called Karamojo. Elephants were reported by the black traders to be very numerous with enormous tusks, and there was no sort of administration to hamper the hunter with restrictions and game laws. Above all there appeared to be no other person hunting elephants in this Eldorado except the natives, and they had no firearms. My informants told me that the starting point for all safaris (caravans) was Mumias, a native town and Government Post at the foot of Mount Elgon, which formed the last outpost of civilisation for a traveller proceeding North.

At the time of which I write Mumias was a town of some importance. It was the base for all trading expeditions to the Lake Rudolph basin, Turkana, Dabossa and the Southern Abyssinia country. In the first few years of the trade in ivory this commodity was obtained for the most trifling sums; for instance, a tusk worth £50 or £60 could be bought for two or three shillings' worth of beads or iron wire. As time went on and more traders flocked to Karamojo to share in the huge profits of the ivory trade, competition became keener. Prices rose higher and higher. Where once beads and iron wire sufficed to buy a tusk, now a cow must be paid. Traders were obliged to go further and further afield to find new territory until they came in violent contact with raiding parties of Abyssinians away in the far North.

When most of the dead ivory in the country had been traded off the only remaining source was the yearly crop of tusks from the elephants snared and killed by the native Karamojans. For these comparatively few tusks competition became so keen and prices so high that there was no longer any profit when as much as eight or ten cows had to be paid for a large tusk, and the cows bought down at the base for spot cash and at prices of from £2 to £5 each. Hence arose the idea in the brains of two or three of the bolder spirits among the traders to take by force that which they could no longer afford to buy. Instead of traders they became raiders. In order to ensure success to a raid an alliance would be made with some tribe which was already about equal in strength to its neighbours through centuries of intertribal warfare. The addition of three or four hundred guns to the tribe's five or six thousand spearmen rendered the result of this raid by the combined forces almost beyond doubt, and moreover, conferred upon the raiders such complete domination of the situation that they were able to search out and capture the young girls, the acquisition of which is the great aim and object of all activity in the Mohammedan mind.

Complete and magnificent success attending the first raiding venture the whole country changed magically. The hitherto more or less peaceful looking trading camps gave place to huge armed Bomas surrounded by high thorn fences. Everyone—trader or native—went about armed to the teeth. Footsore or sick travellers from caravans disappeared entirely, or their remains were found by the roadside. Native women and cattle were heavily guarded, for no man trusted a stranger.

Into this country of suspicion and brooding violence I was about to venture. As soon as my intention became known among the traders at Mumias I encountered on every side a firm barrage of lies and dissuasion of every sort. The buying of pack donkeys was made impossible. Guides were unobtainable. Information about the country north of Turkwell was either distorted and false or entirely withheld. I found that no Mohammedan boy would engage with me. The reason for all this apparently malicious obstruction on the part of the trading community was not at the time known to me, but it soon became clear when I had crossed the Turkwell and found that the peaceful, polite and prosperous looking trader of Mumias became the merciless and bloody Dacoit as soon as he had crossed that river and was no longer under European control. Numbering among them, as they did, some pretty notorious ex-slavers, they knew how unexpectedly far the arm of the law could sometimes reach and they no doubt foresaw that nothing but trouble would arise from my visit to the territory they had come to look upon as theirs by right of discovery. It surprises me now, when I think of how much they had at stake, that they resorted to no more stringent methods than those related above to prevent my entry into Karamojo. As it was I soon got together some bullocks and some pagan boys. The bullocks I half trained to carry packs and the Government Agent very kindly arranged that I should have eight Snider rifles with which to defend myself, and to instill confidence among my Baganda and Wanyamwere and Kavirondo boys. The Sniders looked well and no one knew except myself that the ammunition for them was all bad. And then I had my personal rifles, at that time a.303 Lee-Enfield, a 275 Rigby-Mauser and a double 450-.400, besides a Mauser pistol which could be used as a carbine and which soon acquired the name of "Bom-Bom" and a reputation for itself equal to a hundred ordinary rifles.

While searching through some boxes of loose ammunition in the store at Mumias in the hope of finding at least a few good rounds for my Snider carbines I picked up a Martini-Henry cartridge, and while looking at its base it suddenly struck me that possibly it could be fired from a Snider. And so it proved to be. The base being .577 calibre fitted perfectly, but the bullet, being only .450 bore, was scarcely what you might call a good fit for a .577 barrel, and there was, of course, no accuracy to the thing at all. But it went off with a bang and the propensity of its bullet to fly off at the most disconcerting angles after rattling through the barrel from side to side seemed just to suit the style of aiming adopted by my eight askaris (soldiers), for on several occasions jackal and hyena were laid low while prowling round the camp at night.

Bright and early next morning my little safari began to get itself ready for the voyage into the Unknown. The loads were got out and lined up. First of all an askari, with a Snider rifle very proud in a hide belt with five Martini cartridges gleaming yellow in it. He had carefully polished them with sand for the occasion. Likewise the barrel of the old Snider showed signs of much rubbing, and a piece of fat from the tail of a sheep dangled by a short string from the hammer. Then my chop-boxes, and camp gear borne by porters, followed by my boy Suede and Sulieman, the cook, of cannibal parentage be it whispered. As usual, all the small loads seemed to be jauntily and lightly perched on the massive heads and necks of the biggest porters, while the big loads looked doubly big in comparison to the spindly shanks which appeared below them. One enormous porter in particular drew my attention. He was capering about in the most fantastic manner with a large box on his head. From the rattle which proceeded from the box I perceived that this was the cook's mate, and as I possessed only a few aluminium cooking pots, his was perhaps the lightest load of any, and I vowed that he should have a good heavy tusk to carry as soon as possible. This I was enabled to do soon after passing the Turkwell, and this splendid head-carrier took entire charge of a tusk weighing 123 lb., carrying it with pride for several hundred weary miles on a daily ration of 1 lb. of mtama grain and unlimited buck meat.

Usually when a safari started from Mumias for the "Barra"—as the bush or wilderness is called—the townsfolk would turn out with drums and horns to give them a send off, but in our case we departed without any demonstration of that sort. We passed through almost deserted and silent streets, and we struck out for the Turkwell, the trail skirting the base of Elgon for six days, as we travelled slowly, being heavily laden. I was able to find and shoot enough haartebeeste and oribi to keep the safari in meat, and after two or three days' march the boys became better and better and the bullocks more and more docile. I purposely made the marches more easy at first in order to avoid sore backs, and it was easy to do so, as there were good streams of water crossing our path every few miles.

On the seventh day we reached the Turkwell River. After descending several hundred feet from the high plateau we crossed by the ford and pitched camp on the opposite or north bank. The Turkwell has its sources in the crater of Elgon and its slopes. Its waters reach the dry, hot plains of Karamojo after a drop of about 9,000 ft. in perhaps twenty or thirty miles. In the dry season—when it is fordable almost anywhere—it totally disappears into its sandy river bed while still some days' march from its goal, Lake Rudolph.

It is a queer and romantic river, for it starts in lava 14,000 ft. above sea-level, traverses bitterly cold and often snow-covered heath land, plunges down through the dense bamboo belt, then through dark and dripping evergreen forest to emerge on the sandy plains of Karamojo. From this point to Rudolph its banks are clothed with a more or less dense belt of immense flat-topped thorn trees interspersed with thickets of every kind of thorny bush, the haunt of rhino, buffalo and elephant. Throughout its entire course its waters were drunk, at the time of which I write, by immense herds of elephant during the dry season. Even after disappearing underground, elephant and natives easily procured water by simply making holes in the soft clean sands of its river bed.

At that time the Turkwell formed the northern boundary of European rule. North of it was no rule but disrule. The nearest cultivated settlement of Karamojo natives was at Mani-Mani, some 150 miles to the north, but scattered about in the bush were many temporary settlements of poor Karamojans who got their living by hunting and snaring everything from elephant downwards.

Dreadful tales of murders of peaceful travellers had been related by Swahilis, and we were careful not to let anyone straggle far from the main body. At night my eight askaris mounted guard and kept a huge fire going. Their vigilance was extraordinary, and their keenness and cheerfulness, fidelity and courage of a very high order, showing them to be born soldiers. Their shooting was simply atrocious, in spite of practice with a .22 I had, but notwithstanding their inability to align and aim a rifle properly, they used sometimes to bring off the most brilliant shots under the most impossible conditions of shooting light, thereby showing a great natural aptitude to point a gun and time the shot.

While we were drying out the gear that had got wet while crossing the Turkwell two natives strolled into the camp. These were the first Karamojans we had seen, and I was very much interested in them. They showed great independence of bearing as they stood about leaning on their long thrusting spears. I had some difficulty in getting into conversation with them, although I had an excellent interpreter. They seemed very taciturn and suspicious.

However, I got it explained to them that I had come for one purpose only, i.e., to hunt elephant. They admitted that there were plenty of elephant, but when I asked them to show me where to look for them they merely asked me how I proposed to kill them when I did see them. On showing them my rifle they laughed, and said they had seen Swahili traders using those things for elephants and, although they killed men well enough, they were useless against elephant. My answer to this was that I had procured some wonderful medicine which enabled me to kill the largest-sized elephant with one shot, and that if they would like to see this medicine working all they had to do was to show me where the elephant were and that I would do the rest and they should have as much meat as they wanted. They retorted that if my medicine was truly sufficiently powerful to kill an elephant instantaneously, then they could not believe that it would fail to show me their whereabouts also. This grave fault in my medicine had to be explained, and I could only say that I grieved heartily over the deficiency, which I attributed to the jealousy of a medicine man who was a rival of him who had given me the killing medicine. This left them not altogether satisfied, but a better impression was produced when I presented them with a quarter of buck meat, while telling them that I killed that kind of meat every day. They went off without holding out any hope of showing me elephant, and I thought that I had seen the last of them. I sat until late in my long chair by the camp fire under a brilliant sky and wonderful moon listening to the talk of my Nzamwezi boys and wondering how we were going to fare in the real wild land ahead of us.

An early start was made next morning and we had covered perhaps six or seven miles when the two natives, visitors to our camp of yesterday, came stalking along appearing to cover the ground at a great rate without showing any hurry or fuss. I stopped and called the interpreter and soon learned that four large elephants had that morning passed close to their camp in the bush and that when they left to call me the elephants could still be heard in the vicinity. At once I was for going, but the interpreter and the headman both cautioned me against treachery, declaring that it was only a blind to separate us preparatory to a general massacre. This view I thought a bit far fetched, but

I ordered the safari to get under weigh and to travel well together until they reached the first water, where they were immediately to cut sufficient thorn trees to completely encircle themselves in camp, to keep a good look-out and to await my coming.

Taking my small boy and the gigantic cook's mate—whose feather-weight load I had transferred to the cook's head—I hastily put together a few necessities and hurried off with the two Karamojans at a great pace. We soon struck off from the main trail and headed for the Turkwell Valley. Straight through the open thorn bush we went, the elephant hide sandals of my native guides crunching innumerable darning-needle-sized thorns underfoot, the following porters with their light loads at a jog trot, myself at a fast but laboured walk, while the guides simply soaked along with consummate ease.

Supremely undemonstrative as natives usually are, there was yet observable a kind of suppressed excitement about their bearing, and I noticed that whenever a certain bird called on the right hand the leader would make a low remark to his companions with an indescribably satisfied kind of gesture, whereas the same calling on the left hand drew no notice from them beyond a certain increased forward resolution and a stiff ignoring of it.

The significance of these signs were lost on me at that time, but I was to come to learn them well in my later dealings with these tribes. They were omens and indicated success or failure to our hunting.

On the whole they were apparently favourable. At any rate, the pace never slackened, and I was beginning to wish for a slowing down. As we drew nearer the Turkwell Valley signs of elephant became more and more numerous. Huge paths worn perfectly smooth and with their edges cut as clear as those of garden walks by the huge pads of the ponderous animals began to run together, forming more deeply worn ones converging towards the drinking places on the river. Occasionally the beautiful lesser koodoo stood watching us or loped away, flirting its white fluffed tail. Once we passed a rhino standing motionless with snout ever directed towards us. A small detour round him as we did not wish to get mixed up with his sort and on again. Halt! The little line bunches up against the motionless natives.

A distant rumble resembling somewhat a cart crossing a wooden bridge, and after a few seconds of silence the crash of a broken tree.

Elephant! Atome! (in Karamojo). Word the first to be learned and the last to be forgotten of any native language. A kind of excitement seizes us all; me most of all, the Karamojans least. Now the boys are told to stay behind and to make no noise. They are at liberty to climb trees if they like. I look to my .303, but, of

course, it had been ready for hours. Noting that the wind—what there was of it— was favourable, the natives and I go forward, and soon we come upon the broken trees, mimosa and white thorn, the chewed fibrous balls of sansivera, the moist patches with froth still on them, the still steaming and unoxidised spoor, and the huge tracks with the heavily imprinted clear-cut corrugations of a very recently passing bunch of bull elephants. In numbers they were five as nearly as I could estimate. Tracking them was child's play, and I expected to see them at any moment. It was, however, much longer than I anticipated before we sighted their dull grey hides. For they were travelling as well as feeding. It is remarkable how much territory elephant cover when thus feeding along. At first sight they seem to be so leisurely, and it is not until one begins to keep in touch with them that their speed is realised. Although they appear to take so few steps, each step of their lowest gait is about 6 ft. Then, again, in this feeding along there is always at least one of the party moving forward at about 3½ miles per hour, although the other members may be stopping and feeding, then catching up again by extending the stride to 7 ft. or more.

As soon as they were in sight I got in front of the Karamojans and ran in to about 20 yds. from the stern of the rearmost animal. Intense excitement now had me with its usual signs, hard breathing through the mouth, dry palate and an intense longing to shoot.

As I arrived at this close proximity I vividly remember glancing along the grey bulging sides of the three rearmost animals, who all happened to be in motion at the same time in single file, and remarking a tusk of an incredible length and size sweeping out from the grey wall. I instantly determined to try for this one first. With extraordinary precautions against making a noise, and stoopings and contortions of the body, all of which after-experience taught me were totally unnecessary, I got away off at right-angles to the file of elephants and could now grasp the fact that they were all very large and carried superb ivory.

I was now almost light-headed with excitement, and several times on the very verge of firing a stupid and hasty shot from my jumping and flickering rifle. So shaky was it when I once or twice put it to my shoulder that even in my then state of mind I saw that no good could come of it. After a minute or two, during which I was returning to a more normal state, the animal with the largest tusks left the line slightly, and slowly settled into a halt beside a mimosa bush. I got a clear glimpse at his broadside at what looked about 20 yds., but was really 40 yds., and I fired for his heart. With a flinch, a squirm and a roar he was soon in rapid motion straight away, with his companions in full flight ahead of him. I was rather surprised at this headlong flight after one shot as I had expected the elephant here to be more unsophisticated, but hastily concluding that the Swahili traders must have been pumping lead into them more often than one imagined, I legged it for the cloud of dust where the fleeting animals had disappeared. Being clad in running shorts and light shoes, it was not long before I almost ran slap up against a huge and motionless grey stern. Recoiling very rapidly indeed from this awe-inspiring sight, I saw on one side of it an enormous head and tusk which appeared to stick out at right-angles. So drooping were the trunk and ears and so motionless the whole appearance of what had been a few seconds ago the very essence of power and activity that it was borne straight to even my inexperienced mind that here was death. And so it was, for as I stared goggle-eyed the mighty body began to sway from side to side more and more, until with a crash it fell sideways, bearing earthwards with it a fair sized tree. Straight past it I saw another elephant, turned almost broadside, at about 100 yds. distance, evidently listening and obviously on the point of flight. Running a little forward so as to get a clear sight of the second beast, I sat quickly down and fired carefully at the shoulder, when much the same performance took place as in the first case, except that No. 2 came down to a slow walk after a burst of speed instead of to a standstill as with No. 1.

Ranging rapidly alongside I quickly put him out of misery and tore after the others which were, of course, by this time, thoroughly alarmed and in full flight. After a mile or two of fast going I found myself pretty well done, so I sat down and rolled myself a cigarette of the strong black shag so commonly smoked by the Swahilis. Presently my native guides came with every appearance of satisfaction on their now beaming faces.

After a few minutes' rest we retracked the elephant back to where our two lay dead. The tusks of the first one we examined were not long but very thick, and the other had on one side a tusk broken some 2 ft. outside the lip, while on the other was the magnificent tusk which had filled me with wonder earlier on. It was almost faultless and beautifully curved. What a shame that its companion was broken!

As we were cutting the tail off, which is always done to show anyone finding the carcase that it has been killed and claimed, my good fellows came up with the gear and the interpreter. Everyone, including myself, was in high good humour, and when the Karamojans said that their village was not far off we were more pleased than ever, especially as the sun was sinking rapidly. After what appeared to the natives no doubt as a short distance, but what seemed to my sore feet and tired legs a very long one, we saw the welcome fires of a camp and were soon sitting by one while a group of naked savages stood looking silently at the white man and his preparations for eating and sleeping. These were simple enough. A kettle was soon on the fire for tea, while some strips of sun-cured haartebeeste biltong writhed and sizzled on the embers. Meanwhile my boys got the bed ready by first of all cutting the grass and smoothing down the knobs of the ground while another spread grass on it to form a mattress. Over this the canvas sheet and blankets and with a bag of cartridges wrapped in a coat for a pillow the bed was complete. Then two forked sticks stuck in the ground close alongside the bed to hold the rifle and all was ready for the night.

II. IVORY AND THE RAIDERS

After a hearty supper of toasted biltong and native flour porridge, washed down with tea, I cleaned my rifle, loaded it and lay down utterly tired out and soon dropped off to the music of hyenas' howling. As soon as ever it was light enough to see, we left for the dead elephant, and the way did not seem half so long in the fresh morning air as it had appeared the evening before. We quickly arrived, followed by all the villagers, men, women and children, everyone in high spirits at the sight of the mountains of meat. In this country the meat of elephants is esteemed more highly than that of any other animal, as it contains much more fat. The Karamojan elephants are distinguished for their bodily size, the quality and size of their ivory and for the quantity of fat on them.

I was anxious to get the tusks out as rapidly as possible in order to rejoin my caravan, so I divided the Karamojans into two gangs and explained to them that no one was to touch the carcases until the tusks were out, but that then they could have all the meat. They set to with a will to get all the skin and flesh off the head. It is necessary to do this so as to expose the huge bone sockets containing the ends of the tusks. About a third of their length is so embedded, and a very long, tedious and hard job it is to get all the skin and gristle cut away. Nothing blunts a knife more quickly than elephant hide, because of the sand and grit in its loose texture.

When the skull is clean on one side the neck should be cut. This alone is a herculean task. The vertebra severed, the head is turned over by eight or ten men, and the other side similarly cleaned. When both sockets are ready an axe is used to chop them away chip by chip until the tusk is free. This chopping

should always be done by an expert, as otherwise large chips off the tusk itself are liable to be taken by the axe.

This chopping out of ivory is seldom resorted to by natives, requiring as it does so much hard work. They prefer to leave the sun and putrefaction to do the work for them. On the third day after the death the upper tusk can usually be drawn without difficulty from the socket and the underneath one on the following day.

On this particular occasion no one was at all adept at chopping out, and it was hours before the tusks were freed. Later on my Wanzamwezi boys became very expert indeed at this job, and twelve of them, whose particular job it became, could handle as many as ten bull elephants in a day provided they were not too distant one from the other and that they had plenty of native assistance.

While the chopping out was going on I had leisure to watch the natives, and what struck me first was the remarkable difference between the men and the women. The former were tall, some of them quite 6 ft. 4 ins., slim and well made, while the latter were distinctly short, broad, beefy and squat. The married ones wore aprons of dressed buckskin tied round the waist by the legs of the skin and ornamented with coloured beads sewn on with sinew thread. The unmarried girls wore no skins at all and had merely a short fringe of black thread attached to a string round the waist and falling down in front. As regards hair, all the women wore it plaited and falling down all round the head and giving somewhat the appearance of "bobbed" hair. Some of the men wore the most extraordinary-looking periwigs made up of their own and also their ancestors' hair mixed with clay so as to form a kind of covering for the top of the head and falling down the back of the neck. In this pad of human felt were set neat little woven sockets in such a way as to hold upright an ostrich feather in each.

The people with whom we are dealing at the moment were poor and therefore hunters. Africans differ from us entirely on the question of hunting; whereas among us it is the well-off who hunt, among them it is the poor. Having nothing but a few goats and sheep, these hunters inhabit the bush, shifting their village from site to site according to the movements of the game.

Their system of taking game is the snare; their only weapon a spear. The art of snaring has been brought to a unique development by these people, for they have snares varying in size for all animals from elephant down to dik-dik.

The snare for elephant is a great hawser, 4½ ins. in diameter, of twisted antelope or giraffe hides. One may find in the same rope haartebeeste hide, eland, zebra, rhinoceros, buffalo and giraffe hide. If made of haartebeeste alone no less than eleven or twelve skins are required. The skins are scraped and pounded with huge wooden mallets for weeks by the women before being twisted or "laid" into the rope which is to form the snare. The running nooses at both ends are beautifully made. Besides the snare there is a thing like a cart wheel without any hub and with scores of thin spokes meeting in the centre where their points are sharp. The snare is laid in the following manner:

A well frequented elephant path is chosen and somewhere near the spot decided upon for the snare a large tree is cut. Judgment in the choosing of this must be exercised as if it is too heavy the snare will break, and if too light the snared elephant will travel too far. A tree trunk which ten or twelve men can just stagger along with seems to be the thing. This log is then brought to the scene of action and at its smaller end a deep groove is cut all round to take the noose at one end of the rope. After this noose has been fitted and pulled and hammered tight—no easy matter—the log is laid at right angles to the path with the smaller end pointing towards it. A hole a good bit larger than an elephant's foot is then dug in the path itself to a depth of two feet or so. Over this hole is fitted the cart wheel. Round the rim the large noose of the snare is laid and the whole covered carefully over with earth to resemble the path again. The snare is now laid, and if all goes well some solitary old bull comes wandering along at night, places his foot on the earth borne by the sharp spokes of the hubless wheel, goes through as the spokes open downwards, lifts his foot and with it the wheel bearing the noose well up the ankle, strides forward and tightens the noose. The more he pulls the tighter draws the noose until the log at the other end of the snare begins to move. Now alarmed and presently angry, he soon gets rid of the cart wheel, but as its work is already done, that does not matter. The dragging log is now securely attached to the elephant's leg, and it is seldom that he gets rid of it unless it should jamb in rocks or trees. Soon he becomes thoroughly alarmed and sets off at a great pace, the log ploughing along behind him. Should a strong, vigorous young bull become attached to a rather light log, he may go twenty or thirty miles.

As soon as it becomes known to the natives that an elephant has been caught, everyone within miles immediately seizes all his spears and rushes to the spot where the snare had been set and from there eagerly takes up the trail of the log. When they come up with the somewhat exhausted animal they spear it to death. Then every scrap of meat is shared among the village which owns the snare, the tusks becoming the property of the man who made and laid the snare. The spearing of an elephant, with its enormously thick hide, is no easy matter, as the animal can still make short active rushes. Casualties are not infrequent, and should anyone be caught he is, as a rule, almost certain to be killed.

While the tusk-getting operations were going on I took the opportunity to examine the respective positions-of the heart, lungs and brain in relation to the conspicuous points of the animal's exterior, such as the eye, the ear, the line of the fore leg and the point of the shoulder. In order to fix the position of the heart and lungs I made some boys get the stomach and intestines out. This was a terrific job, but we were ably assisted by the powerful native women. The "innards" of elephant are very greatly prized by all natives who eat elephant. The contents of the stomach must have weighed a ton, I should think, and I saw the intestine or sack which contains the clear pure water so readily drunk by the hunter during the dry season when he finds himself far from water. It is from this internal tank that the elephant can produce water for the purpose of treating himself to a shower bath when there is no water. He brings it up into his throat, whence it is sucked into the trunk and then delivered where required. The first time I saw an elephant doing this I thought he must be standing by a pool of water from which he was drawing it. I was many weary miles from water and the sun was scorching, and I and the boy with me were very thirsty, so we hastened towards the elephant, which moved on slowly through the bush. Very soon we arrived at the spot where we had seen him at his shower bath, but no spring or pool could I find. I asked the Karamojan about it and he then told me, with a smile at my ignorance, that the nearest water was at our camp and that all elephant carried water inside them and need not replenish their stock for three days. Coming up with the elephant I killed him and got Pyjalé (my Karamojan tracker) to pierce its water tank, and sure enough water, perfectly clear barring a little blood, gushed out, which we both drank greedily. It was warm certainly, but quite tasteless and odourless and very wholesome and grateful.

When everything had been got out, except the lungs and heart, I had spears thrust through from the direction from which a bullet would come. I meanwhile peered into the huge cavity formed by the massive ribs and when a spear pierced a lung or the heart, I immediately examined its situation and tried to commit it to my memory. One thing I noticed was that with the animal lying on its side the heart did not occupy the cavity which was obviously intended for it when upright, therefore an allowance had to be made. Another thing I was impressed with was the size of the arteries about the heart. It extended the killing area a considerable distance above the heart, and I have often since killed elephant with a shot above the heart. About the situation of the brain I also learned a lot. I thought I had its position fixed to a nicety in my mind, but I subsequently found that all I had learned was one of the many positions the brain does not occupy. And it was by a series of these misplacings that I finally came to know where the brain really does lie. It is a small object contained in a very large head. It lies so far from the exterior that a very slight and almost unnoticeable change of angle causes the bullet to miss it completely.

From this my first dealing with Karamojans it began to be borne in on me that they were not so bad as the Swahili traders had tried to make out. And my subsequent dealings with them confirmed this impression. As far as I was concerned I had hardly any trouble with them. But at the same time some terrible massacres took place while I was in their country. These affairs were the most completely successful operations I have ever heard of from the native point of view. On three occasions massacres of well-armed trading caravans were attempted, and on two there were no survivors among the traders and no casualties among the natives, while on the third there was one trader survivor who escaped. I will describe later on the methods employed by the natives so successfully, for it was not until my Karamojan friend Pyjalé came to me that I heard the inside of the thing. For the next few days nothing of note happened except that we passed the remains of two black men by the roadside—stragglers from some trading caravan probably, judging by the bits of cloth lying about. Now here was a state of things requiring explanation. We were now close to Mani-Mani, the up-country base for all trading caravans. Mani-Mani was also a populous centre for Karamojans, with whom the traders were perforce at peace. And yet here on the roads were two murdered men obviously belonging to the traders. On my arrival at Mani-Mani I found the explanation. It was thus: Among Karamojans, as among Masai, Somals and other tribes, a young man is of no consideration, has no standing with the girls, until he has killed someone. It does not matter how he kills him, he may be asleep or unarmed. When he has "done someone in," either man or woman, other than Karamojan of course, he has the right to tattoo the right side of his body for a man victim and the left side for a woman. Moreover, at the dances he mounts a very tall ostrich feather dipped blood red, and then he is looked upon as a man. He may and does now demand anything from the unmarried girls. He may flog them should they resist. And this atrocious incitement to murder is the cause of death to any leg-weary straggler from caravans. That the Swahili leaders never made these wayside murders a casus belli shows them to be what they are, callous snivellers. That they could have put down this custom was shown when some of my boys lost their way among the villages. As soon as it was reported to me I at once got together five of my askaris and raced off among the herds of Karamojan cattle. We rounded up a huge mob and held them more or less in one place. Spearmen rushed about, women holloaed, and shields were produced from every hut. I was so hot and angry—thinking that the missing boys had been murdered—that I was eager to begin by attacking straightaway. It looked as if about 400 spearmen were assembled and I meant to give them a genuine shaking up with my 10-shot .303, followed by my 10-shot Mauser pistol. I felt confident that as soon as I let loose on them and killed one or two the others would run like rabbits. It never came to a fight, for some old unarmed men and women came tottering up, picking grass at every step, biting it in two and casting the bits to the winds. This meant peace; peace at any price. Where were my porters? They did not know, really they did not. But they would be all right. Nobody would harm them. I told them to go and produce every one of them unharmed or I would take and kill all their cattle and a lot of them besides. Moreover, if any armed man approached anywhere near to the cattle I would shoot him dead. The cattle would remain there—between ourselves we could not have handled them—until the porters were produced.

And produced they were, very quickly. They had merely lost their way among the villages and had been guided back.

I did not regret having had this opportunity of showing the natives that as far as my people were concerned we were prepared to fight savagely for any member of the safari and not—as did the traders—let stragglers be murdered without even a protest. The noise of this affair travelled far and probably saved us a lot of trouble in our after dealings.

Another reason for this apathy on the part of the Swahili leaders was, I think, that the certainty of murder awaiting anyone on the road prevented desertion. They were enabled by this means to keep their boys for years without payment of wages. So long as they could prevent the boys from reaching Mumias alive there was no redress. Hence it was difficult for the Government representative at Mumias to get reliable information of the internal state of Karamojo.

On our arrival at Mani-Mani we were met by one Shundi—a remarkable man. Kavirondo by birth, he had been captured early in life, taken to the coast and sold as a slave. Being a man of great force of character he had soon freed himself by turning Mohammedan. Thence onward fortune had smiled upon him until at last here he was, the recognised chief Tajir (rich man) of all the traders. Having naturally the intelligence to recognise the value of bluff and from his primitive ancestors the nerve to carry it off, he was at this time the greatest of all the traders. Just as he had been a leader while slave-raiding was the order of the day, so now he led when ivory had given place to slaves as a commodity. One other thing makes him conspicuous, at any rate, in my mind, and that was the fact that he had owned the slave who had laid low the elephant which bore the enormous tusks, one of which now reposes in the South Kensington Museum. These tusks are still, as far as I know, the record. The one which we have in London scales 234 lb. or thereabouts. According to Shundi his slave killed it with a muzzle-loader on the slopes of Kilimandjaro.

Shundi was accompanied by a large body of traders of all sorts. There were Arabs, Swahilis, one or two Persians and a few African born Baluchis, and a pretty tough lot they looked. Beside their mean and cunning air Shundi—the great coal-black Bantu—appeared like a lion among hyenas. What an extraordinary calm and dignity some of these outstanding black men have. Here was a kin spirit to Buba Gida.

They hated my appearing in their country, but did not show it. Shundi took it in the spirit that what had to be had to be, but some of the lesser villains were obviously nervous. They pretended to wish me to camp inside the town, but I preferred to remain outside. The town was of very considerable size, although the buildings were of a temporary construction. I remarked an  extraordinary number of women about and thought that I recognised Masai types among them. This was so, as I afterwards learnt that Shundi alone had over eighty women, many of whom were Masai from Kilimandjaro.

With native politeness gifts of food, etc., were offered and presently all withdrew, intimating that they would return when I had rested.

They must have been feeling rather uncomfortable about the appearance in their midst of a white man, possibly an agent of that detestable Government so troublesome about raiding. I did not actually know at the time, but learnt afterwards that at the very moment of my arrival in their midst they had an enormous raid on the Turkana underway.

In the afternoon they came again and we had the usual ceremonial palaver. Every one was strictly guarded, but they made a distinct effort to embroil me with the natives in the hope, I suppose, of getting me so mixed up in some shooting affair that I would become more or less one of themselves. I refused to have anything to do with their intrigues. I got little information regarding elephant from these people. In fact, neither side could quite overcome a severely suppressed but quite strong hostility to the other.

I stayed a few days at Mani-Mani as there were repairs to be attended to and man and beast required a rest. The first sign of trouble soon appeared, caused, I feel certain, by Swahili intrigue. It was the dry season and all animals were watered once a day at the wells dug in the otherwise dry river-bed. My animals were being watered as usual. That is, water was drawn from the well in buckets and emptied into a watertight ground sheet laid over a suitable depression in the sand. Word was suddenly brought to me that the natives refused to allow my animals to be watered. I went at once to the scene and asked the natives what all the trouble was about. There were about forty young bloods leaning against their spears and they laughed in the most insolent manner without giving me any answer. I turned to my herds and beckoned them to bring up the animals. As they began to do so three of the bloods strode over and began flogging the thirsty bullocks in the face and driving them off. It was now or never, first impression and so on. I seized from the nearest Karamojan his cutting-edged club, sprang over to one of the bullock obstructors and dealt him the hardest blow on the head I possibly could. I was fairly hefty, in good training, and meant all I knew. To my astonishment the native turned on me a smile instead of dropping dead or at least stunned, while the club flew to atoms. I had hit his shock-absorbing periwig, previously described. I might as well have hit a Dunlop Magnum.

I must confess it was rather a set-back. However, one good effect it had was that everyone, except myself, roared with laughter, and then when even I began to see the humour of it I spotted a mischievous devil calmly jabbing his spear through our priceless waterproof ground sheet. This would not do, so I drew my Mauser pistol. Now these natives were then at a most dangerous stage of ignorance with regard to firearms. Their experience of them had been gathered on raids with the Swahilis, and they all firmly held the conviction that all you had to do to avoid being struck by the bullet was to duck when you saw the smoke. While I was fitting the wooden holster to the Mauser they watched me carefully. They had probably never seen such a gun before if they even recognised it as such. When therefore I had it fitted up and was covering them no one moved. They were waiting, I suspect, for the smoke. And when they heard the particularly vicious bang of the little Mauser and saw no smoke, the laugh this time was rather on them, and especially on the gentleman who had been so busy with his spear and my ground sheet; for he now stood looking at a half severed and completely spoilt spear in his hand with a ridiculous air of surprised injury. In a few seconds the humour of this phase struck all concerned, although the natives began to edge nervously away. All their swagger was gone now. I had been approaching the fellow with the damaged spear, and now suddenly set upon him, relying upon my herds to help me. Never have I felt anything like the sinewy strength of that greasy native; he was all but off when the boys secured him just in time. Seeing some flourishing of spears going on among the others, I began pasting dust about them with the little Mauser. Seeing no smoke again, yet getting whing whang right and left of them, they turned and bolted. I got in another clip of ten and kept them dodging dust-bursts for 400 or 500 yds.

On returning I put it out among the natives that our prisoner would be released when ten goats and sheep had been paid by his family as a fine. They were soon forthcoming.

Up till now I had been looked upon by the natives as a sort of poor Arab. In this idea they were no doubt helped by the traders. They had never seen white men, and they saw my mean little safari and drew their own conclusions from appearances. But after the affair at the water hole I was treated with much greater respect, and with a kind of good-humoured indulgence, much as a very persistent headstrong child might be looked upon. And eventually, after a few more "incidents," we became fast friends and they would do almost anything for me or for my people. One instance of this I may as well here record, although it happened long afterwards.

Away down in civilised parts I had left two aged Wanyamwezi boys in charge of my cattle ranch. This was situated a few miles from Nandi Boma (Government Post). At the Boma post office I had left directions for my letters to be forwarded to another Boma on the slopes of Elgon, where I used to send every six months or so to get them. All my letters went as directed until there occurred a change of District Commissioner. Now one of my old pensioners looking after the ranch had orders to report every fortnight to the D.C. that all was well or otherwise. In pursuit of these instructions the old boy appeared one day before the new D.C., who asked him who he was. He said he belonged to me, naming me. The D.C. said he had some letters for me, and told the boy to take them to me, thinking that I was at the ranch a few miles off, instead of which I was actually over 600 miles away. That dear old man took the letters without a word, went straight back to the ranch and prepared to follow me into what was much of it quite unknown country. He told the other boy, who was also about sixty-five years of age, that he would have to look after everything himself as he was going after the Bwana (master). Being a thrifty old soul, he had by him much stock of dry smoked beef from cows which had died. His preparations were, therefore, almost complete. An inveterate snuff-taker, he had only to grind up a good quantity for the journey and he was ready. Shouldering his Snider and with the packet of letters cunningly guarded against wet, off he set through the wilderness, steering due north. Sleeping by night alone by his camp fire and travelling the whole of the day, he came wandering through what would have been to anyone else hostile tribe after hostile tribe. Countries where if I sent at all I sent at least five guns as escort he came through without trouble. How often he must have been looked upon by the lecherous eyes of would-be bloods as fair game for their spears and as means of gaining the coveted tattoo marks and the blood red ostrich feather. But so sublimely unconscious was he of any feeling of nervousness and so bold and confident his bearing that nothing happened. Being old and wise, he courted the routes which led through the most populous centres instead of dodging along the neutral zones between tribes as a nervous man would have done. Had he done this he would to a certainty have been killed. Wherever he went he slept in the largest village, demanded and got the best of everything, and eventually reached me intact. It was a splendid effort. He walked into camp as if he had left it five minutes before, and he still had smoked beef and snuff when he arrived. The dear old hoarder had lived to some purpose on the natives as he passed through. He arrived, if you please, escorted by a number of Karamojan big-men, this dingy and, I have to say it, very dirty old man. The letters, alas! proved to be most uninteresting in themselves, but, nevertheless, they formed a link with civilisation. They were chiefly bills from unscrupulous

Coast merchants being rendered for the third and fourth time although already paid at least once.

The newspapers were, of course, very old, but produced an extraordinary feeling of uneasiness or disquietude. Leading the life I then was, with its freedom from financial care—money was valueless and never handled—from responsibility—there was no law in the land except that of force—it had rather the effect of a sudden chill to read of strikes, famines, railway accidents, unemployment, lawsuits, and the other thousand and one unhappinesses usually contained in newspapers. Although I read them, every word, including the advertisements—here again remedies for ills—I felt distinctly perturbed for two or three days after. The happiest literature I ever had in the bush was "Pickwick Papers," and the happiest newspaper the dear old Field.

III. THE COMING OF PYJALÉ

From Mani-Mani we moved on to Bukora, another section of Karamojans. I was warned by the Swahilis that Bukora was a very bad country. The people were very rich in cattle and correspondingly insolent. Everyone who passed through Bukora had trouble. Either stock was stolen or porters murdered.

I cannot say that I believed all this, or perhaps I would not have been so ready to go there. But that there was some truth in their statements I soon found. In fact, there were moments when it was touch and go. Looking back on it calmly I can see that nothing but chance luck saved us. It was thus: We pushed our way smartly right into the middle of Bukora, intending to camp near some large village. But to our disappointment the catchments of water were nearly dry. What remained in them was merely mud. We were obliged therefore to move on to some wells on the outskirts of the villages. This is always a bad place to be attacked in. Natives are much more willing to attack people outside than when they are right in their midst. When you are close alongside a village and there is any question of hostilities, the people of that particular village feel that they will probably come in for more than their share of the trouble when it begins. They have their goods and chattels there, their corn, cows, babies, fowls, etc. For these reasons they are against hostilities. Another advantage to the travellers when close to stockaded villages—as these were—is that such a village can be rushed and then held against the rest of the tribe.

However, I was young and without much thought of anything in those days, and camp by the wells I would. We accordingly did so. And presently the camp began to fill with apparently friendly natives. They dropped in by twos and threes and stood around, each man with two spears. I thought they seemed a nice friendly, sociable crowd, and took little further heed of them. Then comes my headman, a Swahili, to me. "Bwana, there is no good brewing. These people mean trouble. Look around, do you see a single woman anywhere?" I laughed and asked him what he thought they would do. He said that at a given prearranged signal they would start spearing everyone. And then it dawned on me how absurdly easy it would be for them to do so. When you came to look around with this thought in your mind it became apparent that every man was being marked by several spearmen. If he moved they also lounged about until they were again close to him. I must say they appeared to me to act the indifference part very well. When I had convinced myself that something of this nature really was afoot, I naturally got close to my shooting irons, ready to take a hand when the fun started. In those days I always wore fifty rounds in my belt.

Now I thought that if I could only supply something sufficiently distracting the affair might never begin. There over the plains were plenty of game. I took my rifle and got the interpreter to tell the Karamojans to come as I was going killing meat. They came at once in fair numbers. They had already heard of my wonderful rifles, and wherever I went I always had an audience eager to see them or the Bom-bom (Mauser pistol) at work.

Hardly had we gone a few hundred yards, and while we were still in full view of the camp, when a herd of zebra came galloping across our front. They had been alarmed by some abnormal movement of natives and had somehow got mixed up and lost.

They came well spaced apart and just right for my purpose. I shot one after the other as hard as I could fire. I was using a 10 shot .303, and when I had fired the ten shots the survivors of the herd were too far off. I was careful not to reload in the ordinary way, for I carried another charged magazine. Consequently the natives thought I might have any number of shots left in this quite new and terrifying weapon. No smoke and such a rapid fire of death—they had never seen the like. Bing! bing! bing! bing! bing! they kept saying to themselves, only much more rapidly than the actual rate of fire. And the zebras, strong brutes, knocked right down one after the other. No! this was something new. They had better be careful about fooling around with this red man. He was different from those red men among the Swahilis, who used to fire great clouds of smoke and hit nothing.

After an episode of this kind one feels somehow that a complete mental transformation has taken place. One is established right above these, in some ways, finer but less scientific people. But this knowledge comes to both at the same time. I now ordered these previously truculent, now almost servile, savages to flay, cut up and carry to camp every bit of meat and skin. When I saw anyone sneaking a bit of fat or what-not I blackguarded him soundly. I rushed the whole regiment back to camp loaded with several tons of meat, many of them forgetting their spears in their hurry. But had I ventured to bullyrag them like this before the zebra incident I would have had a spear thrust for answer and right quickly too.

I now began to push enquiries about elephant, but with no great success at first. One day a Bukora boy came to camp and while in conversation with some of my people casually told them that he had recently returned from no man's land, where he and some friends of his had been looking for Kumamma. The Kumamma were their neighbours to the west. They had been looking for them in order to spear them, should things be right—that meaning should the enemy be in sufficiently small force for them to easily overcome. When the numbers are at all equal, both sides retire smartly to the rear. This is the normal kind of state in which these tribes live. It leads to a few deaths certainly, but it keeps the young men fit and out of other mischief. Every young man goes looking for blood frequently, and as they carry no food except a few handfuls of unground millet simply soaked in water, and as they never dare to sleep while in the neutral zone, it acts as a kind of field training.

This youth, then, had seen no Kumamma but had seen elephant. My boys told me this and I tried to get the lad to go with us to hunt. He said he would come back and let me know. He did so and brought a friend. This friend of his was a most remarkable-looking man. Strange as it may seem, he had a most intellectual head. He was a man of perhaps thirty-five years of age, most beautifully made and tattooed for men victims only, I was relieved to see. Pyjalé was his name, and now began a firm and long friendship between this distinguished savage and myself. I cannot say that I have ever had the same feelings for any man as I came to have for Pyjalé. He was, I found, a thorough man, courageous, quiet, modest, with a horror of humbug and untiring in our common pact, the pursuit of elephant. He was with me during the greater part of my time in Karamojo, and although surrounded by people who clothed themselves, never would he wear a rag even. Nor would he sleep comfortably as we did on grass and blankets. The bare hard ground out by the camp fire with a hole dug for his hip bone and his little wooden pillow had been good enough for him before and was good enough now. No one poked fun at Pyjalé for his nakedness; he was the kind who do not get fun poked at them.

Pyjalé was game to show us elephants, but said we would have to travel far. His intelligence was at once apparent by his saying that we ought to take tents as the rains might come any day. He was right, for come they did while we were hunting.

I took to Pyjalé right at the start and asked him what I should do about the main safari. He said I could leave it where it was; no one would interfere with it. If I liked I could leave the ivory in one of the villages. This I gathered was equivalent to putting one's silver in the bank at home. And so it is, bizarre as it may seem. You may leave anything with natives—ivory, beads, which are money, trade goods, stock, anything—and not one thing will they take provided you place it in their care. But if you leave your own people to look after it they will steal it, given the chance.

Thinking that it might save trouble I put all my trade goods and ivory in a village, and leaving the safari with plenty of rations, I left for a few days' hunting, taking a sufficient number of porters to bring home any ivory we were likely to get. This was necessary at this time as the natives did not yet follow me in hundreds wherever I went, as they did later on.

We trekked hard for three days and came once more in sight of the Debasien range, but on its other side. On the night of the third day the rains burst upon us. The light calico bush tents were hastily erected in a perfect gale and downpour. Even Pyjalé had to shelter.

In the morning Pyjalé said we were certain to see elephant if we could only cross a river which lay ahead of us. When we reached its banks it was a raging torrent, red with mud and covered with patches of white froth. There was nothing for it but to camp and wait until the spate subsided.

While this was being done I saw a snake being carried down by the swollen river. Then I saw another and another. Evidently banks were being washed away somewhere.

A boy pointed to my shorts and said that a doodoo (insect) had crawled up the inside of one of my legs. Thinking, perhaps, it was a fly, or not thinking at all, perhaps, I slapped my leg hard with open hand and got a most frightful sting, while a huge scorpion dropped half crushed to the ground. But not before he had injected quite sufficient poison into me. "Insect," indeed! how I cursed that boy. And then, by way of helping me, he said that when people were stung by these big black scorpions—like mine—they always died. He was in a frightful state. And then another fool boy said: "Yes, no one ever recovered from that kind." I shouted for whisky, for you certainly could feel the poison going through the circulation. I knew that what the boys said was bunkum, but still I drank a lot of whisky. My leg swelled and I could not sleep that night, but I was quite all right next day.

The river had gone down somewhat, so I proposed to cross. No one was very eager to go across with a rope. A rope was necessary, as some of the boys could not swim and the current was running too strong for them to walk across the bottom under water, carrying stones to keep them down, as they usually did.

I carried at that time a Mexican raw hide lariat and thought that this stretched across would do nicely for the boys to haul themselves over by. So I took one end to the other side and made it fast, when the safari began to come over. Once the plunge had been taken I found that more of them could swim than they had led me to believe. Then the inevitable—when raw hide gets wet—happened and the rope parted. As luck would have it there was a boy about mid-stream at the instant. The slippery end slid through his fingers and he went rapidly down-stream. His head kept going under and reappearing I noticed, but thought that, as he had a smile on his face each time he came up, he was another humbug pretending to be unable to swim. His friends, who knew perfectly well that he could not swim a yard, said, of course, not a word. And it was not until he gushed water at the mouth instead of air that I realised he was drowning. I ran down the bank while another boy plunged in at the crossing place. I reached the boy first by a second and we soon had him towing to bank. Black men are good to save, they never seem to realise their close call and do not clutch and try to climb out on you. While towing to the bank I felt something on my head and put up a hand to brush it off. Horrors, a snake! It was merely trying to save itself on anything above water level, but I did not realise this. Whenever I knocked it off it seemed to come again. Luckily we just then reached the bank or in another instant I would have abandoned my drowning porter to save myself from that beastly serpent. It was all very silly, and the snake was nearly at its last gasp, but I did not see the humour at the moment. Needless to say, the boy was perfectly all right in ten minutes after vomiting up a bucket or two of water.

While we were getting ready again for the march we heard elephant. To my inexperienced ear the sound seemed to come from some bush 400 yds. or 500 yds. away. But Pyjalé said, to my astonishment, that they were a long way off and that unless we hurried we should not see them before sundown. As the sun then indicated about one o'clock, I thought he was wrong. But he was not; for it was half an hour from sunset when we saw them, still far away. I remember looking industriously about all those miles expecting momentarily to see elephant, while Pyjalé soaked along ahead of me without a glance aside. The only explanation of this extraordinary sound-carrying that has ever occurred to me is humidity of atmosphere. During the dry season the earth becomes so hot that when the first rains fall much is evaporated in steam and the humidity is remarkable.

Here we were face to face with such a gathering of elephant as I had never dared to dream of even. The whole country was black with them, and what lay beyond them one could not see as the country was dead flat. Some of them were up to their knees in water, and when we reached their tracks the going became very bad. The water was so opaque with mud as to quite hide the huge pot-holes made by the heavy animals. You were in and out the whole time. As we drew nearer I thought that we ought to go decently and quietly, at any rate make some pretence of stalking them, if only out of respect to them. But no, that awful Pyjalé rushed me, splashing and squelching right up to them. He was awfully good, and I began to learn a lot from him. He treated elephant with complete indifference. If he were moved at all, and that was seldom, he would smile.

I was for treating them as dangerous animals, especially when we trod on the heels of small bogged-down calves and their mothers came rushing back at us in the most alarming fashion, but Pyjalé would have none of it. Up to the big bulls would he have me go, even if we had to go under infuriated cows. He made me kill seven before sundown stopped the bloodshed.

With great difficulty we found a spot a little higher than the surrounding country and fairly dry. As usual at these flood times the little island was crawling with ants of every description. How comes it that ants do not drown, although they cannot swim? They appear to be covered with something which repels water.

Scorpions and all kinds of other horrors were there also. One of the boys was bitten and made a fearful fuss all night about it.

I expected to do well on the morrow, but when it came, behold, not an elephant in sight. Such are the surprises of elephant hunting. Yesterday when light failed hundreds upon hundreds in sight and now an empty wilderness.

We had not alarmed them, as I noticed that when a shot was fired only the animals in the vicinity ran and that for a short distance only. There were too many to stampede even had they been familiar with firearms. And the noise was such as to drown the crack of a 303 almost immediately.

I asked Pyjalé what he thought about it. He said that at the beginning of the rains elephant wandered all over the country. You could never tell where they might be. With water and mud and green food springing up everywhere they were under no necessity to frequent any one district more than another. Pyjalé's advice was to get the ivory out and take it home, and then he would show me a country where we were certain to get big bulls. Accordingly the boys set about chopping out while I went for a cruise around to make certain there was nothing about.

I saw nothing but ostrich, giraffe and great herds of common and Topi haartebeeste. On crossing some black-cotton soil I noticed that it clung to the boots in a very tiresome way. Each time you lifted a foot, 10 lb. or 15 lb. of sticky mud came with it. At this stage the ground was still dry underneath, only the top few inches being wet. From the big lumps lying about where antelope had passed it was obvious that they had, too, the same trouble as I was having, i.e., mud clinging to the feet.

But on watching Pyjalé it appeared that it did not stick to naked human feet to anything like the same extent. Pyjalé told me, and I afterwards saw it actually done, that it was possible to run down ostrich and the heavy antelope, such as eland, when the ground was in this state.

Returning we found the boys well on with their chopping out. Towards evening we started for home, being much troubled with swollen rivers. Most of the boys walked through the rivers when we could find a place where the current was not too strong. The heavy tusks, of course, kept them on the bottom. But it was a curious sight to see them calmly marching in deeper and deeper until their heads went right under, reappearing again close to the other bank. Of course, the distance they thus traversed was only a few yards, but for fellows who cannot swim it was not bad.

One camp from home (the safari) we slept near some flooded wells. The boys took their tusks to scrub them with sand and water, the better to make an appearance on the morrow when we should rejoin the safari. This is always a source of joy to Wanyamwezi, to carry ivory to the base. When allowed to do so they will spend hours dancing and singing their way into the camp. The women turn out, everybody makes a noise of some kind, from blowing a reed pipe, to trumpeting on a water buck horn or beating a drum or a tin, in fact anything so that it produces noise.

While they were scrubbing the tusks one of these slipped from the boy's hands into a well. I heard of it and went to see what could be done. To test the depth I tried one of Pyjalé's 9 ft. spears. No good. Then I tied another to it, but even then I could not touch bottom. Pyjalé said the bottom was very far. Then I looked at one of my boys squatting on the edge of the well. He had been a coast canoe-man shark-fisher—than whom no finer watermen exist—and knew what I meant without a word passing. He tied his cloth between his legs and stripped his upper body. Then jumping into the air he twisted half round and went down head first into the very middle of the well. It seemed ages before his head reappeared. At last it did so, but only for an instant. Down again; apparently he had not found it the first time. After another long wait he came up with the tusk and swimming or treading water. Eager hands clutched the tusk and drew it out, the boy crawled out himself. This particular tusk weighed 65 lb., the length being almost the diameter of the well, so it had to be brought up end on. How he did it I cannot imagine. The water was the colour of pea-soup, and a scrubbed tusk is like a greasy pole to hold. Of course, it would not weigh 65 lb. when submerged, but it was a pretty good effort I thought. I know I would not have gone 20 ft. or 30 ft. down that well for any number of tusks.

These boys have the most extraordinary lungs. I once sent one of them down to disentangle the anchor of a motor launch, which had got foul of something. There were about four fathoms of chain and the boy went down this hand over hand. I only wanted him to clear the anchor, when we would heave it up in the ordinary way. But presently up the chain came the boy and the anchor.

On the morrow we entered Bukora again, with fourteen fine white tusks. We had a great reception at our camp. The natives, too, were rather astonished at our rapid success. Pyjalé stalked along without any show of feeling.

The boys who had stayed behind had nothing to report except the loss of three of our sheep by theft. Now it was essential to nip this kind of thing in the bud. I did nothing that day, merely sending Pyjalé to his home with a handsome present. I knew he would put it round as to the kind of people we were. Natives always exaggerate enormously when back from a scurry in the bush, and his account of our doings would probably have made me blush had I heard it.

Next day when Pyjalé came with a pot of fresh cow's milk as a present, I asked him if he had heard anything about our sheep. He said no. I asked him to point me out the village which had stolen them. He said they would kill him if he did so. Therefore he knew. I then said that he need not go with me, if only he would indicate it. He said the village with the three tamarind trees was where the thieves lived.

I went over quietly, as if looking for guinea-fowl, in the evening. The village was quite close to our camp. When their stock began to come in I signalled up some boys. We walked up deliberately to the herds, no one taking any great notice of us. I separated out a mob of sheep and goats and we started driving them towards camp, but very quietly and calmly. It is wonderful how imitative Africans are. If you are excited they at once become so. If you are calm and deliberate, so are they.

A more dramatic thing would have been to take the cattle. But these native cattle are not used to boys wearing clothes, as mine did, and we found at Mani-Mani that they became excited and difficult to handle unless they see their black naked owners about. Pyjalé I had carefully left out of this business.

As soon as our object dawned upon the Karamojans there was the usual commotion. Women wha! wha! wha-ed while rushing from the huts with shields; warriors seized these and rushed with prodigious speed directly away from us; while we pushed our two or three hundred hostages slowly along.

Arrived at camp we just managed to squeeze them all into the bullock boma. There were noises all round us now. The boys were uneasy; there is always something in the alarm note when issued by hundreds of human throats. Dark was soon on us and we sat up by the camp fires till fairly late. Nothing happened, as I anticipated. Discretion had won. They hated that little bom-bom so.

What I wanted now was that they should come. I wanted to tell them why I had taken their sheep. No one appeared, but I consoled myself with the thought that they jolly well knew why I had taken them.

Presently there appeared to be great signs of activity in one of the nearer villages. Native men kept coming from all directions. My boys were all eyes for this, to them, impending attack. I thought they must be born fools to try anything of that sort in broad daylight. Night was their best chance.

Pyjalé had been absent, so I hoped that he was at the meeting. Presently he appeared. He said they had had a discussion and had concluded not to attack us. I told him to go straight back and invite them all to come; I wanted to be attacked. And moreover, if my sheep were not instantly brought I would proceed to kill the hostage sheep we held, and that then I would proceed to hunt the thieves.

This acted like magic; I suppose they thought that as I had known the village of the thieves, I also probably knew the actual men themselves. Our sheep were very soon brought and the hostages released.

I took the opportunity when the natives were there to impress upon them that we did not want anything from them. All we wanted was to hunt elephant in peace, but at the same time I hinted that we could be very terrible indeed. I got some of the older men to dry up and sit down, in a friendly way, and we had a good talk together. I now brought out the card to which I owed all my success in killing elephant in Karamojo. I offered a cow as reward for information leading to my killing five or more bull elephant. This was an unheard of reward. There a cow of breeding age is simply priceless. Normally natives never kill or sell she-stock of any kind and cows could only be obtained by successful raiding. Now among Africans there are numbers of young men who just lack the quality which brings success to its lucky owner, just as there are in every community, and to these young men my offer appealed tremendously. That they believed in my promise from the very start was, I thought, a great compliment, not only to me, but to their astuteness in perceiving that there was a difference between white men and Swahilis.

When my offer had gone the rounds the whole country for many miles round was scoured for elephant, with the result that I never could have a day's rest. Everyone was looking for elephant. But had the reward been trade goods scarcely a soul would have bothered about it.

The first man to come was remarkable looking enough to satisfy anybody. A terrible looking man. A grotesquely hideous face above a very broad and deep chest, all mounted on the spindliest of knock-kneed legs. Chest, arms, shoulders, stomach and back heavily tattooed, denoting much killing. By reputation a terrific fighter, and very wealthy.

At first I thought that he was come to show me elephant. That was his intention, he said, but first he wanted to become my blood-brother. He said he could see that I was a kindred spirit and that we two should be friends. He said he had no friends. How was that? I asked. Pyjalé answered in a whisper that the lion never made friends of jackals and hyenas. And so we became friends. I was not going through the blood-brotherhood business, with its eating of bits of toasted meat smeared with each other's blood, sawing in two of living dogs or nonsense of that kind. I took his hand and wrung it hard, and had it explained to him that among us that was an extraordinarily potent way of doing it. That seemed to satisfy the old boy, for the act of shaking hands was as strange to him as the act of eating each other's blood is to us.

He started off then and I said: "What about those elephant?" "Wait," was the answer, and off he went, to return shortly with a fat bullock. And then I found that my friend was the wealthiest cattle owner anywhere about—a kind of multi-millionaire. I thought to myself, well, he will not look for elephant. Nor did he; but he had sons without number, being much married, whom he scattered far and wide to look for them. He had arranged the thing most perfectly. We went with food for a few days and returned laden with ivory. Besides which we had some of the jolliest nights in the bush.

This great man being now my friend, our troubles were at an end. Wherever we went we were followed by scores of the young unmarried girls and one old maid—the only one I have come across in Karamojo. She was so outstandingly above the average in good looks, so beautifully made and so obviously still quite young, that I often asked why she should remain a spinster. They told me that no man would marry her because she was so beautiful. But why should that be a bar? We white men like our wives to be beautiful. They thought this strange, even for white men. They said they never married very beautiful women as all men wanted them. They also gave as another reason that these very attractive women wanted all men. And I must say that our camp beauty gave decided colour to this latter statement.

No sooner were we arrived back with our imposing line of beautiful tusks than other natives clamoured to take us to elephant. They wanted me to go there and then, but I needed a rest.

In the evening I presented my friend with a heifer, when to my astonishment he refused it. He said he wanted nothing from his friend. I was rather suspicious about this at first, but I need not have been, as I subsequently found this man to be thoroughly genuine. I am convinced that he would have given me anything. It is a big affair in their lives, this blood-brotherhood. Apparently we now owned everything in common. He offered me any of his daughters in marriage, and, thank goodness, never asked me for my rifle. From now on he followed me about like a faithful dog, some of his young wives attending to his commissariat arrangements wherever he was. He even took my name, which was Longelly-nyung or Red Man. And he began now to call his young male children, of whom he was very fond, by the same name. He was a delightfully simple fellow at heart and as courageous as a lion, as I had proof later.

After a few more journeys to the bush lasting from four to ten days, I found suddenly that I had as much ivory as I could possibly move. And this, while still on the fringe of Karamojo. I decided to return to Mumias, sell my ivory, fit out a real good expedition capable of moving several tons of ivory, and return to Karamojo fitted out for several years in the bush.

CHAPTER 18

THE THAK MAN-EATER

By Jim Corbett

Peace had reigned in the Ladhya valley for many months when in September '38 a report was received in Naini Tal that a girl, twelve years of age, had been killed by a tiger at Kot Kindri village. The report, which reached me through Donald Stewart, of the Forest Department, gave no details, and it was not until I visited the village some weeks later that I was able to get particulars of the tragedy. It appeared that, about noon one day, this girl was picking up windfalls from a mango tree close to and in full view of the village, when a tiger suddenly appeared. Before the men working near by were able to render any assistance, it carried her off. No attempt was made to follow up the tiger, and as all signs of drag and blood trail had been obliterated and washed away long before I arrived on the scene, I was unable to find the place where the tiger had taken the body to.

Kot Kindri is about four miles southwest of Chuka, and three miles due west of Thak. It was in the valley between Kot Kindri and Thak that the Chuka man-eater had been shot the previous April.

My most direct route to Kot Kindri was to go by rail to Tanakpur, and from there by foot via Kaldhunga and Chuka. This route, however, though it would save me a hundred miles of walking, would necessitate my passing through the most deadly malaria belt in northern India, and to avoid it I decided to go through the hills to Mornaula, and from there along the abandoned Sherring road to its termination on the ridge above Kot Kindri.

While my preparations for this long trek were still under way a second report reached Naini Tal of a kill at Sem, a small village on the left bank of the Ladhya and distant about half a mile from Chuka.

The victim on this occasion was an elderly woman, the mother of the Headman of Sem. This unfortunate woman had been killed while cutting brushwood on a steep bank between two terraced fields. She had started work at the further end of the fifty-yard-long bank, and had cut the brushwood to within a yard of her hut when the tiger sprang on her from the field above. So sudden and unexpected was the attack that the woman only had time to scream once before the tiger killed her, and taking her up the twelve-foot-high bank crossed the upper field and disappeared with her into the dense jungle beyond. Her son, a lad some twenty years of age, was at the time working in a paddy field a few yards away and witnessed the whole occurrence, but was too frightened to try to render any assistance. In response to the lad's urgent summons the Patwari arrived at Sem two days later, accompanied by eighty men he had collected. Following up in the direction the tiger had gone, he found the woman's clothes and a few small bits of bone. This kill had taken place at 2 p.m. on a bright sunny day, and the tiger had eaten its victim only sixty yards from the hut where it had killed her.

On receipt of this second report, Ibbotson, Deputy Commissioner of the three Districts of Almora. Naini Tal, and Gathwal, and I held a council of war, the upshot of which was that Ibbotson, who was on the point of setting out to settle a land dispute at Askot on the border of Tibet, changed his tour program and, instead of going via Bagashwar, decided to accompany me to Sem, and from there go on to Askot.

The route I had selected entailed a considerable amount of hill-climbing so we eventually decided to go up the Nandhour valley, cross the watershed between the Nandhour and Ladhya, and follow the latter river down to Sem. The Ibbotsons accordingly left Naini Tal on 12 October, and the following day I joined them at Chaurgallia.

Going up the Nandhour and fishing as we went—our best day's catch on light trout rods was a hundred and twenty fish—we arrived on the fifth day at Durga Pepal. Here we left the river, and after a very stiff climb camped for the night on the watershed. Making an early start next morning we pitched our tents that night on the left bank of the Ladhya, twelve miles from Chalti.

The monsoon had given over early, which was very fortunate for us, for owing to the rock cliffs that run sheer down into the valley, the river has to be crossed every quarter of a mile or so. At one of these fords my cook, who stands five feet in his boots, was washed away and only saved from a watery grave by the prompt assistance of the man who was carrying our lunch basket.

On the tenth day after leaving Chaurgallia we made camp on a deserted field at Sem, two hundred yards from the hut where the woman had been killed, and a hundred yards from the junction of the Ladhya and Sarda Rivers.

Gill Waddell, of the Police, whom we met on our way down the Ladhya, had camped for several days at Sem and had tied out a buffalo that MacDonald of the Forest Department had very kindly placed at our disposal; and though the tiger had visited Sem several times during Waddell's stay, it had not killed the buffalo.

The day following our arrival at Sem, while Ibbotson was interviewing Patwaris, Forest Guards, and Headmen of the surrounding villages, I went out to look for pug marks. Between our camp and the junction, and also on both banks of the Ladhya, there were long stretches of sand. On this sand I found the tracks of a tigress, and of a young male tiger—possibly one of the cubs I had seen in April. The tigress had crossed and recrossed the Ladhya a number of times during the last few days, and the previous night had walked along the strip of sand in front of our tents. It was this tigress the villagers suspected of being the man-eater, and as she had visited Sem repeatedly since the day the Headman's mother had been killed they were probably correct.

An examination of the pug marks of the tigress showed her as being an average-sized animal, in the prime of life. Why she had become a man-eater would have to be determined later, but one of the reasons might have been that she had assisted to eat the victims of the Chuka tiger when they were together the previous mating season, and having acquired a taste for human flesh and no longer having a mate to provide her with it, had now turned a man-eater herself. This was only a surmise, and proved later to be incorrect.

Before leaving Naini Tal I had written to the Tahsildar of Tanakpur and asked him to purchase four young male buffaloes for me, and to send them to Sem. One of these buffaloes died on the road, the other three arrived on the 24th, and we tied them out the same evening together with the one MacDonald had given us. On going out to visit these animals next morning I found the people of Chuka in a great state of excitement. The fields round the village had been recently plowed, and the tigress the previous night had passed close to three families who were sleeping out on the fields with their cattle; fortunately in each case the cattle had seen the tigress and warned the sleepers of her approach. After leaving the cultivated land the tigress had gone up the track in the direction of Kot Kindri, and had passed close to two of our buffaloes without touching either of them.

The Patwari, Forest Guards, and villagers had told us on our arrival at Sem that it would be a waste of time tying out our young buffaloes, as they were convinced the man-eater would not kill them. The reason they gave was that this method of trying to shoot the man-eater had been tried by others without success, and that in any case if the tigress wanted to eat buffaloes there were many grazing in the jungles for her to choose from. In spite of this advice, however, we continued to tie out our buffaloes, and for the next two nights the tigress passed close to one or more of them, without touching them.

On the morning of the 27th, just as we were finishing breakfast, a party of men led by Tewari, the brother of the Headman of Thak, arrived in camp and reported that a man of their village was missing. They stated that this man had left the village at about noon the previous day, telling his wife before leaving that he was going to see that his cattle did not stray beyond the village boundary, and as he had not returned they feared he had been killed by the man-eater.

Our preparations were soon made, and at ten o'clock the Ibbotsons and I set off for Thak, accompanied by Tewari and the men he had brought with him. The distance was only about two miles but the climb was considerable, and as we did not want to lose more time than we could possibly help we arrived at the outskirts of the village out of breath and in a lather of sweat.

As we approached the village over the scrub-covered flat bit of ground which I have reason to refer to later, we heard a woman crying. The wailing of an Indian woman mourning her dead is unmistakable, and on emerging from the jungle we came on the mourner—the wife of the missing man—and some ten or fifteen men, who were waiting for us on the edge of the cultivated land. These people informed us that from their houses above they had seen some white object, which looked like part of the missing man's clothing, in a field overgrown with scrub thirty yards from where we were now standing. Ibbotson, Tewari, and I set off to investigate the white object, while Mrs. Ibbotson took the woman and the rest of the men up to the village.

The field, which had been out of cultivation for some years, was covered with a dense growth of scrub not unlike chrysanthemum, and it was not until we were standing right over the white object that Tewari recognized it as the loincloth of the missing man. Near it was the man's cap. A struggle had taken place at this spot, but there was no blood. The absence of blood where the attack had taken place and for some considerable distance along the drag could be accounted for by the tigress's having retained her first hold, for no blood would flow in such a case until the hold had been changed.

Thirty yards on the hill above us there was a clump of bushes roofed over with creepers. This spot would have to be looked at before following up the drag, for it was not advisable to have the tigress behind us. In the soft earth under the bushes we found the pug marks of the tigress, and where she had lain before going forward to attack the man.

Returning to our starting point we agreed on the following plan of action. Our primary object was to try to stalk the tigress and shoot her on her kill: to achieve this end I was to follow the trail and at the same time keep a lookout in front, with Tewari—who was unarmed—a yard behind me keeping a sharp lookout to right and left, and Ibbotson a yard behind Tewari to safeguard us against an attack from the rear. In the event of either Ibbotson or I seeing so much as a hair of the tigress, we were to risk a shot.

Cattle had grazed over this area the previous day, disturbing the ground, and as there was no blood and the only indication of the tigress's passage was an occasional turned-up leaf or crushed blade of grass, progress was slow. After carrying the man for two hundred yards the tigress had killed and left him, and had returned and carried him off several hours later, when the people of Thak had heard several sambur calling in this direction. The reason for the tigress's not having carried the man away after she had killed him was possibly because his cattle may have witnessed the attack on him, and driven her away.

A big pool of blood had formed where the man had been lying, and as the blood from the wound in his throat had stopped flowing by the time the tigress had picked him up again, and further, as she was now holding him by the small of the back, whereas she had previously held him by the neck, tracking became even more difficult. The tigress kept to the contour of the hill, and as the undergrowth here was very dense and visibility only extended to a few yards, our advance was slowed down. In two hours we covered half a mile, and reached a ridge beyond which lay the valley in which, six months previously, we had tracked down and killed the Chuka man-eater. On this ridge was a great slab of rock, which sloped upwards and away from the direction in which we had come. The tigress's tracks went down to the right of the rock and I felt sure she was lying up under the overhanging portion of it, or in the close vicinity.

Both Ibbotson and I had on light rubber-soled shoes—Tewari was bare-footed—and we had reached the rock without making a sound. Signing to my two companions to stand still and keep a careful watch all round, I got a foothold on the rock, and inch by inch went forward. Beyond the rock was a short stretch of flat ground, and as more of this ground came into view, I felt certain my suspicion that the tigress was lying under the projection was correct. I had still a foot or two to go before I could look over, when I saw a movement to my left front. A goldenrod that had been pressed down had sprung erect, and a second later there was a slight movement in the bushes beyond, and a monkey in a tree on the far side off the bushes started calling.

The tigress had chosen the spot for her after-dinner sleep with great care, but unfortunately for us she was not asleep; and when she saw the top of my head—I had removed my hat—appearing over the rock, she had risen and taking a step sideways, had disappeared under a tangle of blackberry bushes. Had she been lying anywhere but where she was she could not have got away, no matter how quickly she had moved, without my getting a shot at her. Our so-carefully-carried-out stalk had failed at the very last moment, and there was nothing to be done now but find the kill, and see if there was sufficient of it left for us to sit up over. To have followed her into the blackberry thicket would have been useless, and would also have reduced our chance of getting a shot at her later.

The tigress had eaten her meal close to where she had been lying, and as this spot was open to the sky and to the keen eyes of vultures she had removed the kill to a place of safety where it would not be visible from the air. Track-

ing now was easy, for there was a
blood trail to follow. The trail led
over a ridge of great rocks and fifty
yards beyond these rocks we found
the kill.

I am not going to harrow your
feelings by attempting to describe
that poor torn and mangled thing;
stripped of every stitch of clothing and atom of dignity, which only a few
hours previously had been a Man, the father of two children and the bread-
winner of that wailing woman who was facing—without any illusions—the
fate of a widow of India. I have seen many similar sights, each more terrible than the one preceding it, in the thirty-two years I have been hunting
man-eaters, and on each occasion I have felt that it would have been better to
have left the victim to the slayer than recover a mangled mass of flesh to be a
nightmare ever after to those who saw it. And yet the cry of blood for blood,
and the burning desire to rid a countryside of a menace than which there is
none more terrible, is irresistible; and then there is always the hope, no matter
how absurd one knows it to be, that the victim by some miracle may still be
alive and in need of succour.

The chance of shooting—over a kill—an animal that has in all probability become a man-eater through a wound received over a kill, is very remote,
and each succeeding failure, no matter what its cause, tends to make the animal more cautious, until it reaches a state when it either abandons its kill after
one meal or approaches it as silently and as slowly as a shadow, scanning every
leaf and twig with the certainty of discovering its would-be slayer, no matter
how carefully he may be concealed or how silent and motionless he may be;
a one in a million chance of getting a shot, and yet, who is there among us
who would not take it?

The thicket into which the tigress had retired was roughly forty
yards square, and she could not leave it without the monkey's seeing her
and warning us, so we sat down back to back, to have a smoke and listen

if the jungle had anything further to tell us while we considered our next move.

To make a machan it was necessary to return to the village, and during our absence the tigress was almost certain to carry away the kill. It had been difficult to track her when she was carrying a whole human being, but now, when her burden was considerably lighter and she had been disturbed, she would probably go for miles and we might never find her kill again, so it was necessary for one of us to remain on the spot, while the other two went back to the village for ropes.

Ibbotson, with his usual disregard for danger, elected to go back, and while he and Tewari went down the hill to avoid the difficult ground we had recently come over, I stepped up onto a small tree close to the kill. Four feet above ground the tree divided in two, and by leaning on one half and putting my feet against the other, I was able to maintain a precarious seat which was high enough off the ground to enable me to see the tigress if she approached the kill, and also high enough, if she had any designs on me, to see her before she got to within striking distance.

Ibbotson had been gone fifteen or twenty minutes when I heard a rock tilt forward, and then back. The rock was evidently very delicately poised, and when the tigress had put her weight on it and felt it tilt forward she had removed her foot and let the rock fall back into place. The sound had come from about twenty yards to my left front, the only direction in which it would have been possible for me to have fired without being knocked out of the tree.

Minutes passed, each pulling my hopes down a little lower from the heights to which they had soared, and then, when tension on my nerves and the weight of the heavy rifle were becoming unbearable, I heard a stick snap at the upper end of the thicket. Here was an example of how a tiger can move through the jungle. From the sound she had made I knew her exact position, had kept my eyes fixed on the spot, and yet she had come, seen me, stayed some time watching me, and then gone away without my having seen a leaf or a blade of grass move.

When tension on nerves is suddenly relaxed, cramped and aching muscles call loudly for ease, and though in this case it only meant the lowering of the rifle onto my knees to take the strain off my shoulders and arms, the movement, small though it was, sent a comforting feeling through the whole of my body. No further sound came from the tigress, and an hour or two later I heard Ibbotson returning.

Of all the men I have been on shikar with, Ibbotson is by far and away the best, for not only has he the heart of a lion, but he thinks of everything, and with it all is the most unselfish man that carries a gun. He had gone to fetch a rope and he returned with rugs, cushions, more hot tea than even I could drink, and an ample lunch; and while I sat—on the windward side of the kill—to refresh myself, Ibbotson put a man in a tree forty yards away to distract the tigress's attention, and climbed into a tree overlooking the kill to make a rope machan.

When the machan was ready Ibbotson moved the kill a few feet—a very unpleasant job—and tied it securely to the foot of a sapling to prevent the tigress's carrying it away, for the moon was on the wane and the first two hours of the night at this heavily wooded spot would be pitch dark. After a final smoke I climbed onto the machan, and when I had made myself comfortable Ibbotson recovered the man who was making a diversion and set off in the direction of Thak to pick up Mrs. Ibbotson and return to camp at Sem.

The retreating party were out of sight but were not yet out of sound when I heard a heavy body brushing against leaves, and at the same moment the monkey, which had been silent all this time and which I could now see sitting in a tree on the far side of the blackberry thicket, started calling. Here was more luck than I had hoped for, and our ruse of putting a man up a tree to cause a diversion appeared to be working as successfully as it had done on a previous occasion. A tense minute passed, a second, and a third, and then from the ridge where I had climbed onto the big slab of rock a kakar came dashing down towards me, barking hysterically. The tigress was not coming to the kill but had gone off after Ibbotson. I was now in a fever of anxiety, for it was quite evident that she had abandoned her kill and gone to try to secure another victim.

Before leaving, Ibbotson had promised to take every precaution, but on hearing the kakar barking on my side of the ridge he would naturally assume the tigress was moving in the vicinity of the kill, and if he relaxed his precautions the tigress would get her chance. Ten very uneasy minutes for me passed, and then I heard a second kakar barking in the direction of Thak; the tigress was still following, but the ground there was more open, and there was less fear of her attacking the party. The danger to the Ibbotsons was, however, not over by any means for they had to go through two miles of very heavy jungle to reach camp; and if they stayed at Thak until sundown listening for my shot, which I feared they would do and which as a matter of fact they did do, they would run a very grave risk on the way down. Ibbotson fortunately realized the danger and kept his party close together, and though the tigress followed them the whole way—as her pug marks the following morning showed—they got back to camp safely.

The calling of kakar and sambur enabled me to follow the movements of the tigress. An hour after sunset she was down at the bottom of the valley two miles away. She had the whole night before her, and though there was only one chance in a million of her returning to the kill I determined not to lose that chance. Wrapping a rug around me, for it was a bitterly cold night, I made myself comfortable in a position in which I could remain for hours without movement.

I had taken my seat on the machan at 4 p.m., and at 10 p.m. I heard two animals coming down the hill towards me. It was too dark under the trees to see them, but when they got to the lee of the kill I knew they were porcupines. Rattling their quills, and making the peculiar booming noise that only a porcupine can make, they approached the kill and, after walking round it several times, continued on their way. An hour later, and when the moon had been up some time, I heard an animal in the valley below. It was moving from east to west, and when it came into the wind blowing downhill from the kill it made a long pause, and then came cautiously up the hill. While it was still some distance away I heard it snuffing the air, and knew it to be a bear. The smell of blood was attracting him, but mingled with it was the less welcome smell of a human being, and taking no chances he was very carefully stalking the kill. His nose, the keenest of any animal's in the jungle, had apprised him while he was still in the valley that the kill was the property of a tiger. This to a Himalayan bear who fears nothing, and who will, as I have on several occasions seen, drive a tiger away from its kill, was no deterrent, but what was, and what was causing him uneasiness, was the smell of a human being mingled with the smell of blood and tiger.

On reaching the flat ground the bear sat down on his haunches a few yards from the kill, and when he had satisfied himself that the hated human smell held no danger for him he stood erect and turning his head sent a long-drawn-out cry, which I interpreted as a call to a mate, echoing down into the valley. Then without any further hesitation he walked boldly up to the kill, and as he noted it I aligned the sights of my rifle on him. I know of only one instance of a Himalayan bear eating a human being; on that occasion a woman cutting grass had fallen down a cliff and been killed, and a bear finding the mangled body had carried it away and had eaten it. This bear, however, on whose shoulder my sights were aligned, appeared to draw the line at human flesh, and after looking at and smelling the kill continued his interrupted course to the west. When the sounds of his retreat died away in the distance the jungle settled down to silence until interrupted, a little after sunrise, by Ibbotson's very welcome arrival.

With Ibbotson came the brother and other relatives of the dead man, who very reverently wrapped the remains in a clean white cloth and, laying it on a cradle made of two saplings and rope which Ibbotson provided, set off for the burning that on the banks of the Sarda, repeating under their breath as they went the Hindu hymn of praise 'Ram nam sat hai' with its refrain, 'Satya bol gat hai.'

Fourteen hours in the cold had not been without its effect on me, but after partaking of the hot drink and food Ibbotson had brought, I felt none the worse for my long vigil.

II.

After following the Ibbotsons down to Chuka on the evening of the 27th, the tigress, sometime during the night, crossed the Ladhya into the scrub jungle at the back of our camp. Through this scrub ran a path that had been regularly used by the villagers of the Ladhya valley until the advent of the man-eater had rendered its passage unsafe. On the 28th the two mail-runners who carried Ibbotson's dak on its first stage to Tanakpur got delayed in camp, and to save time took, or more correctly started to take, a short cut through this scrub. Very fortunately the leading man was on the alert and saw the tigress as she crept through the scrub and lay down near the path ahead of them.

Ibbotson and I had just got back from Thak when these two men dashed into camp, and taking our rifles we hurried off to investigate. We found the pug marks of the tigress where she had come out on the path and followed the men for a short distance, but we did not see her, though in one place where the scrub was very dense we saw a movement and heard an animal moving off.

On the morning of the 29th, a party of men came down from Thak to report that one of their bullocks had not returned to the cattle-shed the previous night, and on a search being made where it had last been seen a little blood had been found. At 2 p.m. the Ibbotsons and I were at this spot, and a glance at the ground satisfied us that the bullock had been killed and carried away by a tiger. After a hasty lunch Ibbotson and I, with two men following carrying ropes for a machan, set out along the drag. It went diagonally across the face of the hill for a hundred yards and then straight down into the ravine in which I had fired at and missed the big tiger in April. A few hundred yards down this ravine the bullock, which was an enormous animal, had got fixed between two rocks and, not being able to move it, the tiger had eaten a meal off its hind quarters and left it.

The pug marks of the tiger, owing to the great weight she was carrying, were splayed out and it was not possible to say whether she was the man-eater or not; but as every tiger in this area was suspect I decided to sit up over the kill. There was only one tree within reasonable distance of the kill, and as the men climbed into it to make a machan the tiger started calling in the valley below. Very hurriedly a few strands of rope were tied between two branches, and while Ibbotson stood on guard with his rifle I climbed the tree and took my seat on what, during the next fourteen hours, proved to be the most uncomfortable as well as the most dangerous machan I have ever sat on. The tree was leaning away from the hill, and from the three uneven strands of rope I was sitting on there was a drop of over a hundred feet into the rocky ravine below.

The tiger called several times as I was getting into the tree and continued to call at longer intervals late into the evening, the last call coming from a ridge half a mile away. It was now quite evident that the tiger had been lying up close to the kill and had seen the men climbing into the tree. Knowing from past experience what this meant, she had duly expressed resentment at being disturbed and then gone away, for though I sat on the three strands of rope until Ibbotson returned next morning, I did not see or hear anything throughout the night.

Vultures were not likely to find the kill, for the ravine was deep and overshadowed by trees, and as the bullock was large enough to provide the tiger with several meals we decided not to sit up over it again where it was now lying, hoping the tiger would remove it to some more convenient place where we should have a better chance of getting a shot. In this, however, we were disappointed, for the tiger did not again return to the kill.

Two nights later the buffalo we had tied out behind our camp at Sem was killed, and through a little want of observation on my part a great opportunity of bagging the man-eater was lost.

The men who brought in the news of this kill reported that the rope securing the animal had been broken, and that the kill had been carried away up the ravine at the lower end of which it had been tied. This was the same ravine in which MacDonald and I had chased a tigress in April, and as on that occasion she had taken her kill some distance up the ravine I now very foolishly concluded she had done the same with this kill.

After breakfast Ibbotson and I went out to find the kill and see what prospect there was for an evening sit-up.

The ravine in which the buffalo had been killed was about fifty yards wide and ran deep into the foothills. For two hundred yards the ravine was straight, and then bent round to the left. Just beyond the bend, and on the left-hand side of it, there was a dense patch of young saplings backed by a hundred-foot ridge on which thick grass was growing. In the ravine, and close to the saplings, there was a small pool of water. I had been up the ravine several times in April and had failed to mark the patch of saplings as being a likely place for a tiger to lie up in, and did not take the precautions I should have taken when rounding the bend, with the result that the tigress, who was drinking at the pool, saw us first. There was only one safe line of retreat for her and she took it. This was straight up the steep hill, over the ridge, and into sal forest beyond.

The hill was too steep for us to climb, so we continued on up the ravine to where a sambur track crossed it, and following this track we gained the ridge. The tigress was now in a triangular patch of jungle bounded by the ridge, the Ladhya, and a cliff down which no animal could go. The area was not large, and there were several deer in it which from time to time advised us of the position of the tigress, but unfortunately the ground was cut up by a number of deep and narrow rain-water channels in which we eventually lost touch with her.

We had not yet seen the kill, so we re-entered the ravine by the sambur track and found the kill hidden among the saplings. These saplings were from six inches to a foot in girth, and were not strong enough to support a machan, so we had to abandon the idea of a machan. With the help of a crowbar, a rock could possibly have been pried from the face of the hill and a place made in which to sit, but this was not advisable when dealing with a man-eater.

Reluctant to give up the chance of a shot, we considered the possibility of concealing ourselves in the grass near the kill, in the hope that the tigress would return before dark and that we should see her before she saw us. There were two objections to this plan: (a) if we did not get a shot and the tigress saw us near her kill she might abandon it, as she had done her other two kills; and (b) between the kill and camp there was very heavy scrub jungle, and if we tried to go through this jungle in the dark the tigress would have us at her mercy. So very reluctantly we decided to leave the kill to the tigress for that night, and hope for the best on the morrow.

On our return next morning we found that the tigress had carried away the kill. For three hundred yards she had gone up the bed of the ravine stepping from rock to rock, and leaving no drag marks. At this spot—three hundred yards from where she had picked up the kill—we were at fault, for though there were a number of tracks on a wet patch of ground, none of them had been made while she was carrying the kill. Eventually, after casting round in circles, we found where she had left the ravine and gone up the hill on the left.

This hill up which the tigress had taken her kill was overgrown with ferns and goldenrod and tracking was not difficult, but the going was, for the hill was very steep and in places a detour had to be made and the track picked up further on. After a stiff climb of a thousand feet we came to a small plateau, bordered on the left by a cliff a mile wide. On the side of the plateau nearest the cliff the ground was seamed and cracked, and in these cracks a dense growth of sal, two to six feet in height, had sprung up. The tigress had taken her kill into this dense cover and it was not until we actually trod on it that we were aware of its position.

As we stopped to look at all that remained of the buffalo there was a low growl to our right. With rifles raised we waited for a minute and then, hearing a movement in the undergrowth a little beyond where the growl had come from, we pushed our way through the young sal for ten yards and came on a small clearing, where the tigress had made herself a bed on some soft grass. On the far side of this grass the hill sloped upwards for twenty yards to another plateau, and it was from this slope that the sound we had heard had come. Proceeding up the slope as silently as possible, we had just reached the flat ground, which was about fifty yards wide, when the tigress left the far side and went down into the ravine, disturbing some kaleege pheasants and a kakar as she did so. To have followed her would have been useless, so we went back to the kill and, as there was still a good meal on it, we selected two trees to sit in, and returned to camp.

"Hainan Silver Kaleege" by George Edward Lodge, circa 1921

After an early lunch we went back to the kill and, hampered with our rifles, climbed with some difficulty into the trees we had selected. We sat up for five hours without seeing or hearing anything. At dusk we climbed down from our trees, and stumbling over the cracked and uneven ground eventually reached the ravine when it was quite dark. Both of us had an uneasy feeling that we were being followed, but by keeping close together we reached camp without incident at 9 p.m.

The Ibbotsons had now stayed at Sem as long as it was possible for them to do so, and early next morning they set out on their twelve days' walk to keep their appointment at Askot. Before leaving, Ibbotson extracted a promise from me that I would not follow up any kills alone, or further endanger my life by prolonging my stay at Sem for more than a day or two.

After the departure of the Ibbotsons and their fifty men, the camp, which was surrounded by dense scrub, was reduced to my two servants and myself—my coolies were living in a room in the Headman's house—so throughout the day I set all hands to collecting driftwood, of which there was an inexhaustible supply at the junction, to keep a fire going all night. The fire would not scare away the tigress but it would enable us to see her if she prowled round our tents at night, and anyway the nights were setting in cold and there was ample excuse, if one were needed, for keeping a big fire going all night.

Towards evening, when my men were safely back in camp, I took a rifle and went up the Ladhya to see if he tigress had crossed the river. I found several tracks in the sand, but no fresh ones, and at dusk I returned, convinced that the tigress was still on our side of the river. An hour later, when it was quite dark, a kakar started barking close to our tents and barked persistently for half an hour.

My men had taken over the job of tying out the buffaloes, a task which Ibbotson's men had hitherto performed, and next morning I accompanied them when they went out to bring in the buffaloes. Though we covered several miles I did not find any trace of the tigress. After breakfast I took a rod and went down the junction, and had one of the best day's fishing I have ever had. The junction was full of big fish, and though my light tackle was broken frequently I killed sufficient mahseer to feed the camp.

Again, as on the previous evening, I crossed the Ladhya, with the intention of taking up a position on a rock overlooking the open ground on the right bank of the river and watching for the tigress to cross. As I got away from the roar of the water at the junction I heard a sambur and a monkey calling on the hill to my left, and as I neared the rock I came on the fresh tracks of the tigress. Following them back I found the stones still wet where she had forded the river. A few minutes' delay in camp to dry my fishing line and have a cup of tea cost a man his life, several thousand men weeks of anxiety, and myself many days of strain, for though I stayed at Sem for another three days I did not get another chance of shooting the tigress.

On the morning of the 7th, as I was breaking camp and preparing to start on my twenty-mile walk to Tanakpur, a big contingent of men from all the surrounding villages arrived, and begged me not to leave them to the tender mercies of the man-eater. Giving them what advice it was possible to give people situated as they were. I promised to return as soon as it was possible for me to do so.

I caught the train at Tanakpur next morning and arrived back in Naini Tal on 9 November, having been away nearly a month.

III.

I left Sem on the 7th of November and on the 12th the tigress killed a man at Thak. I received news of this kill through the Divisional Forest Officer, Haldwani, shortly after we had moved down to our winter home at the foot of the hills, and by doing forced marches I arrived at Chuka a little after sunrise on the 14th.

It had been my intention to breakfast at Chuka and then go on to Thak and make that village my headquarters, but the Headman of Thak, whom I found installed at Chuka, informed me that every man, woman, and child had left Thak immediately after the man had been killed on the 12th, and added that if I carried out my intention of camping at Thak I might be able to safeguard my own life, but it would not be possible to safeguard the lives of my men. This was quite reasonable, and while waiting for my men to arrive, the Headman helped me to select a site for my camp at Chuka, where my men would be reasonably safe and I should have some privacy from the thousands of men who were now arriving to fell the forest.

On receipt of the Divisional Forest Officer's telegram acquainting me of the kill, I had telegraphed to the Tahsildar at Tanakpur to send three young male buffaloes to Chuka. My request had been promptly complied with and the three animals had arrived the previous evening.

After breakfast I took one of the buffaloes and set out for Thak, intending to tie it up on the spot where the man had been killed on the 12th. The Headman had given me a very graphic account of the events of that date, for he himself had nearly fallen a victim to the tigress. It appeared that towards the

afternoon, accompanied by his granddaughter, a girl ten years of age, he had
gone to dig up ginger tubers in a field some sixty yards from his house. This
field is about half an acre in extent and is surrounded on three sides by jungle,
and being on the slope of a fairly step hill it is visible from the Headman's
house. After the old man and his granddaughter had been at work for some
time, his wife, who was husking rice in the courtyard of the house, called out
in a very agitated voice and asked him if he was deaf that he could not hear the
pheasants and other birds that were chattering in the jungle above him. Fortunately for him, he acted promptly. Dropping his hoe, he grabbed the child's
hand and together they ran back to the house, urged on by the woman who
said she could now see a red animal in the bushes at the upper end of the field.
Half an hour later the tigress killed a man who was lopping branches off a tree
in a field three hundred yards from the Headman's house.

From the description I had received from the Headman I had no difficulty in locating the tree. It was a small gnarled tree growing out of a three-

foot-high bank between two terraced fields, and had been lopped year after year for cattle fodder. The man who had been killed was standing on the trunk holding one branch and cutting another, when the tigress came up from behind, tore his hold from the branch and, after killing him, carried him away into the dense brushwood bordering the fields.

Thak village was a gift from the Chand Rajas, who ruled Kumaon for many hundreds of years before the Gurkha occupation, to the forefathers of the present owners in return for their services at the Punagiri temples. (The promise made by the Chand Rajas that the lands of Thak and two other villages would remain rent-free for all time has been honored by the British Government for a hundred years.) From a collection of grass huts the village has in the course of time grown into a very prosperous settlement with masonry houses roofed with slate tiles, for not only is the land very fertile, but the revenue from the temples is considerable.

Like all other villages in Kumaon, Thak during its hundreds of years of existence has passed through many vicissitudes, but never before in its long history had it been deserted as it now was. On my previous visits I had found it a hive of industry, but when I went up to it on this afternoon, taking the young buffalo with me, silence reigned over it. Every one of the hundred or more inhabitants had fled, taking their livestock with them—the only animal I saw in the village was a cat, which gave me a warm welcome; so hurried had the evacuation been that many of the doors of the houses had been left wide open. On every path in the village, in the courtyard of the houses, and in the dust before all the doors I found the tigress's pug marks. The open doorways were a menace, for the path as it wound through the village passed close to them, and in any of the houses the tigress may have been lurking.

On the hill thirty yards above the village were several cattle shelters, and in the vicinity of these shelters I saw more kaleege pheasants, red jungle fowl, and white-capped babblers than I have ever before seen, and from the confiding way in which they permitted me to walk among them it is quite evident that the people of Thak have a religious prejudice against the taking of life.

From the terraced fields above the cattle shelters a bird's-eye view of the village is obtained, and it was not difficult, from the description the Headman had given me, to locate the tree where the tigress had secured her last victim. In the soft earth under the tree there were signs of a struggle and a few clots of dried blood. From here the tigress had carried her kill a hundred yards over a plowed field, through a stout hedge, and into the dense brushwood beyond. The foot-prints from the village and back the way they had come showed that the entire population of the village had visited the scene of the kill, but from the tree to the hedge there was only one track, the track the tigress had made when carrying away her victim. No attempt had been made to follow her up and recover the body.

Scraping away a little earth from under the tree I exposed a root and to this root I tied my buffalo, bedding it down with a liberal supply of straw taken from a near-by haystack.

The village, which is on the north face of the hill, was now in shadow, and if I was to get back to camp before dark it was time for me to make a start. Skirting round the village to avoid the menace of the open doorways, I joined the path below the houses.

This path after it leaves the village passes under a giant mango tree from the roots of which issues a cold spring of clear water. After running along a groove cut in a massive slab of rock, this water falls into a rough masonry trough, from where it spreads onto the surrounding ground, rendering it soft and slushy. I had drunk at the spring on my way up, leaving my foot-prints in this slushy ground, and on approaching the spring now for a second drink, I found the tigress's pug marks superimposed on my foot-prints. After quenching her thirst the tigress had avoided the path and had gained the village by climbing a steep bank overgrown with strobilanthes and nettles, and taking up a position in the shelter of one of the houses had possibly watched me while I was tying up the buffalo, expecting me to return the way I had gone; it was fortunate for me that I had noted the danger of passing those open doorways a second time, and had taken the longer way round.

When coming up from Chuka I had taken every precaution to guard against a sudden attack, and it was well that I had done so, for I now found from her pug marks that the tigress had followed me all the way up from my camp, and next morning when I went back to Thak I found she had followed me from where I had joined the path below the houses, right down to the cultivated land at Chuka.

Reading with the illumination I had brought with me was not possible, so after dinner that night, while sitting near a fire which was as welcome for its warmth as it was for the feeling of security it gave me, I reviewed the whole situation and tried to think out some plan by which it would be possible to circumvent the tigress.

When leaving home on the 22nd I had promised that I would return in ten days, and that this would be my last expedition after man-eaters. Years of exposure and strain and long absences from home—extending as in the case of the Chowgarh tigress and the Rudraprayag leopard to several months on end were beginning to tell as much on my constitution as on the nerves of those at home, and if by the 30th of November I had not succeeded in killing this man-eater, others would have to be found who were willing to take on the task.

It was now the night of the 24th, so I had six clear days before me. Judging from the behavior of the tigress that evening she appeared to be anxious to secure another human victim, and it should not therefore be difficult for me, in the time at my disposal, to get in touch with her. There were several methods by which this could be accomplished, and each would be tried in turn. The method that offers the greatest chance of success of shooting a tiger in the hills is to sit up in a tree over a kill, and if during that night the tigress did not kill the buffalo I had tied up at Thak, I would the following night, and every night thereafter, tie up the other two buffaloes in places I had already selected, and failing to secure a human kill it was just possible that the tigress might kill one of my buffaloes, as she had done on a previous occasion when the Ibbotsons and I were camped at Sem in April. After making up the fire with logs that would burn all night I turned in, and went to sleep listening to a kakar barking in the scrub jungle behind my tent.

While breakfast was being prepared the following morning I picked up a rifle and went out to look for tracks on the stretch of sand on the right bank of the river, between Chuka and Sem. The path, after leaving the cultivated land, runs for a short distance through scrub jungle, and here I found the tracks of a big male leopard, possibly the same animal that had alarmed the kakar the previous night. A small male tiger had crossed and recrossed the had many times during the past week, and in the same period the man-eared had crossed only once, coming from the direction of Sem. A big bear had traversed the sand a little before my arrival, and when I got back to camp the contractors complained that while distributing work that morning they had run into a bear which had taken up a very threatening attitude, in consequence of which their labor had refused to work in the area in which the bear had been seen.

Several thousand men—the conductors put the figure at five thousand—had now concentrated at Chuka and Kumaya Chak to fell and saw up the timber and carry it down to the motor road that was being constricted and all the time this considerable labor force was working they shouted at the tops of their voices to keep up their courage. The noise in the valley resulting from axe and saw, the crashing of giant trees down the steep hillside, the breaking of rocks with sledge hammers, and combined with it all the shouting of thousands of men, can better be imagined than described. That there were many and frequent alarms in this nervous community was only natural, and during the next few days I covered much ground and lost much valuable time in investigating false rumors of attacks and kills by the man-eater, for the dread of the tigress was not confined to the Ladhya valley but extended right down the Sarda through Kaldhunga to the gorge, an area of roughly fifty square miles in which an additional ten thousand men were working.

That a single animal should terrorize a labor force of these dimensions in addition to the residents of the surrounding villages and the hundreds of men who were bringing foodstuffs for the laborers or passing through the valley with hill produce in the way of oranges (purchasable at twelve annas a hundred), walnuts, and chilies to the market at Tanakpur is incredible, and would be unbelievable were it not for the historical, and nearly parallel, case of the man-eaters of Tsavo, where a pair of lions, operating only at night, held up work for long periods on the Uganda Railway.

To return to my story. Breakfast disposed of on the morning of the 25th, I took a second buffalo and set out for Thak. The path, after leaving the cultivated land at Chuka, skirts along the foot of the hill for about half a mile before it divides. One arm goes straight up a ridge to Thak and the other, after continuing along the foot of the hill for another half-mile, zigzags up through Kumaya Chak to Kot Kindri.

At the divide I found the pug marks of the tigress and followed them all the way back to Thak. The fact that she had come down the hill after me the previous evening was proof that she had not killed the buffalo. This, though very disappointing, was not at all unusual; for tigers will on occasions visit an animal that is tied up for several nights in succession before they finally kill it, for tigers do not kill unless they are hungry.

Leaving the second buffalo at the mango tree, where there was an abundance of green grass, I skirted round the houses and found No. 1 buffalo sleeping peacefully after a big feed and a disturbed night. The tigress, coming from the direction of the village as her pug marks showed, had approached to within a few feet of the buffalo, and had then gone back the way she had come. Taking the buffalo down to the spring I let it graze for an hour or two, and then took it back and tied it up at the same spot where it had been the previous night.

The second buffalo I tied up fifty yards from the mango tree and at the spot where the wailing woman and villagers had met us the day the Ibbotsons and I had gone up to investigate the human kill. Here a ravine a few feet deep crossed the path, on one side of which there was a dry stump, and on the other an almond tree in which a machan could be made. I tied No. 2 buffalo to the stump, and bedded it down with sufficient hay to keep it going for several days. There was nothing more to be done at Thak, so I returned to camp and, taking the third buffalo, crossed the Ladhya and tied it up behind Sem, in the ravine where the tigress had killed one of our buffaloes in April.

At my request the Tahsildar of Tanakpur had selected three of the fastest young male buffaloes he could find. All three were now tied up in places frequented by the tigress, and as I set out to visit them on the morning of the 26th I had great hopes that one of them had been killed and that I should get an opportunity of shooting the tigress over it. Starting with the one across the Ladhya, I visited all in turn and found that the tigress had not touched any of them. Again, as on the previous morning, I found her tracks on the path leading to Thak, but on this occasion there was a double set of pug marks, one coming down and the other going back. On both her journeys the tigress had kept to the path and had passed within a few feet of the buffalo that was tied to the stump, fifty yards from the mango tree.

On my return to Chuka a deputation of Thak villagers led by the Headman came to my tent and requested me to accompany them to the village to enable them to replenish their supply of foodstuffs, so at midday, followed by the Headman and his tenants, and by four of my own men carrying ropes for a machan and food for me, I returned to Thak and mounted guard while the men hurriedly collected the provisions they needed.

After watering and feeding the two buffaloes I retied No. 2 to the stump and took No. 1 half a mile down the hill and tied it to a sapling on the side of the path. I then took the villagers back to Chuka and returned a few hundred yards up the hill for a scratch meal while my men were making the machan.

It was now quite evident that the tigress had no fancy for my fat buffaloes, and as in three days I had seen her tracks five times on the path leading to Thak, I decided to sit up over the path and try to get a shot at her that way. To give me warning of the tigress's approach I tied a goat with a bell round its neck on the path, and at 4 p.m. I climbed into the tree. I told my men to return at 8 a.m. the following morning, and began my watch.

At sunset a cold wind started blowing and while I was attempting to pull a coat over my shoulders the ropes on one side of the machan slipped, rendering my scat very uncomfortable. An hour later a storm came on, and though it did not rain for long it wet through to the skin, greatly adding to my discomfort. During the sixteen hours I sat in the tree I did not see or hear anything. The men turned up at 8 a.m. I returned to camp for a hot bath and a good meal, and then, accompanied by six of my men, set out for Thak.

The overnight rain had washed all the old tracks off the path, and two hundred yards above the tree I had sat in I found the fresh pug marks of the tigress, where she had come out of the jungle and gone up the path in the direction of Thak. Very cautiously I stalked the first buffalo, only to find it lying asleep on the path; the tigress had skirted round it, rejoined the path a few yards further on and continued up the hill. Following on her tracks I approached the second buffalo, and as I got near the place where it had been tied two blue Himalayan magpies rose off the ground and went screaming down the hill.

The presence of these birds indicated (a) that the buffalo was dead, (b) that it had been partly eaten and not carried away, and (c) that the tigress was not in the close vicinity.

On arrival at the stump to which it had been tied I saw that the buffalo had been dragged off the path and partly eaten, and on examining the animal

I found it had not been killed by the tigress but that it had in all probability died of snake-bite (there were many hamadryads in the surrounding jungles), and that, finding it lying dead on the path, the tigress had eaten a meal off it and had then tried to drag it away. When she found she could not break the rope, she had partly covered it over with dry leaves and brushwood and continued on her way up to Thak.

Tigers as a rule are not carrion eaters but they do on occasions eat animals they themselves have not killed. For instance, on one occasion I left the carcass of a leopard on a fire track and, when I returned next morning to recover a knife I had forgotten, I found that a tiger had removed the carcass to a distance of a hundred yards and eaten two-thirds of it.

On my way up from Chuka I had dismantled the machan I had sat on the previous night, and while two of my men climbed into the almond tree to make a seat for me—the tree was not big enough for a machan—the other four went to the spring to fill a kettle and boil some water for tea. By 4 p.m. I had partaken of a light meal of biscuits and tea, which would have to keep me going until next day, and refusing the men's request to be permitted to stay the night in one of the houses in Thak, I sent them back to camp. There was a certain amount of risk in doing this, but it was nothing compared to the risk they would run if they spent the night in Thak.

My seat on the tree consisted of several strands of rope tied between two upright branches, with a couple of strands lower down for my feet to rest on. When I had settled down comfortably I pulled the branches round me and secured them in position with a thin cord, leaving a small opening to see and fire through. My 'hide' was soon tested, for shortly after the men had gone the two magpies returned, and attracted others, and nine of them fed on the kill until dusk. The presence of the birds enabled me to get some sleep, for they would have given me warning of the tigress's approach, and with their departure my all-night vigil started.

There was still sufficient daylight to shoot by when the moon, a day off the full, rose over the Nepal hills behind me and flooded the hillside with brilliant light. The rain of the previous night had cleared the atmosphere of dust and smoke and, after the moon had been up a few minutes, the light was so good that I was able to see a sambur and her young one feeding in a field of wheat a hundred and fifty yards away.

The dead buffalo was directly in front and about twenty yards away, and the path along which I expected the tigress to come was two or three yards nearer, so I should have an easy shot at a range at which it would be impossible to miss the tigress—provided she came; and there was no reason why she should not do so.

The moon had been up two hours, and the sambur had approached to within fifty yards of my tree, when a kakar started barking on the hill just above the village. The kakar had been barking for some minutes when suddenly a scream which I can only, very inadequately, describe as 'Ar-Ar-Arr' dying away on a long-drawn-out note, came from the direction of the village. So sudden and so unexpected had the scream been that I involuntarily stood up with the intention of slipping down from the tree and dashing up to the village, for the thought flashed through my mind that the man-eater was killing one of my men. Then in a second flash of thought I remembered I had counted them one by one as they had passed my tree, and that I had watched them out of sight on their way back to camp to see if they were obeying my instructions to keep close together.

The scream had been the despairing cry of a human being in mortal agony, and reason questioned how such a sound could have come from a deserted village. It was not a thing of my imagination for the kakar had heard it and had abruptly stopped barking, and the sambur had dashed away across the fields closely followed by her young one. Two days previously, when I had escorted the men to the village, I had remarked that they appeared to be very confident to leave their property behind doors that were not even shut or latched, and the Headman had answered that even if their village remained un tenanted for years their property would be quite safe, for they were priests of Punagiri and no one would dream of robbing them; he added that as long as the tigress lived she was a better guard of their property—if guard were needed—than any hundred men could be, for no one in all that countryside would dare to approach the village, for any purpose, through the dense forests that surrounded it, unless escorted by me as they had been.

The screams were not repeated, and as there appeared to be nothing that I could do I settled down again on my rope seat. At 10 p.m. a kakar that was feeding on the young wheat crop at the lower end of the fields dashed away barking, and a minute later the tigress called twice. She had now left the village and was on the move, and even if she did not fancy having another meal off the buffalo there was every hope of her coming along the path which she had used twice every day for the past few days. With finger on trigger and eyes straining on the path I sat hour after hour until daylight succeeded moonlight, and when the sun had been up an hour, my men returned. Very thoughtfully they had brought a bundle of dry wood with them, and in a surprisingly short time I was sitting down to a hot cup of tea. The tigress may have been lurking in the bushes close to us, or she may have been miles away, for after she had called at 10 p.m. the jungles had been silent.

When I got back to camp I found a number of men sitting near my tent. Some of these men had come to inquire what luck I had had the previous night, and others had come to tell me that the tigress had called from midnight to a little before sunrise at the foot of the hill, and that all the laborers engaged in the forests and on the new export road were too frightened to go to work. I had already heard about the tigress from my men, who had informed me that, together with the thousands of men who were camped round Chuka, they had sat up all night to keep big fires going.

Among the men collected near my tent was the Headman of Thak, and when the others had gone I questioned him about the kill at Thak on the 12th of the month, when he so narrowly escaped falling a victim to the man-eater.

Once again the Headman told me in great detail how he had gone to his fields to dig ginger, taking his grandchild with him, and how on hearing his wife calling he had caught the child's hand and run back to the house—where his wife had said a word or two to him about not keeping his ears open and thereby endangering his own and the child's life—and how a few minutes later the tigress had killed a man while he was cutting leaves off a tree in a field above his house.

All this part of the story I had heard before, and I now asked him if he had actually seen the tigress killing the man. His answer was no; and he added that the tree was not visible from where he had been standing. I then asked him how he knew that the man had been killed, and he said, because he had heard him. In reply to further questions he said the man had not called for help but had cried out; and when asked if he had cried out once he said, 'No, three times,' and then at my request he gave an imitation of the man's cry. It was the same—but a very modified rendering—as the screams I had heard the previous night.

I then told him what I had heard and asked him if it was possible for anyone to have arrived at the village accidentally, and his answer was an emphatic negative. There were only two paths leading to Thak, and every man, woman, and child in the villages through which these two paths passed knew that Thak was deserted and the reason for its being so. It was known throughout the district that it was dangerous to go near Thak in daylight, and it was therefore quite impossible for anyone to have been in the village at eight o'clock the previous night.

When asked if he could give any explanation for screams having come from a village in which there could not—according to him—have been any human beings, his answer was that he could not. And as I can do no better than the Headman, it were best to assume that neither the kakar, the sambur, nor I heard those very real screams—the screams of a human being in mortal agony.

IV.

When all my visitors, including the Headman, had gone, and I was having breakfast, my servant informed me that the Headman of Sem had come to the camp the previous evening and had left word for me that his wife, while cutting grass near the hut where his mother had been killed, had come on a blood trail, and that he would wait for me near the ford over the Ladhya in the morning. So after breakfast I set out to investigate this trail.

While I was fording the river I saw four men hurrying towards me, and as soon as I was on dry land they told me that when they were coming down the hill above Sem they had heard a tiger falling across the valley on the hill between Chuka and Thak. The noise of the water had prevented my hearing the call. I told the men that I was on my way to Sem and would return to Chuka shortly and left them.

The Headman was waiting for me near his house, and his wife took me to where she had seen the blood trail the previous day. The trail, after continuing along a field for a short distance, crossed some big rocks, on one of which I found the hairs of a kakar. A little further on I found the pug marks of a big male leopard, and while I was looking at them I heard a tiger call. Telling my companions to sit down and remain quiet, I listened, in order to locate the tiger. Presently I heard the call again, and thereafter it was repeated at intervals of about two minutes.

It was the tigress calling and I located her as being five hundred yards below Thak and in the deep ravine which, starting from the spring under the mango tree, runs parallel to the path and crosses it at its junction with the Kumaya Chak path.

Telling the Headman that the leopard would have to wait to be shot at a more convenient time, I set off as hard as I could go for camp, picking up at the ford the four men who were waiting for my company to Chuka.

On reaching camp I found a crowd of men round my tent, most of them sawyers from Delhi, but including the petty contractors, agents, clerks, timekeepers, and gangmen of the financier who had taken up the timber and road construction contracts in the Ladhya valley. These men had come to see me in connection with my stay at Chuka. They informed me that many of the hillmen carrying timber and working on the road had left for their homes that morning and that if I left Chuka on 1 December, as they had heard I intended doing, the entire labor force, including themselves, would leave on the same day; for already they were too frightened to eat or sleep, and no one would dare to remain in the valley after I had gone. It was then the morning of 29 November and I told the men that I still had two days and two nights and that much could happen in that time, but that in any case it would not be possible for me to prolong my stay beyond the morning of the first.

The tigress had by now stopped calling, and when my servant had put up something for me to eat I set out for Thak, intending, if the tigress called again and I could locate her position, to try to stalk her; and if she did not call again, to sit up over the buffalo. I found her tracks on the path and saw where she had entered the ravine, and though I stopped repeatedly on my way up to Thak and listened I did not hear her again. So a little before sunset I ate the biscuits and drank the bottle of tea I had brought with me, and then climbed into the almond tree and took my seat on the few strands of rope that had to serve me as a machan. On this occasion the magpies were absent, so I was unable to get the hour or two's sleep the birds had enabled me to get the previous evening.

If a tiger fails to return to its kill the first night it does not necessarily mean that the kill has been abandoned. I have on occasions seen a tiger return on the tenth night and eat what could no longer be described as flesh. On the present occasion, however, I was not sitting over a kill, but over an animal that the tigress had found dead and off which she had made a small meal, and had she not been a man-eater I would not have considered the chance of her returning the second night good enough to justify spending a whole night in a tree when she had not taken sufficient interest in the dead buffalo to return to it the first night. It was therefore with very little hope of getting a shot that I sat on the tree from sunset to sunrise, and though the time I spent was not as long as it had been the previous night, my discomfort was very much greater, for the ropes I was sitting on cut into me, and a cold wind that started blowing shortly after moonrise and continued throughout the night chilled me to the bone. On this second night I heard no jungle or other sounds, nor did the sambur and her young one come out to feed on the fields. As daylight was succeeding moonlight I thought I heard a tiger call in the distance, but could not be sure of the sound or of its direction.

When I got back to camp my servant had a cup of tea and a hot bath ready for me, but before I could indulge in the latter—my forty-pound tent was not big enough for me to bathe in—I had to get rid of the excited throng of people who were clamoring to tell me their experiences of the night before. It appeared that shortly after moonrise the tigress had started calling close to Chuka, and after calling at intervals for a couple of hours had gone off in the direction of the labor camps at Kumaya Chak. The men in these camps hearing her coming started shouting to try to drive her away, but so far from having this effect the shouting only infuriated her the more and she demonstrated in front of the camps until she had cowed the men into silence. Having accomplished this she spent the rest of the night between the labor camps and Chuka, daring all and sundry to shout at her. Towards morning she had gone away in the direction of Thak, and my informants were surprised and very disappointed that I had not met her.

This was my last day of man-eater hunting, and though I was badly in need of rest and sleep, I decided to spend what was left of it in one last attempt to get in touch with the tigress.

The people not only of Chuka and Sem but of all the surrounding villages, and especially the men from Talla Des where some years previously I had shot three man-eaters, were very anxious that I should try sitting up over a live goat, for, said they. 'All hill tigers eat goats, and as you have had no luck with buffaloes, why not try a goat?' More to humor them than with any hope of getting a shot, I consented to spend this last day in sitting up over the two goats I had already purchased for this purpose.

I was convinced that no matter where the tigress wandered to at night her headquarters were at Thak, so at midday, taking the two goats, and accompanied by four of my men. I set out for Thak.

The path from Chuka to Thak, as I have already mentioned, runs up a very steep ridge. A quarter of a mile on this side of Thak the path leaves the ridge, and crosses a more or less flat bit of ground which extends right up to the mango tree. For its whole length across this flat ground the path passes through dense brushwood, and is crossed by two narrow ravines which run east and join the main ravine. Midway between these two ravines, and a hundred yards from the tree I had sat in the previous two nights, there is a giant almond tree; this tree had been my objective when I left camp. The path passes right under the tree and I thought that if I climbed half-way up not only should I be able to see the two goats, one of which I intended tying at the edge of the main ravine and the other at the foot of the hill to the right, but I should also be able to see the dead buffalo. As all three of these points were at some distance from the tree, I armed myself with an accurate .275 rifle, in addition to the 450/400 rifle which I took for an emergency.

I found the climb up from Chuka on this last day very trying, and I had just reached the spot where the path leaves the ridge for the flat ground, when the tigress called about a hundred and fifty yards to my left. The ground here was covered with dense undergrowth and trees interlaced with creepers, and was cut up by narrow and deep ravines, and strewn over with enormous boulders—a very unsuitable place in which to stalk a man-eater. However, before deciding on what action I should take, it was necessary to know whether the tigress was lying down, as she very well might be, for it was then 1 p.m., or whether she was on the move and if so in what direction. So making the men sit down behind me I listened, and presently the call was repeated; she had moved some fifty yards, and appeared to be going up the main ravine in the direction of Thak.

This was very encouraging, for the tree I had selected to sit in was only fifty yards from the ravine. After enjoining silence on the men and telling them to keep close behind me, we hurried along the path. We had about two hundred yards to go to reach the tree and had covered half the distance when, as we approached a spot where the path was bordered on both sides by dense brushwood, a covey of kaleege pheasants rose out of the brushwood and went screaming away. I knelt down and covered the path for a few minutes, but as nothing happened we went cautiously forward and reached the tree without further incident. As quickly and as silently as possible one goat was tied at the edge of the ravine, while the other was tied at the foot of the hill to the right; then I took the men to the edge of the cultivated land and told them to stay in the upper verandah of the Headman's house until I fetched them, and ran back to the tree. I climbed to a height of forty feet, and pulled the rifle up after me with a cord I had brought for the purpose. Not only were the two goats visible from my seat, one at a range of seventy and the other at a range of sixty yards, but I could also see part of the buffalo, and as the .275 rifle was very accurate I felt sure I could kill the tigress if she showed up anywhere on the ground I was overlooking.

The two goats had lived together ever since I had purchased them on my previous visit, and being separate now, were calling lustily to each other. Under normal conditions a goat can be heard at a distance of four hundred yards, but here the conditions were not normal, for the goats were tied on the side of a hill down which a strong wind was blowing, and even if the tigress had moved after I had heard her, it was impossible for her not to hear them. It she was hungry, as I had every reason to believe she was there was a very good chance of my getting a shot.

After I had been on the tree for ten minutes a kakar barked near the spot the pheasants had risen from. For a minute or two my hopes rose sky-high and then dropped back to earth, for the kakar barked only three times and ended on a note of inquiry; evidently there was a snake in the scrub which neither he nor the pheasants liked the look of.

My seat was not uncomfortable and the sun was pleasingly warm, so for the next three hours I remained in the tree without any discomfort. At 4 p.m. the sun went down behind the high hill above Thak and thereafter the wind became unbearably cold. For an hour I stood the discomfort, and then decided to give up, for the cold had brought on an attack of ague, and if the tigress came now it would not be possible for me to hit her. I retied the cord to the rifle and let it down, climbed down myself, and walked to the edge of the cultivated land to call up my men.

V.

There are few people, I imagine, who have not experienced that feeling of depression that follows failure to accomplish anything they have set out to do. The road back to camp after a strenuous day when the chukor bag is full is only a step compared with the same road which one plods over, mile after weary mile, when the bag is empty, and if this feeling of depression has ever assailed you at the end of a single day, and when the quarry has only been chuker, you will have some idea of the depth of my depression that evening when, after calling up my men and untying the goats. I set off on my two-mile walk to camp, for my effort had been not of a single day or my quarry a few birds, not did my failure concern only myself.

Excluding the time spent on the journeys from and to home, I had been on the heels of the man-eater from 23 October to 7 November, and again from 14 to 30 November, and it is only those of you who have walked in fear of having the teeth of a tiger meet in your throat who will have any idea of the effect on one's nerves of days and weeks of such anticipation.

Then again my quarry was a man-eater, and my failure to shoot it would very gravely affect everyone who was working in, or whose homes were in, that area. Already work in the forests had been stopped, and the entire population of the largest village in the district had abandoned their homes. Bad as the conditions were they would undoubtedly get worse if the man-eater was not killed, for the entire labor force could not afford to stop work indefinitely, nor could the population of the surrounding villages afford to abandon their homes and their cultivation as the more prosperous people of Thak had been able to do.

The tigress had long since lost her natural fear of human beings, as was abundantly evident from her having carried away a girl picking up mangoes in a field close to where several men were working, killing a woman near the door of her house, dragging a man off a tree in the heart of a village, and, the previous night, cowing a few thousand men into silence. And here was I, who knew full well what the presence of a man-eater meant to the permanent and to the temporary inhabitants and to all the people who passed through the district on their way to the markets at the foothills or the temples at Punagiri, plodding down to camp on what I had promised others would be my last day of man-eater hunting; reason enough for a depression of soul which I felt would remain with me for the rest of my days. Gladly at that moment would

I have bartered the success that had attended thirty-two years of man-eater hunting for one unhurried shot at the tigress.

I have told you of some of the attempts I made during this period of seven days and seven nights to get a shot at the tigress, but these were by no means the only attempts I made. I knew that I was being watched and followed, and every time I went through the two miles of jungle between my camp and Thak I tried every trick I have learnt in a lifetime spent in the jungles to outwit the tigress. Bitter though my disappointment was, I felt that my failure was not in any way due to anything I had done or left undone.

VI.

My men when they rejoined me said that, an hour after the kakar had barked, they had heard the tigress calling a long way off but were not sure of the direction. Quite evidently the tigress had as little interest in goats as she had in buffaloes, but even so it was unusual for her to have moved at that time of day from a locality in which she was thoroughly at home, unless she had been attracted away by some sound which neither I nor my men had heard; however that may have been, it was quite evident that she had gone, and as there was nothing further that I could do I set off on my weary tramp to camp.

The path, as I have already mentioned, joins the ridge that runs down to Chuka a quarter of a mile from Thak, and when I now got to this spot where the ridge is only a few feet wide and from where a view is obtained of the two great ravines that run down to the Ladhya River, I heard the tigress call once and again across the valley on my left. She was a little above and to the left of Kumaya Chak, and a few hundred yards below the Kot Kindri ridge on which the men working in that area had built themselves grass shelters.

Here was an opportunity, admittedly forlorn and unquestionably desperate, of getting a shot; still it was an opportunity and the last I should ever have, and the question was, whether or not I was justified in taking it.

When I got down from the tree I had one hour in which to get back to camp before dark. Calling up the men, hearing what they had to say, collecting the goats, and walking to the ridge had taken about thirty minutes, and judging from the position of the sun which was now casting a red glow on the peaks of the Nepal hills, I calculated I had roughly half an hour's daylight in hand. This time factor, or perhaps it would be more correct to say light factor, was all-important, for if I took the opportunity that offered, on it would depend the lives of five men.

The tigress was a mile way and the intervening ground was densely wooded, strewn over with great rocks and cut up by a number of deep nullahs, but she could cover the distance well within the half-hour—if she wanted to. The question I had to decide was, whether or not I should try to call her up. If I called and she heard me, and came while it was still daylight and gave me a shot, all would be well; on the other hand, if she came and did not give me a shot some of us would not reach camp, for we had nearly two miles to go and the path the whole way ran through heavy jungle, and was bordered in some places by big rocks, and in others by dense brushwood. It was useless to consult the men, for none of them had ever been in a jungle before coming on this trip, so the decision would have to be mine. I decided to try to call up the tigress.

Handing my rifle over to one of the men I waited until the tigress called again and, cupping my hands round my mouth and filling my lungs to their utmost limit, sent an answering call over the valley. Back came her call and thereafter, for several minutes, call answered call. She would come, had in fact already started, and if she arrived while there was light to shoot by, all the advantages would be on my side, for I had the selecting of the ground on which it would best suit me to meet her. November is the mating season for tigers and it was evident that for the past forty-eight hours she had been rampaging through the jungles in search of a mate, and that now, on hearing what she thought was a tiger answering her mating call, she would lose no time in joining him.

Four hundred yards down the ridge the path runs for fifty yards across a flat bit of ground. At the far right-hand side of this flat ground the path skirts a big rock and then drops steeply, and continues in a series of hairpin bends, down to the next bench. It was at this rock I decided to meet the tigress, and on my way down to it I called several times to let her know I was changing my position, and also to keep in touch with her.

I want you now to have a clear picture of the ground in your mind, to enable you to follow the subsequent events. Imagine then a rectangular piece of ground forty yards wide and eighty yards long, ending in a more or less perpendicular rock face. The path coming down from Thak runs on to this ground at its short or south end, and after continuing down the center for twenty-five yards bends to the right and leaves the rectangle on its long or east side. At the point where the path leaves the flat ground there is a rock about four feet high. From a little beyond where the path bends to the right, a ridge of rock, three or four feet high, rises and extends to the north side of the rectangle, where the ground falls away in a perpendicular rock face. On the near or path side of this low ridge there is a dense line of bushes approaching to within ten feet of the four-foot-high rock I have mentioned. The rest of the rectangle is grown over with trees, scattered bushes, and short grass.

It was my intention to lie on the path by the side of the rock and shoot the tigress as she approached me, but when I tried this position I found it would not be possible for me to see her until she was within two or three yards, and further, that she could get at me either round the rock or through the scattered bushes on my left without my seeing her at all. Projecting out of the rock, from the side opposite to that from which I expected the tigress to approach, there was a narrow ledge. By sitting sideways I found I could get a little of my bottom on the ledge, and by putting my left hand flat on the top of the rounded rock and stretching out my right leg to its full extent and touching the ground with my toes, retain my position on it. The men and goats I placed immediately behind, and ten to twelve feet below me.

The stage was now set for the reception of the tigress, who while these preparations were being made had approached to within three hundred yards. Sending out one final call to give her direction, I looked round to see if my men were all right.

The spectacle these men presented would under other circumstances have been ludicrous, but was here tragic. Sitting in a tight little circle with their knees drawn up and their heads together, with the goats burrowing in under them, they had that look of intense expectancy on their screwed-up features that one sees on the faces of spectators waiting to hear a big gun go off. From the time we had first heard the tigress from the ridge, neither the men nor the goats had made a sound, beyond one suppressed cough. They were probably by now frozen with fear—as well they might be—and even if they were, I take my hat off to those four men who had the courage to do what I, had I been in their shoes, would not have dreamt of doing. For seven days they had been hearing the most exaggerated and blood-curdling tales of this fearsome beast that had kept them awake the past two nights, and now, while darkness was coming on, and sitting unarmed in a position where they could see nothing, they were listening to the man-eater drawing nearer and nearer; greater courage, and greater faith, it is not possible to conceive.

The fact that I could not hold my rifle, a D.B. 450/400, with my left hand (which I was using to retain my precarious seat on the ledge) was causing me some uneasiness, for apart from the fear of the rifle's slipping on the rounded top of the rock—I had folded my handkerchief and placed the rifle on it to try to prevent this—I did not know what would be the effect of the recoil of a high velocity rifle fired in this position. The rifle was pointing along the path, in which there was a hump, and it was my intention to fire into the tigress's face immediately as it appeared over this hump, which was twenty feet from the rock.

The tigress however did not keep to the contour of the hill, which would have brought her out on the path a little beyond the hump, but crossed a deep ravine and came straight towards where she had heard my last call, at an angle which I can best describe as one o'clock. This manoeuver put the low ridge of rock, over which I could not see, between us. She had located the direction of my last call with great accuracy, but had misjudged the distance, and not finding her prospective mate at the spot she had expected him to be, she was now working herself up into a perfect fury and you will have some idea of what the fury of a tigress in her condition can be when I tell you that not many miles from my home a tigress on one occasion closed a public road for a whole week, attacking everything that attempted to go along it, including a string of camels, until she was finally joined by a mate.

I know of no sound more liable to fret one's nerves than the calling of an unseen tiger at close range. What effect this appalling sound was having on my men I was frightened to think, and if they had gone screaming down the hill I should not have been at all surprised, for even though I had the heel of a good rifle to my shoulder and the stock against my cheek I felt like screaming myself.

But even more frightening than this continuous calling was the fading out of the light. Another few seconds, ten or fifteen at the most, and it would be too dark to see my sights, and we should then be at the mercy of a man-eater, plus a tigress wanting a mate. Something would have to be done, and done in a hurry, if we were not to be massacred, and the only thing I could think of was to call.

The tigress was now so close that I could hear the intake of her breath each time before she called, and as she again filled her lungs, I did the same with mine, and we called simultaneously. The effect was startlingly instantaneous. Without a second's hesitation she came tramping with quick steps through the dead leaves, over the low ridge and into the bushes a little to my right front, and just as I was expecting her to walk right on top of me she stopped, and the next moment the full blast of her deep-throated call struck me in the face and would have carried the hat off my head had I been wearing one. A second's pause, then again quick steps; a glimpse of her as she passed between two bushes, and then she stepped right out into the open, and, looking into my face, stopped dead.

By great and unexpected good luck the half-dozen steps the tigress took to her right front carried her almost to the exact spot at which my rifle was pointing. Had she continued in the direction in which she was coming before her last call, my story—if written—would have had a different ending, for it would have been as impossible to slew the rifle on the rounded top of the rock as it would have been to lift and fire it with one hand.

Owing to the nearness of the tigress, and the fading light, all that I could see of her was her head. My first bullet caught her under the right eye and the second, fired more by accident than with intent, took her in the throat and she came to rest with her nose against the rock and knocked me off the ledge, and the recoil from the left barrel, fired while I was in the air, brought the rifle up in violent contact with my jaw and sent me heels over head right on top of the men and goats. Once again I take my hat off to those four men for, not knowing but what the tigress was going to land on them next, they caught me as I fell and saved me from injury and my rifle from being broken.

When I had freed myself from the tangle of human and goat legs I took the .275 rifle from the man who was holding it, rammed a clip of cartridges into the magazine and sent a stream of five bullets singing over the valley and across the Sarda into Nepal. Two shots, to the thousands of men in the valley and in the surrounding villages who were anxiously listening for the sound of my rifle, might mean anything, but two shots followed by five more, spaced at regular intervals of five seconds, could only be interpreted as conveying one message, and that was that the man-eater was dead.

I had not spoken to my men from the time we had first heard the tigress from the ridge. On my telling them now that she was dead and that there was no longer any reason for us to be afraid, they did not appear to be able to take in what I was saying, so I told them to go up and have a look while I found and lit a cigarette. Very cautiously they climbed up to the rock, but went no further for, as I have told you, the tigress was touching the other side of it. Late in camp that night, while sitting round a camp-fire and relating their experiences to relays of eager listeners, their narrative invariably ended up with, 'and then the tiger whose roaring had turned our livers into water hit the sahib on the head and knocked him down on top of us and if you don't believe us, go and look at his face.' A mirror is superfluous in camp and even if I had had one it could not have made the swelling on my jaw, which put me on milk diet for several days, look as large and as painful as it felt.

By the time a sapling had been felled and the tigress lashed to it, lights were beginning to show in the Ladhya valley and in all the surrounding camps and villages. The four men were very anxious to have the honor of carrying the tigress to camp, but the task was beyond them; so I left them and set off for help.

In my three visits to Chuka during the past eight months I had been along this path many times by day and always with a loaded rifle in my hands, and now I was stumbling down in the dark, unarmed, my only anxiety being to avoid a fall. If the greatest happiness one can experience is the sudden cessation of great pain, then the second greatest happiness is undoubtedly the sudden cessation of great fear. One short hour previously it would have taken wild elephants to have dragged from their homes and camps the men who now, singing and shouting, were converging from every direction, singly and in groups, on the path leading to Thak. Some of the men of this rapidly growing crowd went up the path to help carry in the tigress, while others accompanied me on my way to camp, and would have carried me had I permitted them. Progress was slow, for frequent halts had to be made to allow each group of new arrivals to express their gratitude in their own particular way. This gave the party carrying the tigress time to catch us up, and we entered the village together. I will not attempt to describe the welcome my men and I received, or the scenes I witnessed at Chuka that night, for having lived the greater part of my life in the jungles I have not the ability to paint word-pictures.

A hayrick was dismantled and the tigress laid on it, and an enormous bonfire made from driftwood close at hand to light up the scene and for warmth, for the night was dark and cold with a north wind blowing. Round about midnight my servant, assisted by the Headman of Thak and Kunwar Singh, near whose house I was camped, persuaded the crowd to return to their respective villages and labor camps, telling them they would have ample opportunity of feasting their eyes on the tigress the following day. Before leaving himself, the Headman of Thak told me he would send word in the morning to the people of Thak to return to their village. This he did, and two days later the entire population returned to their homes, and have lived in peace ever since.

After my midnight dinner I sent for Kunwar Singh and told him that in order to reach home on the promised date I should have to start in a few hours, and that he would have to explain to the people in the morning why I had gone. This he promised to do, and I then started to skin the tigress. Skinning a tiger with a pocket-knife is a long job, but it gives one an opportunity of examining the animal that one would otherwise not get, and in the case of man-eaters enables one to ascertain, more or less accurately, the reason for the animal's having become a man-eater.

The tigress was a comparatively young animal and in the perfect condition one would expect her to be at the beginning of the mating season. Her dark winter coat was without a blemish, and in spite of her having so persistently refused the meals I had provided for her she was encased in fat. She had two old gunshot wounds, neither of which showed on her skin. The one in her left shoulder, caused by several pellets of homemade buckshot, had become septic, and when healing the skin, over quite a large surface, had adhered permanently to the flesh. To what extent this wound had incapacitated her it would have been difficult to say, but it had evidently taken a very long time to heal, and could quite reasonably have been the cause of her having become a man-eater. The second wound, which was in her right shoulder, had also been caused by a charge of buckshot, but had healed without becoming septic. These two wounds received over kills in the days before she had become a man-eater were quite sufficient reason for her not having returned to the human and other kills I had sat over.

After having skinned the tigress I bathed and dressed, and though my face was swollen and painful and I had twenty miles of rough going before me, I left Chuka walking on air, while the thousands of men in and around the valley were peacefully sleeping.

I have come to the end of the jungle stories I set out to tell you and I have also come near the end of my man-eater hunting career.

I have had a long spell and count myself fortunate in having walked out on my own feet and not been carried out on a cradle in the manner and condition of the man of Thak.

There have been occasions when life has hung by a thread and others when a light purse and disease resulting from exposure and strain have made the going difficult, but for all these occasions I am amply rewarded if my hunting has resulted in saving one human life.

SECTION SIX

REFLECTIONS ON OUR SPORT

CHAPTER 19

HUNTER'S MOON

By Gene Hill

AN ENGLISH astronomer once commented to the effect that the slight changing of the redness of a distant star could alter a hundred years of our mathematical calculations. This was his way of saying that the works of man are insignificant when faced with the whims of nature. Civilizations have been born or lost in earthquakes and the coming and going of volcanos and tidal waves. A degree or two of temperature change over a few thousand years melted away the ice cap that covered much of North America and a slight shifting in the rain patterns of the world has created bare and torrid deserts where years ago lay tropic jungle. Hairy mammoths that were born and raised in long-lost humid swamps are now chipped out of the light blue ice of our polar lands.

And you and I stand now in the coming of the fall speculating on the possibilities of an early frost that hopefully will skim the leaves from tenacious oaks . . . and yet not be severe enough to chill the ground so as to send the woodcock flying on to warmer soils and softer breezes. The slim balance of our sport so hangs on the vagaries of the unseen winds, the unknown seas—mysteries in their causes no less to us than to our apelike ancestors.

Yet, we will grow restive in the weeks ahead. The Hunter's Moon will see the shadow of a sleepless man who paces up and down his plot of grass, a morsel of dog as curious and as expectant as he is, tagging at his heels. He will stare at scudding clouds . . . wet his fingers to predict the vagrant wind . . . and hope that tomorrow will be kind enough to offer him a touch of frost or a heavy rain or a tracking snow. (And don't forget the days you have all three between the dawn and dark!)

But we'll go on out, if I know you, regardless. And come home wet or cold or both ten times to the single day we come home smiling at the red god's toss of dice. But that's all part of sport . . . small creatures are the birds and sheep and deer to us . . . and we, small creatures too, our wishes merely hopes sent up at night, cast out on the winds, in the light of the Hunter's Moon.

CHAPTER 20

LOG FIRES

By Gene Hill

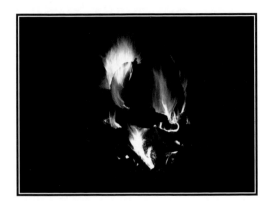

THERE ARE few things most outdoor-minded men pride themselves on more than the ability to build a good fire.

I know I can start with a match, a nice dry chestnut log and a hatchet and bring a quart bucket of cold water to a rolling boil in less than five minutes. This particular accomplishment will not be whispered about in awed tones by my pals, but I take great pleasure in the fact. I think you can tell a lot about a man in the way he behaves around a fire—at home by the fireplace, in a gunning lodge, or the best of all fires—by the edge of a lake with only the wild voiced loons for company. They used to say that if you wanted to draw a crowd, start mixing a martini and suddenly six people would show up and tell you how to do it. But log fires are worse. People are forever poking and messing around with my fires; and never doing much good. I belong to the "start it right and leave it pretty much alone" school. I've just about gotten to the point where I hide my fireplace tools to keep meddlers from fussing around with a perfectly fine fire. To me a good fire doesn't roar and flame. It's obedient and thoughtful. It just burns quietly to provide a little background color to the stories and fill up the lulls in the conversation.

Ever notice how much the hunting dogs love a fire with their menfolk sitting around? Old Tip, my lovely lady Labrador, will snuggle up to a scorcher until I'll swear I can smell her singe. She'll toast one side, then the other. More often than not, when bedtime comes around she looks the other way or pretends she's deep in sleep because she wants to spend the night alone staring at the coals. Good fires make good friends.

And here's an old verse about wood that I've always wanted to memorize and never will:

Beechwood fires are bright and clear
If the logs are kept a year.
Chestnut's only good, they say,
If for long it's laid away.
Birch and fir logs burn too fast,
Blaze up bright and do not last.
Elm wood burns like a churchyard mold;
Even the very flames are cold.
Poplar gives a bitter smoke,
Fills your eyes and makes you choke.
Apple wood will scent your room
With an incense like perfume.
Oak and maple, if dry and old,
Keep away the winter cold.
But ash wood wet and ash wood dry,
A king shall warm his slippers by.

CHAPTER 21

A CHRISTMAS WISH

By Gene Hill

THERE ARE a lot of legends and stories about Christmas wishes . . . and how I wish this year that wishes were real and I had one now and then. My old dog Tip, I know, wishes she could run the fields again instead of having to shuffle slowly at my heels. And I'd like to wipe away the touch of winter that has come to stay forever with some of my old shooting friends. Some folks say to be careful of what I wish for because it might come true. But I don't think you and I would abuse the privilege. I don't know what I'd do if I was rich, so I wouldn't wish for that this Christmas. I'd like to take the friendships that I deeply treasure and really stretch them out for times to come. Old dogs, old friends, old brooks and quail meadows that I have learned to love especially should never change or go away. I think I know the wish that we'd all like to have. A handful of friends . . . a handful of dogs . . . would have their sweetest yesterdays become tomorrows.

CHAPTER 21

TO HUNT:
THE QUESTION OF KILLING

By Tom McIntyre

A T SIXTEEN I HUNTED AND KILLED a barren-ground caribou. He bedded on Alaska tundra under a lead sky, and I bellied to the rim of the basin and shot him through the lungs with a rifle I borrowed from my father. The bull shuddered and rolled to his side, big-hoofed legs stiffening, heavy-antlered head sinking. I rose and bolted another round, setting the safety. Pink blood frothed from his nostrils; and as I walked to him, he gasped, drowning. The big hooves kicked, and a round staring eye clouded from ice-water clear to bottle green. The caribou stopped shuddering. I trembled still.

To arrive at an at best imperfect understanding of the hunt in these latter days, it is almost impossible not to rely on the Spaniard José Ortega y Gasset, again. A cranky, rather more than elitist existentialist critic of "mass man," Ortega y Gasset remained a meritocratic republican. Although quoted to the brink of emesis by hunters desperate to demonstrate their literacy, his book-length essay, Meditations on Hunting, was the 20th-century's most luminous explication of the hunt. And at the heart of Meditations lay the truth that after his spotting, pursuit, and stalking of an animal, "The hunter is a death dealer."

Hunting deals, inescapably, in death. Or more precisely, killing. Killing is what places the hunter (animal and human) apart from every other walker in the woods. Not that this always explains the kill to the satisfaction of our friends, especially those of the more doctrinaire environmentalist or animal-zealot stripe, or often to our own families. Sometimes not even entirely satisfactorily to ourselves.

This killing is, of course, not homicide or the martial hunting of "armed men," but the legal killing in the hunt of wild animals (traditional game animals, ones neither endangered as a species nor representing members of an imperiled population), with the recovery and consumption of the animal's body moral and ethical obligations of that killing. The killing in hunting is not murder incognito—assuming a relative absence of psychopathological impulse. It is killing not for the sake (or thrill) of killing, and therefore causes hunters, oddly, to be excruciatingly tongue-tied about what draws them to the hunt, of which the kill is such an indissoluble component. Partly that's a matter of trying to tell a stranger about rock 'n' roll, but also because, as Ortega y Gasset says, hunting means "accepting reason's insufficiencies." The desire to hunt, which must inevitably lead to killing (at least by intent), comes from a place well before consciousness and words, so that when it arises today it does so almost beyond articulation. Most hunters cannot even say when it began for them, yet some try.

At four I entered a small dark Lascaux of a den in my father's best friend's house. Both men were employed in aerospace, the industry just then becoming the ample bosom of the Southern California economy; but on the paneled walls of the inner space of that den were not heroic photos of rocket launches but the mounted heads of a deer, an elk, and a wild boar, with a black-bear skin on the hardwood floor. There were also the head of a red African forest buffalo and a pair of perfect rose-ivory tusks, my father's friend having taken all his savings, cashed out his wife's life-insurance policy, and gone to (then) French Equatorial Africa to kill an elephant at less than thirty paces in dense jungle. No such icons would ever be found on the avocado-hued walls or aqua pile carpet of our home; and it was inconceivable to me that they could be found anywhere else inside suburban Los Angeles county tract housing.

In later years there would be my walking behind on desultory hunts for farm-raised pheasants set out by the State of California and fetching birds during the once-a-year San Joaquin Valley mourning-dove shoots that my father approached as social requirements rather than outings, "outing" in its earlier connotation representing a letting loose for which my mad parent in his life was never entirely prepared. Through it all my mind grew into its own Lascaux of feathers and horns and tusks, until I was old enough to shoulder my own gun. Then the painted walls expanded only more.

The summer I convinced my father to let me go to the Talkeetna Mountains, taking the rifle he owned but never used, was the summer of '68, of Chicago police in Lincoln Park and Soviet tanks in Wenceslaus Square, which were matters of minor note to me compared to my desire to hunt something "bigger than I." Then, looking at the caribou, the summit of Denali beyond, and the sky above, I realized that everything around me in the hunt was bigger than I, bigger than the caribou, too. It was bigger than both of us.

So, I had killed. What was it, though, I had really done? Killing is the most incomprehensible aspect of the hunt to a large extent because we have almost no widespread experience of the reverential or even prosaic forms of killing animals, no longer sacrificing, or even slaughtering, our own livestock. The writer Reynolds Price said, in one of those plummy commentaries

National Public Radio so dotes on broadcasting, that "death has become almost the last obscenity, the single thing we're loath to discuss in public." This could with all due respect only be the opinion of an intellectual who must prattle on almost ceaselessly with his peers about death. It is based on an assumption that no one outside the cloister of the academy discusses so fraught a subject, when in fact we as a population have become further steeped than Aztec priests in a cult of death. It is impossible not to hear a constant drone about the "end-of-life experience" or oxymoronically termed "living wills," "doctor-assisted suicide," "death with dignity," and the "right to die" (more an obligation, isn't it?). The highest compliment to be paid fashion and food is that they are "to die for." Death be not just proud, these days, but dern-near haughty.

With this peculiar exaltation of death, though, killing, as identified above, remains a conundrum. People can pruriently covet the sight of death at a remove (the fiery crashes on stockcar tracks, exploding space shuttles, fatal accidents memorialized on the Web, network-televised euthanasia, and as Susan Sontag wrote, "What pornography [both rampant and tolerated, I would add] is really about, ultimately, isn't sex but death") while believing it iniquitous, even inhuman, to participate in the killing of the hunt. And yet that killing can never be genuinely understood or experienced without direct participation (which is what makes most writing about it, and almost all visual depictions of it—such as some hideously obscene televised hunting shows dwelling in the depths of the cable morass—abysmal). The best that can be done is to try to answer the questions such killing raises.

Is it fun? Is it wicked? Most important, is there anything erotic about it?

Bull, bedded, belly, shuddering, stiffening, rolled, gasped, trembled—what other conclusion could there be than that killing must be leather-and-latex erotic? This is possible to conclude because (aside from the Freudianization of all human behavior, and the view of some that the hunt is a form of "rapism") hunting and sex can appear to be the last natural acts humans enjoy on earth. Not for nothing is intercourse vulgarly characterized as the "wild thing"; for a great many of us sex is the final bivouac in the wild, our only first-hand experience of it anymore. So sex becomes the template we, knowing no better, place over all wild experience, unable to recall that there was once for humans, and yet for animals, a little more to it than that. Sex in the wild, as it were, is an intense (often perilous) but seasonal activity, and only one of many wild conditions, far more time taken up by gestation, birth, nurturing, feeding, gathering, divination, migrating, concealment, flight—and killing. It is a subsequence of modernism that everything be classified as erotic (and practically a shibboleth of postmodernism that "all sex is rape"); but killing is not a division of a corporation established by Eros: In the wild it is its own going concern.

What about fun?

The correct response given by the more enlightened hunter of the day is that he takes no pleasure in killing. He does it solely in pious acknowledgement of the cost of his food, or as a desperate, unavoidable, altruistic, anguished conservation measure ("thinning the herd"). Which is all, if you will forgive me, more than passing strange. Very few people in the industrialized world are hunters for any reason other than personal choice; far from bumming out its participants, hunting is, in the words of another Spaniard, Felipe Fernández-Armesto, in his history of food, "an attractive way of life, which still exercises a romantic appeal for some people in sedentary and even urban societies: thousands of years of civilization seem insufficient to scratch out the savage under the skin . . ."

Aldo Leopold, the "father of wildlife management," wrote, "We seek contacts with nature because we derive pleasure from them," and hunting is contact with nature at the most elemental level. It is a mistake, though, to equate pleasure with fun, with its implication of frivolousness. Pleasure is a primary constituent of life, and not necessarily just human life. You can see this in real "savages," those indigenous hunters for whom killing is hardly a style-of-life option. What experience I have had of such hunters, for whom killing can be both arduous and precarious, is that they tend to display something akin to sacred delight when an animal is brought down: Why not, when a kill can provide food, clothing, craft material, even objects of veneration,

all in a tidy bundle? Outside the human realm, watch the predators on the
Discovery Channel or Animal Planet, if you cannot witness them elsewhere.
Even in close-up it's hard to detect much solemnity or remorse as the cheetah
tumbles the Thomson's gazelle in a billow of ochre dust, or the croc rolls in
the black river mud, the wildebeest calf in its toothsome grin. There aren't
even crocodile tears.

The question should be whether one hunts for some sort of "joy of
killing." I can say only that I hunt to hunt. I could find far less taxing means
of satisfying an obsessive love of killing, had I one, than by hiking for miles
through chaparral to shoot a plateful of quail. And in fact, the too-easy,
"lucky" kill can rob the hunt of much of its savor. Killing, though, I must admit, does give me pleasure when I do it well. I believe this is the raw response
to good killing by all those who truly love to hunt. I know of nothing we do
that is not, without coercion, finally rooted in pleasure, however postponed
or sublimated or lofty. Denials of the pleasure inherent in the good kill are
less heartfelt than they are hunters' p.c. means of throwing an increasingly
denunciatory public off the scent.

Then does this make it wicked?

In his NPR soliloquy, Price, quoting A. E. Housman's translation of
lines from the Roman poet Horace—Feast then they heart, for what the heart
has had/The fingers of no heir will ever hold—counseled that unless "a heart
craves blood and cruelty, its owner should feed it lavishly." What Price did not
explain was how blood and cruelty are intrinsically linked, making it wrong
to feed with blood—certain kinds, anyway. Blood can be holy, sacrificial, cel-
ebratory, and yet not cruel. Some of the most profound cruelties involve the
shedding of not a single drop.

In our ever-more denatured world, though, we can recognize nothing in
spilled blood but heartlessness. This due not to any special characteristic of
blood so much as of our stunted perception that makes us want to place our
faith in a chimera like the one evoked by such phrases as "cruelty-free" or "no
animals were harmed in the . . . etc." Never mind that it is most often uti-
lized as a marketing ploy by cosmetics companies or a goad animal-rightists

brandish for extorting contributions from media conglomerates; it represents a real desire (perhaps to deny the "savage under the skin"), although one that fails to account for each second of sentient existence that rides upon (or at the very least owes an irredeemable debt to) an innate bow wave of cruelty from which we are powerless to exempt any living creature, ourselves included. Which is not to say that blood/killing cannot be cruel.

In true hunting, though, cruelty is never the goal and is either inadvertent or the result of inexperience. Good hunting means good killing. Good killing means possessing the skill, knowledge, and empathy to be able to inflict a wound that will end an animal's life in a matter of heartbeats, honorably, and with a minimum of sensation, let alone pain. When an animal is killed well, to appropriate (who else?) Hemingway's words, all of him will race all the rest of him to the ground, leaving the hunter with almost no opportunity for regret. Bad killing—fumbled, prolonged, visibly painful—can fill a hunter with physical unease, even disgust, both for the unintended cruelty and the dishonor to the animal. Bad killing, though, to paraphrase Ortega y Gasset a final time, exists only at the expense of good killing.

There was a time when good killing mattered, when men were expected to be good killers. There is D. H. Lawrence's oft-repeated chestnut, referring to James Fenimore Cooper's *Deerslayer*, about how the "essential American soul is hard, isolate, stoic, and a killer." What never gets quoted is Lawrence's next sentence: "It has never yet melted." Maybe not in Lawrence's day; but since then the essential American soul, at least that of sensitized man (I hesitate to use the now rather passé neologism "metrosexual"), has turned into nothing less than a sump of goo.

Killing has never been the exclusive route to manhood (or personhood), but neither has being abstractly repulsed by or irrationally ignorant of it. A soul that has neurotically diagnosed itself as unfit to kill, and wishes to advertise itself as such, can, curiously, all too often be a soul unfit for trustworthiness, commitment, self-sacrifice, and courage, as well.

I kill, and try to kill well, because it is a difficult and complex physical act, involves moral and ethical reflection, compels me to look at death—and life—without an arbiter, and is an authentic thing in a grotesquely inauthentic world.

An end to good killing will lead not to a sounder environment, but will merely be evidence of one too deteriorated to sustain any longer the most primeval of nature's processes. Seeing a better world in the cessation of killing is like the conscious refusal of the "environmental movement's leading intellects" to bear children for the sake of a better planet, because they consider it, puzzlingly, the "most humane thing" to do. Hardly humane; more like unearthly, and an endeavor to prove a negative: That it enriches the world to withhold a child from it. Similarly, how it will be a poorer world that can no longer afford human hunting. (In the end, neither the child nor the hunt is what impoverishes the earth.)

Within his environment all of a caribou's life—all of the life of the caribou I killed—is an anticipation of the hunter, the killer, in whatever shape he assumes (the caribou's existence, in fact, owes itself to being hunted and killed, because that is how the caribou was shaped by evolution: What but the wolf's tooth whittled so fine/The fleet limbs of the antelope? as Robinson Jeffers wrote). If the killer were not me, then it would be the wolf's tooth or Old

Ephraim the grizzly or winter, no animal going gentle into any good night (of them all, death by hunter may actually be gentlest). And yet the caribou never fears dying, is never enthralled by it, never once goes on the FM radio to meditate upon its meaning. If it were possible for death's lovers to tell the caribou how vital (sic) it is to embrace, even cherish death, it probably would shrug, if caribou shrug, and graze on.

Standing beside the body of a dead caribou, the trembling ebbing, I wondered at the thing of killing, which now seemed quite small, too. Against the sweep of the tundra, against the snows of Denali, against the curtain of light that would flourish late in the night sky, it was small and frail. All that I saw was greater than killing—this kind of killing. It made death itself, even my own someday, not some supreme Moloch, but something perceptibly withered and feeble, hardly worth mentioning. Hunting and killing gave me that. It let me shrug, too.

Would I have learned this without first having hunted and killed? There is no way now in which it will ever be possible for me to know.

Editor's Note: Thomas McIntyre's latest book, *Augusts in Africa: Safaris into the Twilight,* is now available wherever books are sold.